GLIMPSES OF HIDDEN INDIA

GLIMPSES OF HIDDEN INDIA

JOHN LAW

GYAN

Published by

GYAN

Gyan Publishing House
5, Ansari Road
Daryaganj, New Delhi-110002
Phone: 011-47034999, 9811692060
E-mail: books@gyanbooks.com

Distribution Network
gyanbooks.com
India, USA, Canada, UK, Australia, France

ISBN: 978-81-212-9278-8 (PB)
First Published, 1908

2nd Impression 2023

Printed at: Gyan Press, Delhi.

GLIMPSES OF HIDDEN INDIA

AUTHOR: JOHN LAW

GLIMPSES OF

HIDDEN INDIA

BY

JOHN LAW

Author of "A CITY GIRL," "GEORGE EASTMONT: WANDERER," Etc.

INDIAN EDITION

THACKER, SPINK & Co.

CALCUTTA, SIMLA, AND BOMBAY.

CONTENTS

GLIMPSES OF HIDDEN INDIA

CHAPTER I

MADRAS AT CHRISTMAS

"IT must be sad to visit a country where the English are so much disliked."

So said a Russian officer, who had been through the siege of Port Arthur. I looked at him with astonishment; but said nothing, for I had always heard that the Russians desire to replace the English in India, and I thought that the sad-eyed officer, who wore deep mourning, was prejudiced by national aspirations and jealousies.

We were returning from Kandy, having visited there the Temple of the Sacred Tooth; and we carried on a desultory conversation in the train.

"Where are you going to?" he asked.

"India," I replied.

And then he said, in French, the words with which I open this book—words so true, so sad, and, at the present time, so full of significance.

I crossed from Colombo to Tuticorin in an English steamer; and I was, I think, the only person on board who did not suffer from sea-sickness, for the twelve hours journey from Ceylon to India is choppy and unpleasant. American and French tourists were my fellow-passengers, people who desired to see the temples and the ruins of Southern India; and at Tuticorin the Frenchmen were met by servants from Pondicherry; and the Americans then raised the question whether English-speaking persons can travel in India without "boys" or "bearers."

"I have never had a valet;" said a young man from Boston, "and I will go from here to Lahore without a servant."

A French priest, who had come to welcome his countrymen, smiled and said :—

"In India no man is so poor that he cannot find someone yet poorer than himself to do his work."

The mail train left Tuticorin at about 9 o'clock, and for a day and a night we passed through desolate, barren country. Occasionally hills were seen, and sometimes a small temple, but hard, dry mud stretched on either side of the railway line, and poverty was written large on Southern India. At the stations, I saw crowds of Indians, and among them Brahmins wearing the Sacred Thread. Most of these people carried a brass *lola* to hold water, a bundle and an umbrella. Small, and very thin they looked, and rather picturesque—more especially the women, who had flowers in their neat black hair and wore many brass ornaments and much imitation jewelry. Nearly all belonged to the peasant castes, and they ran about, talking loud and fast, and shouting to one-another as if the train were on fire. One of the things that amuses me most when I read an article, or a speech, by an English visitor to India, is to hear that

Indians are *silent* people. Mrs. Hobhouse lately made a most extraordinary statement to this effect. Indians are quiet in the presence of strangers, it is true ; but when they are by themselves, they make three times the noise heard among English people. That a soft voice is an excellent thing in women is a thing Indians have yet to learn ; and the uneducated Indian is noisier than half-a-dozen parrots.

I travelled straight to Madras, stopping for meals, to which the few Englishwomen on the train went with uncovered heads and in muslin dresses. Railway carriages in India (first-class) afford every facility for making a toilette; and electric fans and electric lights give an impetus to the feminine desire to "look nice." And the food is fairly good, both in dining-cars and in station dining-rooms: servants are plentiful: ice is abundant.

In Madras, I drove to a hotel, and I stayed there until Christmas Day. Then I accepted an invitation to attend the annual Convention of the Theosophists. I wanted to come in touch with Indians, not to become a unit of the governing community ; and I thought that the Theosophists would introduce me to Hindus and Mahomedans. So, to the disgust of my compatriots in the hotel, after attending a Military Parade Service at St. Mary's Church (which is by-the-way the oldest Anglican Church in India) I drove to Adyar, the beautiful suburb where the Theosophists have their headquarters. On the way, I passed the temple of Mylapore, and I stopped to look at its many-coloured tower. A Hindu, holding a bunch of enormous keys, stood at the entrance; and I was told that no English person might enter. Ten years ago, by removing his shoes, an Englishman could go into a Hindu temple; but now Hindus are much more particular, and even Mrs. Besant, the High Priestess of Theosophists, is seldom allowed to cross the threshold of a Hindu temple. Lord Curzon was refused admittance to the temple at Puri; and Sir Arthur Lawley had to sit down outside a temple at Conjeeveram.

A large tank, covered with the leaves and the flowers of the sacred lotus, was in front of the Mylapore temple; and I stood for a time looking at the flower around which so much mysticism has been woven and listening to the temple bells. that sounded almost exactly like the bells of English churches. And presently I saw a little woman on the roof of a low house, walking up and down, and looking up at the sky.

"Who is that lady?" I asked; and a Hindu answered, in excellent English:—

"Your honour, that is an American lady, who lives here and wants to become a saint."

I learnt later on that the little woman on the roof had come to India as a governess, and is now trying to attain "realization" under the direction of a Hindu guru.

There seems to be in America, at the present time, a strong re-action against materialism, and the eccentric behaviour of some American women in India makes me feel sorry for the West. For instance, I met in Calcutta last year five American women, travelling with a Hindu—a Swami. He treated them like school-children, making them chant Hindu hymns at railway stations. This Swami went to America some years ago, without money, or influence, and has now returned to India to found a paper there with the help of his American constituents.

Leaving Mylapore, I joined a long stream of carriages, carts, bicycles, and pedestrians on the bridge of the Adyar river. "Canterbury Pilgrims," I said to myself and I wished that some modern Chaucer would interpret for me the lives of the people on the road, for I felt the task of understanding the masses around me very difficult.

Has not Mr. Kipling himself said that East and West can never be the same ? But when I quote Mr. Kipling in India, I am told (of course, I know it is a mistake) that he has Eurasian antecedents. Of course, Eurasians out-do English people in drawing a hard, dividing line between India and England. Since the Prince of Wales was in India, Eurasians have taken advantage of the suggestion of His Royal Highness that they should call themselves Europeans ; and, in consequence, India is divided to-day into Englishmen, Europeans and Indians. It would be better, I think, to give to the divisions religious names, and to say that in India are Christians, Hindus, Mahomedans, Jains, Parsis and Buddhists. When Lord Morley told the people of England that India is the only country in which bad manners are a crime, he meant, perhaps, that as the majority of English people in India are third and fourth class, they should try not to offend any well-bred Indians with whom they are brought in contact ; and Indians are never offended when the distinctions drawn have a religious basis.

At the Theosophical Convention, I found a handful of American ladies, a few Englishmen, an Italian artist, a French doctor, a Dutch linguist, a German student, about twenty Parsis, and some hundreds of Hindu Theosophists. A little palm-leaf hut on the roof of the house was given to me; and from that place I watched the Hindus in a miniature village among the palm trees. Hour after hour I sat on the roof, watching and thinking; and the following conclusions shaped themselves in my mind:—

"These people are wanting in what we call "a sense of the ludicrous." See how they wear an English shirt, without a collar, over cloths draped like the robes of Greek statues! They are noisy, because nervous. See how their limbs twitch ! And in their deep, large, dark eyes, I read suspicion, I read craft."

Some months afterwards I told a Brahmin artist my first impressions of his countrymen. He had been educated in Italy and had married a French wife; consequently he had considerable experience of both East and West.

"Your first impressions were not far wrong," he said. "The Englishman is a fine animal. The Hindu is a subtle soul."

Very few, if any, Mahomedans were present at the Convention. European and American Theosophists copy Hindus too closely to please the followers of the Prophet. If anyone says that Hindus and Mahomedans have the same interests in India, he makes a mistake. Mahomedans are playing a world-wide game to-day, and that game keeps them loyal to England in India, and very quiet. The reception given by the King-Emperor and the people of England to the Young Turkey Movement has pleased Mahomedans in India, and made them feel grateful; and, at the same time, it has shewn how far Mahomedans and Hindus in India are apart.

The morning after my arrival at Adyar, at an early hour, Mrs. Besant gave a lecture in a crowded hall; the house-party sitting on chairs, and the Hindus on the floor. She spoke with her usual force and eloquence on God, the Soul, and kindred subjects. What she said was but the A, B, C, of the Hindu religion; and some Brahmins did not hesitate to tell me, after her lecture was over, that her good intentions are of more value to India than her religious teachings. The Theosophists from the West listened with breathless interest; but the Hindus were critically kind, smilingly lenient. When the lecture was over, the crowd dispersed; the house-party going to breakfast, and to the fine Oriental Library established by Col. Olcott, and the majority of the listeners returning to the daily routine of their lives in Madras.

The Convention was made peculiarly pathetic by the fact that Col. Olcott, the President-Founder of the Theosophical Society, had returned from America in a dying condition. His history is well known. About thirty years ago, he and Madame Blavatsky arrived in Ceylon penniless; and after reviving there the religion of Buddha, travelled on to India, and established themselves at Adyar, where the Theosophists have now large estates. Opinions vary very much about Madame Blavatsky; but few doubt the zeal and the ability of the American Colonel who organised the Theosophical Society—a Society that now boasts of having branches from Norway to New Zealand. It was announced that Col. Olcott would be brought to the hall to bid farewell to the people assembled there; and on the last day of the Convention, a sad little procession came out of the private apartments of the Theosophists. The old man was carried in a chair, a doctor walking on one side of him, a hospital nurse on the other; and with him were, also, Mrs. Besant and two American ladies—mediums. His white hair and long white beard gave him a venerable appearance. Death was written on his face; the unmistakable tints of dissolution had replaced the ruddy colour that had characterised him while he was in good health. He spoke in a feeble voice for a few minutes; and was afterwards carried out of the hall, while the Hindu Theosophists prostrated themselves before him and kissed his hands. Later on he said good-bye to the European and American Theosophists; and they spoke then in whispers of the preparations he was making for his cremation, even ordering the sandal-wood and the spices, and arranging who should carry him from the house to the burning place. Three months later, I was invited to attend his obsequies. I received a message from Adyar, saying that Col. Olcott had "passed on;" and that the cremation would take place that afternoon. It was Sunday, so newspapers could not announce the ceremony; and when I drove to Adyar, I found few pilgrims on the road. In the lecture-hall, however, a good many Hindus had assembled, also some English friends of the dead man. There he lay on a low bier; face uncovered, body hidden by the Stars and Stripes. On his breast many flowers had been heaped up, his long white beard was pillowed on the petals of sweet-scented roses. He seemed to be only asleep. On a table, beside him, copies of all the sacred books of the world had been placed—typifying his desire to unite in one the various creeds of mankind, and his conviction that all religions have the same basis. Fragrant incense was by his head, also sacred fire to light the funeral pile. Strange talk was going in the hall about "Mahatmas" seen by the American mediums; and all eyes turned to well-dressed American ladies who vouched for the truth of these statements.

Mrs. Besant, in a white, semi-Indian costume, with black beads round her neck, and shoeless feet, moved noiselessly about, giving directions to silent Hindus. Then the ceremony commenced. A Buddhist spoke;

also a Parsi. A Christian said a few words. A Hindu made a prayer. Finally, Mrs. Besant gave an oration, ending with the assurance that the "Masters" had come that morning from the snowy Hymalayas to fetch their disciple home.

It was a strange scene!

The dead American, who had seen active service in his own land. The English, white-robed priestess of Theosophy, who is much like a Hindu as she can possibly be, and who claims to have had Brahminical antecedents. A young officer of the English Army. An Italian doctor. A Sanskrit scholar. Half-a-dozen English friends of the dead man, who had come out of respect for his memory. A few Parsis in shiny black hats. Some hundreds of Hindu Theosophists. As Colonel Olcott had received the Sacred Thread, Brahmins carried him to the place under the palm-trees where the cremation would take place. True, he had scandalized the orthodox on more than one occasion by eating meat at Government House, Madras; but he was the only American to whom the Sacred Thread had been given, and he had done much in India to revive the Hindu religion. So Brahmins lifted the bier and bore it out of the house.

And then a strange thing happened.

The dead man had tried to educate the children of the lowest castes in Madras; and these children had been brought by their teachers to the cocoanut plantation and had been made to wait there until Mrs. Besant's oration was over. Directly the bier was carried out of the house, these children were set loose; and each child—holding a flag and a candle—raised a loud shout, and rushed forward with wild excitement.

So the dead man was carried along, amid the merry children, just as he would have wished; for he had said:-

"Put crackers under my arms, and let people have a good laugh when this worn-out body is burnt."

The bier was placed on the rich, red earth, and the Theosophists gathered round to look for the last time on the familiar face of their late President. Mrs. Besant bent down and kissed the American's broad white forehead. She took the flowers from his breast and gave them to the people; and they sat down, in a large circle. Sandal-wood was built up over the bier, palm leaves,—bronzed and dried by the sun—were added, much ghee (clarified butter) was poured over the wood, spices and camphor were sprinkled, a sacred flame set fire to the pile, and dense white and grey smoke rose toward the blue sky. Not far off was the sea; and nearer moved the winding river, where fishes could be seen, jumping and glittering in the sunshine. The people sat on, watching the clouds of smoke; and —although leaning against a tree and at some distance,—I was suddenly seized with sickness, for an awful smell came to me—human flesh—burning. The Hindus thought nothing of it; and their European and American copyists talked and even laughed; and I said to myself that habit is indeed a strong thing, for English people can bear to commit the body of a loved relation to the earth, and will visit the grave constantly, and deck it with flowers, while putrefaction and decomposition are going on inside the coffin. English people will not think of anything unpleasant, if they can possibly help it. With Hindus it is different. They turn their beliefs, feelings, hopes and fears inside out. They live and die scientifically; while we—a nation of yesterday—are like children—we hide our heads, and fancy if we see nothing, nothing is there to be seen.

CHAPTER II

THE CONQUEST OF INDIA BY THE ENGLISH

FEW things astonished me more in Madras than the ignorance of the people there concerning the oldest place of English historical interest in India—Fort St. George. Indians said to me:—

"We would like to see Fort St. George; but we do not care to ask the Commandant a favour that might be misunderstood and refused."

The English people whom I met, showed no interest in the Fort whatsoever; and a local English Colonel, who had held a responsible position there for more than a year, confessed that he knew nothing about its history and that he could not find the places where Clive tried to shoot himself and La Bourdonnais received as hostages, on behalf of the King of France, the children of the Governor in 1746. I went to look at the register of Clive's marriage with Margaret Maskelyne in the Fort Church; and I was told that Clive's descendants are the only persons who ask to see the book. And I pointed out to uninterested officials the place where Clive sat at dinner while he was a clerk in the service of the Saib Company; and the spot on which he tried, three times, to shoot himself.

"I must be reserved for something great!" he said to the clerk who came into the room shortly afterwards, and who fired, without any difficulty, the pistol that refused to blow out the brains of the man "who gave England India."

That happened 150 years ago; but Englishmen in India talk as if England had held India from time immemorial; and while Indians now study those 150 years with the greatest care, the majority of Englishmen in India are woefully ignorant of all that took place in them, except, perhaps, the Mutiny. Many old people in India saw the Mutiny, and talk graphically about it; but the 100 years before the Mutiny—the time the English spent in conquering India—that period is little known to, and little thought about by the ruling community.

English people in India remind me of a small boy who was taken to have tea in the refreshment-room of the British Museum. He had seen statues and mummies, sculptures and marbles; and he asked the waiter, who brought him some cake :—

"Is this cake very old, too?"

"Old!" snapped the waiter "It was baked to-day."

So, in India, the ruling community seem to think that as India is very old, its present rulers must be very old, too. An English acorn fell into Indian soil 150 years ago; and Englishmen speak of the acorn as if it were a tree, while Indians call it "only a sapling."

Let me briefly trace the conquest of India by the English.

One hundred and fifty years ago English settlers in India were traders, servants of the so-called Saib Company; and England had never thought of conquering a country almost as large as Europe, and with as many different nations and rulers as we find in Europe at present. It was Robert Clive, who, about the year 1750, saw that the Governor of the French trading settlements in India had conceived the idea of founding a European empire in Asia; and who set himself to defeat the projects of Dupleix. At Pondicherry, the largest of the moribund French settlements in India, may be seen to-day a statue of Dupleix—a man of unbounded ambition, a born intriguer, married to an Indian lady of rank, who initiated him into the manners and customs of the native Courts and carried on his correspondence with the Indian rulers in the vernaculars. By the siege of the Fort of Arcot, Clive turned the eyes of England on India as a country to be exploited, and, if possible, conquered. The Fort of Arcot is now marked by fragments of a ruined wall and picnics are held in a room over an archway where Clive (so it is said) spent many hours in contemplation.

What was India like when French and English traders there grew tired of commerce and lusted for conquest ?

I will quote from a book much read by Indians to-day, called :—" *Empire in Asia* : How we came by it. : A Book of Confessions by W. M. Torrens, M. P." published in 1872. The author says :—

" India in the days of Walpole, and the elder Pitt, was still ruled, like Europe, by a number of distinct and independent Governments, differing in origin, creed, power, and civilization, frequently at feud with one another, and often suffering from over-weening vanity and ambition, just as if they had been blessed with the paternal sway of most Christian Kings, august and apostolic Kaisers, or most religious and gracious Sovereigns of immortal memory ; but they were practically self-ruled and locally free. Even in states of a secondary rank, dependent upon the superior will of Peishwa or Padishah the people of each separate province still saw in the midst of them the camp and the court of the prince they obeyed and whatever may have been the burdens on their industry, they could not but be conscious that its produce was lavished or husbanded within their borders.

The whole of the vast region lying between the Afghan hills and those of Burmah, and from the Himalayas to Cape Comorin, 1,500,000 square miles, with upwards of 200,000,000 inhabitants, consists to-day of revenue districts under an English Minister, or of mediatised States dependent for their continuance in that equivocal condition on his will.

No change like this, effected within a century, is to be found in the chronicles of conquest."

How was the conquest brought about ?

The tragedy of the "Black Hole" called Clive to Bengal at the close of 1756; and the battle of Plassey determined that not France, but England should found an empire in Asia. The enormous wealth taken at Moorshedabad, after the battle of Plassey, raised Calcutta from a struggling trade centre to its present proud position, and made it the capital of British India. At Moorshedabad may still be seen the ruins of the house in which Omichund was undeceived about the red and the white papers; the place where Suraja Dowla was murdered; and a piece of the throne on which Clive placed Mir Jaffir. The river is washing away these historical landmarks; and, but for Lord Curzon, the battlefield of Plassey would to-day be a wilderness.

If any one does not understand why and how a country almost as large as Europe came so easily into English hands, he has but to study the make-up of Suraja Dowla's army at the battle of Plassey. At that time, women and dancing girls, shop-keepers and musicians formed part of an Indian Camp; and it resembled a moving city. Music went on night and day; soldiers used largely bows and arrows; and the few guns were antique and cumbersome. A curious specimen of an Indian cannon of that time may be seen to-day at Moorshedabad. It has grown into the trunk of a tree, and is held thus in a tight embrace. The Hindu peasants of the district worship it as a symbol of power, smear it with red powder, and put into its mouth ghee and sweetmeats. Hindus were in the Eighteenth Century, as they are to-day, contemplative and peace-loving people; and their ancient civilization knew little about gunpowder and bullets. The presents sent by the Saib Company to Indian Princes show how far India was at that time from the latest scientific improvements; and letters written by Eighteenth Century English kings to Indian rulers demonstrate very plainly the condition of India before the battle of Plassey. What could millions of unarmed people do when troops furnished with the latest weapons of war, and trained on the battle fields of Europe, arrived in India?

"Plassey! Ah! good pig-sticking at Plassey," said an English officer when I asked him about the famous battlefield; and Messrs. T. Cook's agent in Calcutta could give me no information concerning Plassey.

"American tourists never ask to go there," he said.

After the battle of Plassey, Clive returned for a time to England, and his house in Berkeley Square, his carriages and dress showed very plainly the effect that an Eastern life had had upon him.

"We have at last arrived at that critical period which I have long foreseen," he wrote to a friend, "which renders it necessary for us to determine whether we shall take the whole of India for ourselves, for it is mere hyperbole to say:—' To-morrow the whole Mogul Empire is in our power.' After the lengths we have run, the Princes of Hindustan must conclude our views to be boundless. They have such instances of our ambition, that they cannot suppose us capable of moderation. The very Nawabs, whom we might support, would be jealous of our power. We must be Nawabs ourselves in fact, if not in name."

In 1765 Clive returned to India; and he then obtained from the Court of Delhi, for the East India Company, the Dewanny of Bengal, Behar and Orissa. An annual sum was to be paid to the Nawab Nazim of Bengal; but the Company was henceforth to collect and dispose of the revenues of the three Provinces. This has been called "the turning point in India's conquest." The Nawab was to receive 51 lakhs a year. But when he died, the Company reduced the annuity of his successor to 41 lakhs. And so it has gone with this Prince, and with other Princes; and to-day Indian Princes are unable to leave their native country without the permission of the Government of India.

In St. John's Church, Calcutta, I saw the register of Warren Hasting's marriage with the fair and fascinating Baroness Imhoff. A native took me to the Vestry, demanded backsheesh, and left me alone. There I thought much about the first Governor-General of India, the war with the Rohillas, the murder of Nuncomar, the cruel treatment of the Begums of Oude, and Sheridan's magnificent speech in the House of Commons—he was offered one hundred guineas for the copyright, but had forgotten every word of the speech by the following morning—in which he spoke of Warren

Hastings as "a great delinquent, and the greatest of all those who by rapacity and oppression have brought ruin upon the natives of India and disgrace upon the inhabitants of Great Britain."

In the Reading Room of the Madras Museum is a marble statue of Lord Cornwallis, who succeeded Warren Hastings as Governor-General of India in 1786. The pedestal of the statue shows Lord Cornwallis receiving as hostages the sons of Tippoo Saib, embracing them and assuring them of his fatherly care and protection. Tippoo was a religious fanatic, who stood in the way of the Saib Company. So his treasury was emptied and his kingdom was divided among his enemies. The Parliament of the day declared that "the pursuit of conquest and extension of dominion in India are repugnant to the wish, the honour and the policy of the nation;" but Lord Cornwallis was made a Marquis, and the Company gained many lakhs of rupees and a large extent of territory. I have often stood before that statue, thinking of the dramatic scene made famous by the pen of a great artist; and afterwards I have turned to the history of those days and have read how Tippoo's heart was broken. An English officer wrote at that time:—

"Conquest is the policy of England in India; and the British revenue in India can easily be trebled. The dissensions and revolutions of the native governments will point out the time when it is proper for us to become actors. But the time can never come while Tippoo exists."

In vain Tippoo tried "to remove the dust which has obscured the upright mind of the Governor." He stood in the way; and he was crushed.

I went to India with the conviction that the English had done a great work there by bringing order out of chaos. Setting aside the belief held by so many Christians that the Almighty had sent the English to India "to convert the heathen," I believed, because I had been so taught, and had so read, that the English had found Mahomedans and Hindus fighting together in India, and that if England withdrew to-day from her unselfish task of keeping order, then Indians would fight among themselves until Russia, or some other European Power, took the control of Indian affairs. But historical documents have shewn me that during the years of Mahomedan supremacy in India—roughly speaking from the time when William the Conqueror went to England until the battle of Plassey—less fighting was carried on in India than in Europe. The power of the Mahomedan Emperors waxed and waned, and never touched some parts of India; and during that long period, Mahomedans and Hindus were more homogeneous in India than English and Indian people have ever been, or are to-day. It has been considered politic to write of things in India as England would like them to be; but now that our Indian fellow-subjects are greater students of modern Indian history than Englishmen take the trouble to be, it is wiser to state facts than to spread fancies.

I have sat in the Old Church, in Calcutta, and thought about Lord Wellesley, who, with his brother, Colonel Wellesley (afterwards Duke of Wellington), worshipped there about the year 1800. He persuaded the Indian Rulers to receive English Residents at their Courts, also small bodies of English troops, nominally out of regard for the independence and protection of the States. The Princes of India were afraid to refuse his seemingly kind offers; and soon he went on to ask for concessions of land, instead of money, to pay the soldiers. In the same way he tried to obtain a controlling power over all the governments of the Mahratta nation. And meanwhile he imitated the mode of life of the Indian Rulers, and lived with much pomp and glitter. He began his career in India as Lord Mornington, and became while there a Marquis; but he returned home a disappointed man, because the Saib Company did not appreciate his schemes of conquest. In many ways this "glorious little man" reminds us of Lord Curzon; for history says that he was "constitutionally irritable and impatient, full of courtesy and generosity, but unreasonable and wilful, and with talents that scarcely equalled his ambition."

Lord Cornwallis was asked to return to India; and on arriving there, he wrote :—

"I deprecate the almost frenzy which has seized even some of the heads which I thought the soundest in this country for conquest and victory, as opposed to the interests as well as to the laws of our country."

Soon after this letter was written, Lord Cornwallis died in the Province of Benares; and the country then enjoyed six peaceful, uneventful years under Lord Minto.

Not for nothing did the present Viceroy and Her Excellency Lady Minto appear at a fancy-dress ball in Calcutta wearing the costumes of their predecessors of one hundred years ago! The more closely one studies the six years between the administrations of Lord Cornwallis and Lord Moira, the more clearly one sees a close resemblance between the present Viceroy of India and his ancestor and predecessor of the same name. In temperament, and policy, the Viceroy of today is very like the Governor-General under whose rule India breathed and rested at the beginning of the Nineteenth Century.

Lord Minto was succeeded by Lord Moira; an insolvent earl whose creditors sent an attache-extraordinary to Calcutta to receive his salary every quarter. On arriving in Madras, the new Governor-General said soothing words to the Nawab of the Carnatic, who had been the first ally of the English in India, and who was so closely watched that he could not even hunt without permission. The direct descendant of this Nawab now lives in Madras, where he receives a stipend from the Government. His name is the Prince of Arcot; and he is the head of the Mahomedans in Southern India.

Lord Moira spoke "of the natural irritation of those whom we have scourged with nettles;" and sympathised with the Nawab-Vizier of Oude, who was subjected to petty and prying interference, although he had surrendered one-half of his possessions to the East India Company. But soon after his arrival in India, Lord Moira came under the influence of Colonel Metcalfe, who told him that the British Empire in India had arisen from superiority of British military power, and that its stability rested entirely upon the same foundation. "If this foundation is removed, the fabric will fall to the ground," said Col. Metcalfe. "Whatever delusions may prevail in England regarding the affections of Indians, English power in India depends solely on English military superiority. The number of our troops must be permanently augmented. The existence of British Empire in Asia must ever be dependent on the sword."

Lord Moira spent the greater part of his administration in wars with the Goorkhas and the Mahrattas; and having conquered these peoples, he returned to London as the Marquis of Hastings.

He was succeeded by Lord Amherst.

Afterwards came Lord William Bentinck, of whom it has been said:—

" He was nearer to the *beau ideal* of what a Governor-General ought to be than any man that ever filled the office. There have been several good and several great men in the same position, but there has been none like him. A paramount sense of duty to the people of India and a desire to do them good, inspired all his words and actions."

Lord William Bentinck hated to be looked upon as a jailor, and encouraged private reports from the humblest native in the land. English officials did not like him; and a Circuit Judge, who was asked if he were not related to Lady William, replied:—

"No, unfortunately to the brute himself."

He did not encourage the love of display that seems to seize hold of nearly all English people who go to India; and he set his face against extravagance. He was the first Governor-General who admitted Indians to various branches of the Civil Service; and he prepared the way for a free Indian Press.

After him came Lord Auckland, whose ill-fated policy in Afghanistan sent him home with a bad reputation. Lord Ellenborough followed, with orders from Sir Robert Peel to keep the peace, if possible. But the the next step was the conquest of Scinde; of which a friend wrote to Sir Charles Metcalfe (formerly Col. Metcalfe), "Scinde is a bad scene of insolence and oppression. Coming so soon after Afghanistan, it puts one in mind of a bully who had been kicked in the streets and went home to beat his wife."

Lord Hardinge, the next Governor-General, began the conquest of the Sikhs, which ended in the Koh-i-noor, or Mountain-of-Light, being surrendered to the

Queen of England. This precious stone, which was found in the mines of Golconda, is said to bring ill-luck on those who own it. That it was a precursor of sorrow and war is only too true; but to-day it is almost forgotten, having been thrown into the shade by the magnificent present of South Africa to the King-Emperor.

Finally came Lord Dalhousie, who was Governor-General of India for eight years. Lord Dalhousie did more than anyone else to hasten on the Mutiny, for he annexed many small Indian kingdoms under the plea of "lapse to England." He wrote:—

"I take occasion of recording my strong and deliberate opinion that in the exercise of a wise and sound policy, the British Government is bound not to put aside or neglect such lawful opportunities of securing territory or revenue as may from time to time present themselves, whether they rise from the lapse of subordinate States, by the failure of all heirs of every description, whatsoever, or from the failure of heirs natural where the succession can be sustained only by the sanction of the Government being given to the ceremony of adoption, according to Hindu law."

This policy culminated in the public sale of the Nagpore jewels in October 1855. They were advertised in the Calcutta *Morning Chronicle* as "the largest and most valuable collection ever exhibited in Calcutta;" and their sale was regarded in every zenana and every bazaar as a threat, and a warning.

The incorporation of Jhansi followed; and it will be remembered that the widow of the Rajah of Jhansi, Luckshmi Bai, took to horse during the Mutiny and fell by a random shot while leading her angry followers.

The appropriation of the revenues of Oude was the last act of annexation before the Mutiny.

I pass over here the horrors of the Mutiny, and close this letter with a quotation from the Royal Proclamation of the 1st November 1858.

"Whereas for divers weighty reasons, we have resolved to take upon ourselves the Government of India, heretofore administered in trust for us by the Honourable East India Company, we do by these presents notify and declare that we have taken upon ourselves the said Government, and we hereby call upon all our subjects within the said territories to be faithful, and to bear true allegiance to us, our heirs and successors.

We hereby announce to the native Princes of India, that all treaties made with them by the Honourable East India Company are by us accepted, and will be scrupulously maintained, and we look for the like observance on their part. We desire no extension of our territorial possessions; and while we permit no aggression on our dominions, or our rights to be attempted with impunity, we shall sanction no encroachment on those of others. We shall respect the rights, dignity and honour of native Princes as our own.

We hold ourselves bound to the natives of India by the same obligations of duty which bind us to all our other subjects; and those obligations, by the blessing of Almighty God, we shall faithfully and conscientiously fulfil."

CHAPTER III

Liberation

The Theosophists at Adyar did not afford me much assistance. If I had been a member of their Society, it might have been different; but they held out no helping hand to "an enquirer." They had, in an upper room, it was said, portraits of "Masters," turbans, etc., given to Col. Olcott by "Mahatmas." These things, however, did not excite my curiosity; and in the Oriental Library, pundits kept up a perpetual sing-song that made reading to oneself difficult. The story of a Dutch boy, who, a year or so previously had become a Buddhist priest in Ceylon, interested me. He was a pretty boy, I was told, with a pink-and-white face, yellow hair and innocent blue eyes; and on his arrival at Adyar, he wanted to worship Col. Olcott as a living representation of Buddha.

"Get up, you idiot," the bluff American said to him. "Go home to your parents."

The boy wore the Yellow Robe, and desired to beg his way to Buddha Gaya, where he expected to attain Nirvana; but Mrs. Besant, who, it appears, has suffered much from penniless, religious adumbrants, wrote, or wired :—

"Tell him God can be found under every tree."

I had brought with me to Madras an introduction to an Indian doctor, who held a Government appointment; and he plunged me at once into Vedantism. Many modern Hindus call themselves Vedantists, and say that the whole of Vedantism is contained in the Bagavad Gita, and the Upanishads. Fortunately I had been grounded in Buddhism before landing in India ; and I would advise every English student of Eastern religions to begin with Buddha ; for, in my opinion, modern Vedantism is but Buddhism vitalised by modern thought and modern science, and there is only the difference of a name between Nirvana and Brahman.

A description of this doctor and his mode of living will give an idea of the way in which Hindus of the professional classes live at the present time. His house—a three-storied building, with a gabled roof and verandahs—stands in a suburb of Madras that Hindus have kept for themselves by refusing to let, or sell, houses there to Englishmen, or Eurasians. Poor people hang about the entrance, for the doctor has a large practice and many of his uneducated patients attribute to him superhuman powers. His touch is enough to cure some complaints, they say. Turret staircases lead to his office, and in this room I noticed a large collection of photographs, including the King-Emperor, Indian Deities, Native Princes, and modern Scientists. Further on, in a large drawing-room furnished with many mirrors and sofas and chairs, the doctor may be found, reading "A Life of Saint Theresa", perhaps, or glancing at such a book as "Artic Home in the Vedas." But little does he care about the birth-place of the Aryans, and things of that sort. He is a powerfully-built man, and wears the usual Hindu cloth and over it a silk coat. He is clean-shaven, and he puts on a turban when strangers are in the room. Never does the word "I" come from his lips;

and the only thing that seems to irritate him, is the intrusion of a personal element into the conversation. To the pains and sorrows of his patients he listens with sympathy and patience; but directly any mention is made of personal likes and dislikes, ambitions and achievements, he calls the person " empty-headed"—in other words, the self-conscious person seems to him uninteresting and undeveloped.

"There are three sorts of consciousness known to us," he told me. "simple-consciousness, self-consciousness, and cosmic-consciousness, which Vedantists call liberation. We Hindus are all seeking after the last state of consciousness. Old souls are born in India, new souls in America and Europe. See how old men in England amuse themselves with cards and billiards and golf! We Hindus have not patience for such things—they seem to us absurd, childish."

A Hindu woman is subjected to many restrictions, but these do not debar her from attaining liberation, which is the highest aim of an orthodox Hindu man. In the doctor's house I saw a room dedicated to a female saint, a lady who was his guru for many years. The history of this Brahmin lady throws a light on the inner workings of the Hindu mind; and these are said to be understood by one English woman only, by name Margaret Noble, a lady who lived in India for some years and was known there as "Sister Nevidita." Hindus have told me that no learned scholar of the West,—be he philosopher or Christian Bishop,—not even the High Priestess of Theosophists, Mrs. Besant, has come to the core of the Hindu religion; but Sister Nevidita, who helped to establish a home for sick and dying pilgrims at Benares, and did other charitable acts, is a true Vedantist.

The doctor allowed me to see the Chapel dedicated to the Brahmin lady who attained liberation; and the first thing that I noticed there was a picture of Jesus Christ, by an Indian artist.

Vedantists claim to understand Christ better than Christians do; and explain that He was a supreme case of liberation. Did He not say "The kingdom of Heaven is within you"? "I and my Father are One"?

In Calcutta, I met a Brahmin who told me, in a matter-of-fact way:—

"I have never seen Christ myself; but I have a friend who often sees him, and he tells my friend that he finds many of his followers very trying people."

The way in which the ordinary Christian believes in Jesus Christ seems to Vedantists very crude and ignorant ; but for the character and the life of Christ they have the greatest possible admiration and reverence. They say that He was probably taught by Buddhists in early manhood, some of these people having settled in Asia Minor before His birth ; and in this way they account for the many beautiful Buddhist parables and sayings that are found in the New Testament.

The mystical part of Christ's teachings appeals to the Hindu mind; and "*The Light of the World*" is a favourite picture in modern India.

The doctor has a costly crucifix made of gold and silver, in a glass case; and this has been placed under a picture of Krishna, who is represented as playing on his flute and "drawing all the world after him." Krishna, "the Dark God," is very popular in modern India ; and translations of the Bagavad Gita have made him known to many persons in modern America and modern Europe.

In the centre of the room, a marble statue represented the lady Sanyasin, and I was struck by the blissful expression on her face.

"She looks as if life were a big joke !" I exclaimed.

"That is just what attracted me to her first," the doctor said. "I had been called in to see her brother, and he had died, and at the ceremonies accompanying his death, while all wept, she seemed quite unconcerned. In fact, she laughed, scandalizing her relations and friends.

"Why should I be miserable ?" she asked. "He is here, there, everywhere. He is ever-blissful, ever-free, ever-happy. Why should I cry ?"

Yet he had been her only brother, the companion of her youth, and she had loved him devotedly. Some of her relations thought her mad ; but I studied her carefully, and I found that she had attained liberation."

The doctor then related the story of this lady's life.

The only daughter of a Brahmin, whose duties took him much to a temple, she was surrounded from her birth by religious influences. At an early age, she married a man much older than herself. Her husband died before she was twenty. She had no children, and, being a Hindu, she could not marry again. Outwardly her life, from that time until her death, was spent in an uneventful way ; but her spiritual development was rapid and intense.

Her husband's death made her think constantly and deeply about religious matters; and she became possessed by a great desire to escape from re-births and attain the ever-blissful, ever-free, ever-happy state of union with Brahman. At first, she gave herself up to austerities, and worshipped in temples, and she begged her relations to let her give presents to gods and goddesses. She thought that by going into a forest, far from other people, she might attain her great desire; and her mother promised that after the first year of her widowhood was over, she should visit some secluded spot and there seek for Brahman. She read all the books available on religious subjects, and asked questions of Sanyasins who visited her father's house, and she spent all her spare time on the roof of the dwelling, alone, praying. On the roof she meditated, going there before sunrise, and returning at sunset; and there she worshipped a little lingam, the symbol of Siva, the third person of the Hindu Trinity.

> "In those three Persons the one God was shewn
> Each first in place, each last, not one alone,
> Of Brahma, Vishnu, Siva, each may be,
> First, Second, Third, among the blessed Three."

Sometimes she grew impatient because her prayers were not answered quickly and she made and performed vows, such as travelling a long distance by measuring her length on the ground. Sometimes, after her daily bath, before sunrise, she walked many times round a temple. Every day and all day, when she was not working, she went on the roof of the house, to pray and meditate; and her one prayer was for union with Brahman. During her daily life, she kept her God ever in mind. "Now we will do this, or that, and then, my God, we will return to the roof, to pray and meditate," she said.

After a time, she gave up visiting the temple ; for she realized that God is as much in one place as in another. And then, acting on the advice of a female ascetic, whom she visited sometimes in the jungle, she threw away her little lingam. With her mind ever fixed on

Brahman, praying constantly, and with tears, she fell one day into a trance. When she came to herself, her appetite was gone. From that day until the end of her life, many years afterwards, she eat only "trash," that is a little grain, or rice, or some sort of sweetmeat.

"Do not force me to eat," she said to her mother, who was much alarmed by her long fast. "I am like a cat on the outer wall. If I jump out, I shall be a slave all my life; if I jump in, I shall be free and happy. A critical time has come, I feel this, although I cannot explain it. I beg you to leave me alone."

Shortly afterwards, she became for a time dumb, and lay for days without eating or speaking. When, as last, she got up, her self-consciousness had gone, never to return again. She lived from that time until her death on two, or three, spoonsful of rice, daily, and sometimes she went without food for days together. She bathed every day before dawn, and then returned to her room, and sat there, talking to all who came to ask for advice on spiritual subjects, and astonishing even learned Brahmins by the wisdom that flowed from her lips.

"Who is talking?" she asked sometimes, "I don't know who is speaking. Who is it?"

Of time she was unconscious; living or dying were the same to her. Always joyous, free from all sense of limitation, callous to pain, feeling neither hunger nor thirst, she passed many happy years. Then she closed her eyes, and died. Thousands of Hindus followed her to the grave—Sanyasins are buried, not burnt,—and still her followers assemble by her tomb to pray and meditate. The doctor took me to see the ceremony of "Waving the Lights" in a little chapel consecrated to her memory. There many Hindus had gathered together, and I saw lights waved before her picture, also a distribution of fruits and sweets among the children who were present. And finally I drove to the doctor's country house, where many people were fed with rice and curry, after performing their religious ablutions in a large tank near the entrance.

The devout Hindu looks upon a meal as a sacrament. He eats no animal food. Fish and eggs he does not touch. His food is composed of rice, vegetables, ghee and sweetmeats. Coffee and tea have been introduced into India by Europeans, also tobacco and whisky, and the Englishman's greatest crime, in the eyes of devout Hindus, is eating beef. In Puri, one of sacred places of India, which I will describe in another chapter, it is impossible to obtain beef; and if a cow, or a calf, were killed there by an European, there would be a riot, Hindu widows in Puri live upon food offered to Jagannath; and "Move on, that your shadow may not fall on the food of the god", is said to any Englishman there who looks too curiously into a cooking-shop.

The doctor took me to see a man in Madras who has attained liberation. We drove to a bungalow in a part of the city inhabited largely by missionaries; and I am sure those good people have no idea that a man living in their midst claims to be one with the Deity. A house, surrounded by a garden, and looking exactly like the many missionary houses in the neighbourhood, is the home of some well-to-do Hindus, and one of these gentlemen led us to a cocoanut plantation, where, outside a little hut, sat the Sanyasin. He was about thirty, and he looked, as the doctor said, "plumpy." His body was well-nourished, and he seemed to be in excellent health. On his face was a look of contentment; and he smiled benignly on the people who sat in a circle round him. Some of the visitors were reading, others writing, but the greater number were meditating, and only whispers broke the silence, unless a question was put to the Sanyasin. Each person did puja as he came or went away; and I noticed that the visitors were not ignorant people, but highly-educated Hindus. For half-an-hour I watched the Sanyasin; and unless he answered a question, no muscle of his body seemed to move, and his face retained the same expression. His legs and arms were crossed, and his body was upright, and I was told that he remained in the same position both night and day.

" Does he not lie down to sleep?" I asked.

" No, he is always as you see him now. Sometimes he eats nothing for days together. I have known Sanyasins who lived on one grain of rice a day."

So said the doctor ; and he added :—

" Eating is not necessary when liberation is attained."

The moon rose while we sat under the palm trees, watching the Sanyasin, and its calm light fell on a scene with which the ordinary Englishman would have little patience.

"Why does n't he get up and do some work?" the energetic Englishman would ask. But Hindus claim that Sanyasins work incessantly in a state of consciousness that enables them to help their fellow-men much more than the labour agitator, the Salvation Army blood-and-fire soldier, and the scholarly Bishop can help them; and when I spoke to the doctor about "laziness", he told me the following little story:—

" Once upon a time, a sage was living quietly in a corner of a temple. The Manager of the temple property who was a very pious man, had some regard for the sage, and allowed a certain amount of temple rice to be given to him daily—a very small amount, but enough for his frugal wants. This Manager died, and his successor—a younger man—called the sage a 'lazy do-nothing, old scoundrel,' and stopped the supply of temple rice that had satisfied the few wants of the sage for many years. Yet the sage sat quietly in the corner of the temple, and seemed quite happy and quite satisfied. After two days, the Manager came to 'the lazy do-nothing, old scoundrel', and found him as well and peaceful as before. And the sage said:—

"Will you sit down with me?"

The Manager sat down, but soon he became restless. The sage begged him to keep quiet, but he could not do it. Then he began to understand how difficult it is to sit still and do nothing and he doubled the allowance of temple rice and did not call the sage 'a lazy do-nothing, old scoundrel' any more.

The Sanyasin I visited with the doctor, sat with his eyes open; and when he answered a question, I noticed a shadow flitting across his eyes, just as if a delicate shutter were being drawn aside. I was told that he had received no education in the way of reading, writing and arithmetic, but that he could, nevertheless, answer deep and difficult questions put to him by Vedantists, and that he was able to solve the religious difficulties of the people who went to him for advice and counsel.

"The word Veda," said the doctor, "means divine, unwritten knowledge. The Vedic hymns are supposed to have issued like breath from Brahman. Hindus believe that Brahman still breathes divine knowledge into his devotees, and in this way teaches them more than can be learnt in schools and colleges.".

The doctor was fully convinced that anyone can attain liberation who earnestly desires to do so. A man has but to sit down and food will come, if he sets his heart on Brahman. Thus he told me (not as a fact but an illustration) the story of a young man who sat down on a hill to see if God would feed him. A flood rose, and, as Hindus worship floods, bread was carried to him by the rising waters. Hindus are always willing to feed people who give up the life of the senses and become Sanyasins, because they think that such people are dear to God and near to the Kingdom of Heaven. Any man who truly desires to find God, and seeks Him with tears and prayers, will find Him, the doctor said; and having found Him, will care no more for the things of this world, but will become ever-free, ever-blissful, ever-happy. For such a person there will be no more birth, no more death, for he will become one with God, who is Everlasting Life.

" Into that Everlasting Life we Hindus try to enter," the doctor said. " To do so is the object of our lives."

"There is but one Being, without a second. Nothing really exists but Brahman. Whatever appears to exist separately is mere illusion. And in each man is a spark of Brahman, a spark that can be fanned into a flame by the man himself ; and, the self-conscious sheaths that enclose the ego being thus burnt up, the man knows that he is God, and enters into Life Everlasting."

The doctor had studied the lives of Christian saints, and he remarked that while such people are sometimes in ecstasy and sometimes depressed, the Hindu Sanyasin, after liberation, enters a state of perpetual bliss and peace.

" He functions on another plane," explained the doctor. " Poets, composers, and geniuses of all sorts are sometimes taken out of themselves, as it were, and while in that state receive inspiration. The scientific study of liberation is only now beginning; but Prof. James, and other psychologists are now taking an interest in 'cosmic-consciousness,'—the western name for liberation."

India abounds with lazy vagabonds who put on the robe of a Sanyasin and live by begging. One sees them everywhere, especially near temples, and they are usually dirty and lazy, and have long matted hair, the result of some vow made by their parents before they were born. But the Sanyasin whom the doctor took me to see, bathed daily in a tank near his hut, and wore a clean cloth, and had hair that showed careful attention. He was shaven, and altogether a pleasant object to look at. He did not go to a temple, or worship idols. But idols are helps towards liberation. So many Hindus think. They believe that God is everywhere and in everything, and they worship God under the forms of millions of idols, fearing to leave some part of Him unworshipped. They worship animals, snakes, trees, and stones. Yet the most ignorant Hindu is well aware that such things are but symbols of the Deity, and it is no uncommon thing to see a Hindu woman make an idol of clay, do puja to it, break it in pieces and throw it away. As Christians adore the Holy Eucharist and the Crucifix, so do Hindus worship anything and everything as a representation of Brahman. They see God 'in a thousand forms, in phases, colours, fashions infinite;' and highly-educated Hindus assure me that the worship of idols helps them to fix their mind on the Supreme, who is everywhere and in everything.

CHAPTER IV

ENGLISH PEOPLE IN INDIA

THE ruling community in India may be compared with a number of little light islands set in a dark sea. Some of the islands are larger than others, but all have the same external appearance and internal idiocyncrasies. From Viceroy to shopkeeper, and shopkeeper to Tommy Atkins, each English person in India says to himself:—

" I belong to the conquerors of India. "

The more well-bred and highly-educated the English person happens to be, the less does he show by looks, voice and manner that he is a part of the ruling community; but the fact remains that India was won, and is held, by the sword of England. *The Times* reminded Indians of that fact not long ago ; and no Indian denies it.

During the visit of H. R. H. the Prince of Wales to India, English officers said sometimes :—

" We hold the country for England ; yet H. R. H. makes a fuss of every little Indian Prince, and takes no notice of us. "

These gentlemen forgot, perhaps, that they are paid for their services, while from the Princes of India have been taken both power and influence. However, no amount of politeness shewn to Indian Princes will blind English people to the fact that they are puppets. They know their true position very well; but bow to the inevitable. When the Maharajah of Mysore visited Madras, a Salute was fired, and he was taken for a State drive by the Governor, preceded by a scarlet-clad Body-guard. At the same time a paragraph in an Anglo-Indian newspaper said that his Highness wanted to go to England, but that before doing so, he must ask the permission of the Government of India. The greater the fuss made of Indian Princes, the more do they feel in the velvet glove the hand of steel; and while speaking of the British Raj with due loyalty and respect, many of them are sad at heart. Those who have been educated in England do not mind restrictions so much; but one of the richest and most influential of the Indian Princes has never left India because he will not ask permission of the Government of India to do so.

It is a noticeable fact that Indian Princes are almost the only natives who mix freely with the ruling community in British India. The English people they meet at Viceregal functions and whom they invite to their palaces, are men and women of the world, and consequently free from insular prejudices; besides English people are not afraid to "lose caste" by associating with Indians whom the King's representative treats as his equals. With the exception of the Princes, few Indian gentlemen associate with the ruling community; and English people look with suspicion on a compatriot who goes to the homes of Hindus and Mahomedans.

One great difficulty in the way of social intercourse between English people and Indians is the purdah system. The higher the caste, the stricter the purdah. Indian ladies of the highest rank went to the purdah parties given in honour of H.R.H. the Princess of Wales; but many of these ladies had never left home before and will never do so again.

"But for the purdah system, we should long ago have ceased to be a nation," a Hindu said to me; and he added that Hindu women only became purdah after the Mahomedans went to India.

English ladies, who are accustomed to associate with men, and have so many and such varied interests, seldom trouble to visit zenanas, where views of life are necessarily circumscribed and very domestic. The wives of Government officials, female missionaries, and women doctors are the only English people who go now into zenanas; and even these people often find it difficult to penetrate into the homes of high caste Hindus and Mahomedans of rank. I was told by a Maharani in Calcutta, who is out of purdah, that curiosity has taken English ladies sometimes into zenanas and purdah ladies have not enjoyed such visits.

English Army people, who keep very much to themselves while soldiering a place in India, have been described by Mr. Kipling with all the accuracy of genius; and if a passion on the part of some officers' wives for shooting big game *a la* Lady Minto, and a good deal of snobbishness in the behaviour of young officers belonging to certain crack regiments be added to his *Plain Tales from the Hills*, a very good idea can be gained of Army life in India to-day. I was told the story of a young Eurasian officer who shot himself owing to English exclusiveness ; and stories about Lord Kitchener met me at every turn. He has grown very stout in India; and has lost there a good deal of the ferocious appearance made familiar by English photographs. But he is looked upon as the guiding hand of the Viceroy's Council, and people say "That's Kitchener" when deportations and other unpleasant things occur. An amusing instance of his masterly ways took place during the Bengal Railway Strike, when trains were held up and passengers were starved, belated, and put to great inconvenience. At Arkonam, the headquarters of the strikers, while the platform was crowded with hungry, weary passengers, an unexpected Express dashed by the station.

It carried Lord Kitchener's baggage!

His Majesty's Civil Service ranks first in India, although the Army considers itself all-important; and at Christmas Anglo-Indian papers announce in the Presidencies that 'His Excellency the Governor requests the honour of the presence of His Majesty's Civil, Military, Naval and Ecclesiastical Services and the ladies of their families at Government House.' Such invitations are very elastic; and it is amusing to see how many ladies belong to the families of Civil Servants and Clergymen at Christmas! The cost of such balls and receptions is great, for they are carried out in a lavish style; and if Governors and Viceroys did not practise domestic economies they must return home bankrupt.

Lady Curzon, who had money to throw away, was extremely popular in India; and during her fatal illness, prayers for her recovery went up in many Hindu temples and Mahomedan mosques. I was assured by Indians at Delhi, that she wept every night during the great Durbar that hurt the feelings of so many Indian Princes; and that the knowledge of her husband's unpopularity in India hastened her untimely end. A favourite story about her in Anglo-Indian circles concerns a titled Middy, who asked for a dance at a Viceregal ball, saying :—

"A bet is on it,"

"Then let us sit it out," said Lady Curzon.

To Lady Curzon we owe, to a great extent, the preservation of so many historical ruins and art treasures that were falling into decay when her brilliant husband went to India. Her compatriots flocked to see a daughter of the Republic living in Viceregal splendour, and revelled in the remains of Mogul magnificence. I was told that an American lady went twelve times to the Palace during a visit to Delhi, and lavished rupees on attendants who allowed her to sit on the throne of Mahomedan Emperors. Americans are a source of considerable income during the cool season in India; and in the time of Lord Curzon's administration, they made India a place of pilgrimage. Their intense admiration for Hindu and Mahomedan antiquities influenced Lord Curzon, it is said, to undertake the work by which he is gratefully remembered to-day, namely the restoration of mosques and burial grounds, palaces and forts, and the annotation, with cosmopolitan impartiality, of places where people who made history lived and died.

Lady Minto had no easy place to fill when she followed the beautiful Lady Curzon as leader of Society at Simla, and in Calcutta. She seems to have a dual personality, for Lady Minto in a short dress of native cloth, with a gun, is a very different person from the stately and charming Lady Minto at a Viceregal function. Her strict surveillance of household expenditure sets an excellent example to aspiring memsahibs, and her rose-leaf-like daughters are fond of horses, dancing and tennis. Lord Minto bears the character of being 'extremely conscientious.' Anglo-Indians he does not trouble about; but the natives of India are his constant care. He is sometimes called 'the red-tape Governor', because he keeps so closely within his own province. He is neither much liked nor much disliked; while Hindus say of Lord Curzon:—

"He was our greatest friend, because, by the Partition of Bengal, he roused all our dormant antipathy for England."

In discussing Lord Minto's successor, Lord MacDonnell is sometimes mentioned. But many people say that if Sir Arthur Lawley carried heavy enough guns for the position, he would be the most suitable man to succeed Lord Minto, because he knows something about India and its peoples, and he has a genius for governing. He went to Madras during a financial crisis, known locally as 'the Arbuthnot scandal;' and by his firm and just behaviour during that trying business, he won the confidence of both Hindus and Mahomedans. He has just the mixture of firmness and kindness that Indians appreciate; and he carries out the instructions given by Queen Victoria to his predecessor :—

"Be gentle and kind to the people of India."

Lady Lawley has, also, the gift of pleasing; and her unassuming manner and simple mode of living set a valuable example in a country where most English people vie with one another in the number of servants they can keep, and the smartness of their equipages and liveries, and often spend much more than they can afford on display and amusements.

Sir George Clarke has still his spurs to win in India. But he is much liked in the Bombay Presidency ; and at the time of his sad bereavement, prayers for Lady Clarke were offered up by Christians, Parsis, Hindus and Mahomedans. His brilliant daughter, Miss Violet Clarke, took her mother's place during the late Lady Clarke's absence in England, and carried out the Viceregal programme to the entire satisfaction of all concerned. She is much liked by Indian ladies, visiting them in their own homes and being present at their weddings. Rumours are afloat that, owing to stress of work and other things, the Viceroy and the Governors of the Presidencies wish to return to England. But no sane person pays any attention to such floating talk, for they are all men of the same stamp, and they carry out unflinchingly the policy of Lord Morley. Never was a Secretary of State more faithfully represented in India than at the present time; and, whatever may happen, the men at the helm can be trusted to do their duty as Englishmen and Imperialists.

The absence of party politics in India gives to Anglo,-Indian Society an exclusiveness that is not found in any self-governing part of the Empire. No aspiring hotel-keeper, or shopkeeper can force himself and his wife and family into Society in India by adding M. P. to his name, or becoming a Premier or a Minister. Trade is rigidly excluded from Anglo-Indian Society, unless the trader is the head of a large shipping firm, or an important import and export business. Money cannot buy a place in Anglo-Indian Society for the wealthy tradesman; but the poorest lieutenant can write his name in the Visitors Book at any Government House, and obtain invitations to the Viceroy's parties. I met in India a retired Colonel, and he told me that some of his sons are making a bare living in professions and others are earning high salaries in shops, and the former may go to Government House and the Club and the latter may not. Caste is very strong in Anglo-Indian Society, although its rules for eating and marrying are not made of cast iron.

The English communities in India closely resemble one another, in spite of the fact that they are scattered over an area as large as Europe with Russia left out. Imagine an English community in Paris, another in Berlin, and a third in Rome; and then you will have an idea of the distances between the English communities in Calcutta, Bombay and Madras.

Add to these large communities many small ones, and fancy that they are placed in towns and villages dotted over Europe, and remember that each little community is an exact copy of the communities in Paris, Berlin and Rome; and then you will understand how things are in the many little English centres scattered over India.

Again, imagine an English community in India a rose, and pick it to pieces. Pull out the yellow centre, which is made up of the Governor and the Englishmen who hold the highest official positions. Tear off the leaves circling the middle of the flower and lay aside the generals, colonels, majors and others who hold India for England. Go on to the open leaves, which represent clergymen, lawyers, bankers, doctors, editors, professors, planters and merchants; and come finally to the outside petals which are made up of shop-keepers, canvassers, mine and mill managers, hotel-keepers, clerks, actors, teachers, engineers, railway officials, mounted constables, soldiers and others.

The caste system must be catching, for there is in an English community in India a strong tendency to fall into groups. Thus the Indian Medical Service is a close body, and the English people who belong to it are satisfied to know the other members of the I. M. S. and no outsiders. Lawyers associate with lawyers, missionaries with missionaries, engineers with engineers, shopkeepers with shopkeepers. Enter one of these little groups, and you will find in it much social rivalry, egotism and debt.

"Some Englishmen in India remind me of cocoanut trees," remarked a Hindu Zemindar.

"Why?" I asked.

"Because when cocoanuts are over-manured, they bleed," he said.

I have often thought that if English people in India would talk more freely with Indians, then they might become wiser men; for Hindus bring to bear on the English character the wisdom of the ages. They see our virtues—dogged perseverence, pluck, grit, punctuality and truthfulness; but they see our faults too, and we think, perhaps, because they are so often silent in our presence, that they think us generous!—that they think us unselfish!

It is only polite to bear in mind that Indians cannot criticise us without giving offence in high quarters. They must listen to the hasty conclusions of English tourists—conclusions often very offensive to them—and say nothing. As to this book, I, for one, will not add to the mass of ill-will and misunderstanding caused by English people who do not, or will not, think about the feelings, beliefs and, perhaps, prejudices of their Indian fellow-subjects.

Cheap labour is, no doubt, at the root of the "side" put on by so many uneducated English people in India. The station-master's wife, for instance, fancies herself 'a lady' because, instead of cooking the meals, minding the children and washing the clothes, as she was wont to do in Egland, she can find coolies in India eager to do this work for five or six rupees a months. Carriages are, also, very cheap in India, five pounds a month paying for a carriage with two servants in livery. The highly-paid engineer, imported from England, may be seen driving in India with his dusty boots on the seat in front of him, his arms stretched wide apart and his head lying on a cushion. In an European shop, it is diverting to watch the "chartered hands" behind the counters; for they will not lift down a box, or make up a parcel, but call a native to do these things and to carry the purchases to the entrance of the shop, where a peon puts them into the carriage. I happened to be staying for few days in a house adjoining a bungalow hired by a large English shop-manager for his "chartered hands". Each young man there had a "boy' to clean his bicycle and boots and run his errands. Little boys picked up balls that fell out-of-court at tennis and obsequious servants brought ice and cigarettes. "Boy"! "Boy"! was the call from early morning until the shop-sahibs went to sleep; and young men, who in England would have cleaned their own boots or have had them cleaned by a maid-of-all-work, looked languidly on, while "boys" brushed their clothes and laced their shoes.

I asked a Hindu gentleman, who had been to London, what had astonished him most there; and he answered, without hesitation :—

"The maid-of-all-work."

The fact that English artizans and English labourers cannot work in the Indian climate, or compete with the exceedingly low rate of wages given in the overcrowded Indian labour market, seems to throw English working-people out-of-gear in India. "Chartered hands' go there on high salaries, and for a fixed time, and they find themselves in small English communities where all hard manual work is done by Indians of the lowest castes. 'Chartered hands' have generally had a Board School education, and possess little culture and no breeding; and they fancy that they have suddenly become 'ladies and gentlemen,' because they can, for the first time in their lives, perhaps, afford to keep servants. And Indians too often think that all working-people in England are well-off and independent, because the only English working-people they see in India have enough money to dress well, eat well, drink well, and keep coolies to say 'sab' and 'mem'. It is impossible to convey to the mind of an Indian (unless he has been in London) the misery and suffering of very poor English people during an English winter,—misery and suffering unknown and impossible in a hot country.

One of the greatest difficulties in the so-called 'Indian Question' is the climate, because it places in false positions many very common English people —people who cannot understand, or appreciate, Eastern culture, Eastern religions, and Eastern habits, and who are apt to think that everything they do themselves must be admirable because it is British.

Some English employers try to put down snobbishness; and a Calcutta merchant told me that, in his opinion, a book ought to be written on *How to Treat the People of India* and given to every young Englishman at Port Said. "I allow no difference to be made between my chartered hands and my native *employes*" he said; "and if my English boys give themselves airs, I tell then to pack their portmanteaus." The same merchant said that each year English merchants find it harder to make money in India. 'We have to live in a certain style or drop out,' he told me.

'House-keeping becomes daily more expensive; and a memsahib who looks after her own house, loses caste. So we have to let servants rob us. That's the way with native servants.' A Hindu gentleman told me that in his opinion English people made a great mistake about servants, in the first instance, 'We Hindus," he said 'are most particular about the castes we employ to cook our food and wait on us; but English people will take servants of the lowest castes into their kitchens and let them wait at table.'

"Only the lowest castes will break eggs and kill chickens," I suggested.

"That is so," he said.

Certainly the native servants employed by English people are generally thieves and liars; and as servants are the only Indians with whom most English people come closely in contact, it is no unusual thing to hear the vast population of India judged by people whose counterparts can be found only in the slums of European cities. Outside missionary circles, the Christian native servant is considered to be, if possible, a more accomplished liar and thief than the Hindu cook, or dressing-boy. An amusing instance of ready conversion happened to myself shortly after my arrival in India. A peon came to me in trouble about his soul.

"Me be heathen, me be Christian, as you tell me", he said. I advised him to go to the nearest missionary; and he departed, looking crestfallen and disappointed. Afterwards I heard that he had visited other English people with the same story, and on Christmas Day he had presented a lime to the zealous sahibs who had advised him to adopt Christianity. Presenting a lime is considered a mark of respect in Southern India, and to refuse it is an insult; so on Christmas Day servants, postmen, dhobies and others offer limes to English people and then wait about for a present.

"Did I not give you a lime?" asks the dhobie, when his bill is paid and he receives no *backsheesh*.

CHAPTER V

THE EURASIAN COMMUNITY

THE Eurasians are a very unhappy community in India. Long before the conquest of India by England, Portuguese, French, and English people had intermarried and intermixed with Hindus and Mahomedans; and many years previous to the Mutiny an Eurasian community had come into existence. To-day, in Calcutta, and in every other Anglo-Indian centre, large numbers of Eurasians may be seen; and throughout India, in offices and places of business, Eurasians are employed.

The first Eurasian that I met was working in a large Post Office, of which I will not give the name because of all people in this world Eurasians are the most touchy and the quickest to take offence.

While I was waiting for a missing money order, this gentleman asked :—

" Don't you find that Hindus and Mahomedans are very anxious to get in with *us* "?

The speaker was very dark, and I had taken him for a Hindu in English dress, a native Christian, perhaps; and I answered :—

"I am very anxious to become acquianted with Hindus and Mahomedans."

He looked at me with suspicion, waited a minute, and then abruptly asked:—

"How do Indian post offices compare with post offices in England?"

"My experience of Indian post offices is slight," I said; "but I notice that some of them are very slow in the delivery of money sent by telegram, or through the post. I have just left a young Englishman who has lost his boat through the delay of a money order, and I imagine that men in Indian post offices, who are paid monthly, have little idea of the importance attached by English people to be a rapid and businesslike delivery of money."

I was invited to attend a concert at an Anglo-Indian club, the members of which were Eurasians only; and I was told by the secretary:—

"Natives are so anxious to get in with *us*."

And he offered to enroll me as a member of the club, although he knew that no member of it could go to the English club of the place or dine with the English Resident.

Personally I should like Eurasians very much better if they did not insist on being wholly English ; and if they did not irritate Indians by the things they say about Hindus and Mahomedans.

"We ought to have martial law in India" Eurasians have often said in my presence. "Lord Morley and Lord Minto are sowing the wind and will reap the whirlwind. They should blow natives connected with bombs and outrages from the mouths of cannon. Hanging is too good for the wretches. They are all tarred with the same brush."

Eurasians like to call themselves 'the domiciled community,' and this annoys English people born in India, and I have noticed that new-comers exhibit much less antagonism towards Eurasians than is shewn by domiciled English persons. The latter smart under the fact that English people are brought to

India and placed over their heads, and there certainly is a prejudice against what is called in India 'a native-born Englishman.'

Often I have read in the advertisement columns of Anglo-Indian newspapers, 'No Eurasian need apply;' and under the heading of 'Situations Wanted', I have seen the signature 'Pure European.' Sometimes 'A fair Eurasian' is asked for; and I have noticed that the children of Eurasian parents vary very much in colour, one child being whiter than an English boy or girl, perhaps, and the rest of the family very dark, or nearly black. Some Eurasian girls are pretty, large dark eyes being set in an olive complexion and curly black hair; but the ordinary, poor Eurasian has a down-trodden expression, and is careless about hair and clothes, shoes and socks. The worst cases of poverty in Indian cities are found among Eurasians who want to live in English style and have only enough money to live as poor Hindus and Mahomedans do; and in Indian cities I have seen 'Homes for Eurasians' in which betel was allowed, also the hucca, and the food supplied was only rice and curry. But to ask a poor Eurasian to sit on the floor, or to speak to such a person in any language but English, would be considered an unpardonable insult; and very few Eurasians can be engaged as household servants, because they will not associate with Indian servants, but want separate rooms and separate food. I think I am right in saying that there is not a single Eurasian in India who does not profess to belong to the Christian religion; and the words Indians dislike most—'native' and 'heathen'—are constantly on the lips of Eurasians. I met several Eurasian missionaries, and, although darker than many Hindus and Mahomedans, they spoke as if no drop of 'heathen' blood were in their veins. Of the English missionaries they seemed to be very jealous, saying that such missionaries are no longer wanted in India, and the work of 'converting the heathen' ought to be left to people born in the country. The high salaries paid to English missionaries, and the trips home that such missionaries consider necessary for their health, the Eurasian missionaries seem to think needless expenses; and they call the English missionaries 'stuck up' and 'stand off,' and consequently 'un-Christlike.' I have seen letters on this subject in Anglo-Indian papers, and these endorsed the statements made to me by Eurasian missionaries trained in India by the London Missionary Societies.

Now that fares to England are cheap, an Englishman rarely chooses a wife in India. Almost every steamer brings brides—sometimes five or six—and it is no unusual thing to hear the banns of an Englishman published in an Anglo-Indian Church, and people asked to say whether there be any just cause or impediment why so-and-so 'Bachelor of this Parish' shall not be united in Holy Matrimony with 'Dash-Dash, Spinster, now on the High Seas'? Some friend of the bridegroom, or the wife of the clergyman of the parish, receives the bride on her arrival, and shortly afterwards she is married. She brings her trousseau, and also sometimes the wedding-cake, and the Captain, or an Officer of the steamer on which she had made the voyage, is often asked to give her away. I am now speaking of girls who come out to marry young Englishmen in shops and offices, young men with high salaries and good prospects. Such brides are placed in the care of the Captain, or the

Stewardess; and after a merry voyage become memsahibs in villas and boarding-houses, and quickly fall into the routine of the little circles to which their husbands belong.

When the voyage to England took months instead of days, Englishmen in India looked for wives in the country; and stories are still told of the portionless girls who were then sent to India to find husbands, and who, if unsuccessful, were shipped back to England as 'returned empties'. In those days the Government went into the matrimonial business, and in a suburb of an Indian city, I saw in a large compound, a magnificent house where the illegitimate daughters of English Officers who were killed during the Mutiny, had been received, educated, and, if possible, married. Balls were given to which young Englishmen were invited; and everything that the Government of the day could do to find husbands for its protegees was done. At the present time, only two or three very old ladies inhabit this place; and when they die, it will lapse to the Government.

The most noticeable thing about the ordinary Eurasian is that he claims to be wholly English, Scotch, Portuguese, French, or Dutch, and ignores altogether his Indian ancestry. Yet his colour, eyes and hair remind one more of the Indian than the European, and if he did not insist so much on being altogether of Europe, it would, I believe, be better for him. His attitude towards Hindus and Mahomedans makes him much disliked by Indians; and I have often asked myself:—

"If England left India, what would become of Eurasians?"

It is usual to blame the English alone for the large and ever-increasing Eurasian community in India. But this is a mistake. The English deserve three-quarters of the blame, but not all of it. Unmarried English soldiers are the chief cause of the Eurasian element in India, female native Camp followers being allowed—many people say 'encouraged'—by the Military Authorities. On this subject I shall have more to say later on. I will only remark here that although Hindu women of the Four Great Castes are carefully guarded in India, Panchama, or Fifth Caste women, are treated as beasts of burden. I am told that originally all Hindus belonged to the Four Great Castes, and that the so-called Panchama Caste came into existence because some Hindus neglected their duties, committed sins, and thereby fell out of the Four Great Castes. Among the Panchamas the missionaries work ; and in the Fifth Caste only have missionaries made many converts. From the Pancham Caste English people take most of their servants ; and the bitterest pang of the Eurasian is that chiefly Panchama women have succumbed to the English. Indians—both Hindus and Mahomedans—do not hesitate to throw this fact in the faces of Eurasians; and hence, to a great extent, the exceeding bitterness of the Eurasian towards the Indian.

Mahomedan women, of all classes, have been carefully secluded ever since the English went to India; and in the Eurasian community we do not find the traits of Persia and Arabia, but the features of Hindus.

I talked one day with an English missionary about Eurasians, and he said:—

"We cannot be too kind, or too considerate, in matters where Eurasians are concerned; for we brought them here, and in language, religion and education, they are more akin to us than to the natives of India. Their ancestors have been, in many cases, respectably married for generations. They are often well-educated, and intelligent, and they are more loyal than the English themselves in all matters in which England is concerned. I confess that they are hyper-sensitive, exacting, jealous; but we must try to put ourselves in their places and remember that the sins of the fathers have been visited upon the children from generation to generation."

It is impossible not to feel sorry for some of the well-bred, highly-educated Eurasian families with whom English people refuse to associate; more especially when the girls have been educated in England. On returning home, such girls naturally desire to enter local social circles; and the hard and fast line drawn between Eurasians and English people in Anglo-Indian Society is felt by them very keenly.

I met in an Indian city two charming English ladies, and the younger one remarked:—

"I hate India!"

"Why, I thought India was 'the ladies paradise' said an old gentleman, who happened to be present.

I was told that the elder lady had met a wealthy Eurasian in England, and had married him there, and on coming to India, she had found herself outside English Society. And the younger lady—her sister—could not go into local Society, although all the appendages of a good social position were at her command—a large house, horses, carriages, and plenty of servants. Consequently the girl hated India, and was counting the days until she could return to England.

In places where English communities are small, peculiarly painful cases of English exclusiveness came to my notice. For instance, in one place, an Eurasian lawyer had the entire English practice, but he could not go to the English club, and his wife and daughters lived in London. I met several well-to-do Eurasians whose families were in England; and these gentlemen told me that they must remain grass-widowers until their daughters were married. The Eurasian lawyer already mentioned had no friends among the highly-educated Hindus and wealthy Mahomedans in the place where he had lived all his life; and he made his religion (Christianity) an excuse for keeping apart from the people of India. His only associates were English missionaries; and his hobby was gardening.

In a little Dutch cemetery in India, I have seen on tombstones the surnames of Eurasian families; and such Portuguese names as 'Perera' and 'De Silva' are common among these people. English Christian names—such as Peter, Joseph, Martin, etc.,—have been used as surnames by Eurasians for generations, and 'de' is a favourite appendage to an Eurasian name, spelt with a capital D. Many Eurasians, in fact most, I think, are Roman Catholics; and as Roman Catholic priests are scattered all over India, Eurasians have ample opportunities for carrying on the religion of their adventurous forefathers.

CHAPTER VI

Hindu Lawyers

I met in India several Hindu lawyers.

One of these gentlemen invited me to his house, and introduced me to his wife, who received me in a drawing-room furnished in English style. I was told that the children of the family were taught by an Eurasian governess and that a pundit instructed them in religion and Sanskrit. The little girls drove out in an open carriage and the boys attended a Government College. The whole family had an English varnish; but an early visit found the lawyer sitting on the verandah of his house with no covering but a waistcloth, and although he drove to the High Court in a brougham, his coat was thrown off directly he returned home. He sat on the floor while eating his food, and used his fingers instead of a knife and fork, and he was waited upon by his wife, who had her meals afterwards with the little girls. The eldest boy was treated by his mother and sisters as a superior being, because he was almost a man. This lawyer had read the latest English books, and was quite up-to-date in European politics, and his children devoured English novels. Each Christmas he took his wife to a reception and a ball at Government House, and every summer he accompanied her to a Viceregal garden-party at the same place; but these were (so he told me) the only occasions on which he met English people in a social way. He worked with English lawyers at the Law Courts, but he did not associate with these Englishmen after office hours, and he was not a member of the Club. No English lady had called on his wife. His children had no English associates. The whole family spoke English perfectly; but of English manners and customs they had little experience.

In this house I felt, rather than heard, the undercurrent of dislike for England that is so strong everywhere to-day among Hindus. I avoided, as far as possible, all mention of things English; but I told the lawyer that, in country places, children came out of huts and threw stones at me and boys drove cattle in my way, if they had the opportunity, and a dozen other things that showed anti-English feeling. He smiled; and when I declined invitations to dinner at his house—knowing that he and his family would not eat with a *feringhi*—he smiled again.

"Our social customs are made of cast iron," he said.

A younger lawyer, to whom I was introduced, asked many questions about English manners and customs.

"I should like to call on English people," he told me "but I am afraid of making mistakes. If an English lady comes into the room, ought I to stand up? Our ladies wait on us—my mother would not allow me to fetch a glass of water for myself—; but at Government House I see English gentlemen fetching ices and cups of tea for ladies, and His Excellency the Governor will allow any lady to precede him into a room."

"You see," he continued, "my dress is English (he wore a white shirt, without a collar or a tie, over a white cloth, and patent leather shoes without socks); and I would like to associate with English people. All that we Indians ask is that the English will settle down here with us. But the English do not treat us as equals. If I visit an Englishman, and his wife comes into the room, I am never sure that I shall be introduced. I notice that whenever I go to see an Englishman, his wife wants something in the room! With our ladies, it is different. They are never anywhere about, if, by any chance, an Englishman comes to visit us."

"Does your wife know any English ladies?" I asked.

"No," he replied. "She speaks very little English. I have sometimes thought," he went on to say, "that English ladies, who live here like princesses, and keep so many servants, might learn the languages of India. Our ladies have scarcely a spare minute, unless their husbands are princes. Our ladies must look after the house, see that the children attend to their religious duties and take their ceremonial baths, watch the servants, superintend the cooking, wait on their lords, and say their prayers. Very few of our girls have time to learn English properly. So why do not English ladies, who have so much leisure, learn the languages of India?"

"Of which there are five hundred and thirty-nine," I suggested.

"That is true," he said. "But each large district in India has its own language; and the wife of an English official seldom goes to more than one part of India. Some of the grandest English ladies in Calcutta have never been to Bombay, and I am told that very grand English ladies in Bombay; have not seen Madras."

"All Mahomedans speak Hindustani," I remarked.

"Yes," he said, "but Mahomedans form only one-fifth of the population of India, and nearly all the other people in this country are Hindus. And we have a common language—a language English people seldom take the trouble to learn—I mean Sanskrit."

"Sanskrit is the most scientific, and, also, the most difficult language in the world," I said.

"Well, it can be learnt—even by women—even by European women," said the lawyer. And he instanced Mrs. Schrader, the wife of a German scholar in India, who is said to have learnt Sanskrit in a year and a half.

There was a pause in the conversation; for I wondered what he would like to say next.

"Have you ever been in the kitchen of an hotel for Englishmen in India?" he asked, after a short silence.

"No, never." I replied.

"Well then don't."

"Why?"

"Because you would never touch food in India again. The native cooks employed are of the lowest castes, and often they are covered with vermin, I don't wonder that English people fall ill in India. I have seen cooks in hotel-kitchens suffering from small-pox, and dropping vermin on the dishes. You can form no idea of the filth of an hotel-kitchen unless you have been inside it."

I remembered that an English lady had told me the same things—a lady whose husband rented a bungalow in the compound of an hotel managed by a native, and frequented by English people; and I remembered, too, the look of horror that had passed over the face of a 'twice born' hotel proprietor when I asked :—'Do you eat the food cooked in your hotel?'

"Why do English ladies leave everything to their servants?" the lawyer asked. "If our ladies did not look after our homes, things would be with us as they are in English houses. By buying bad ghee, servants make a fortune out of English people. We, who know that ghee is the essence of meat, are most particular about ghee. We buy ghee in the country, and keep it for months. English people let their servants buy ghee in any dirty boutique, or bazaar."

"Is that so?" I asked, remembering that a memsahib had told me that the most expensive part of housekeeping in India is the daily supply of ghee for the kitchen.

I waited again for the lawyer to speak ; and presently he said, in a confidential voice:—

" What astonishes me most about English people in India is the way the sexes dance together. I don't think dancing immoral myself, but I confess I don't understand it. At Government House, I see an A.D.C. introduce a gentleman to a lady, and immediately afterwards the gentleman takes the lady in his arms and dances with her. What happens afterwards? Does she introduce him to her father and brothers? Does he marry her?"

Flirting Indians find even harder to understand than dancing. This western fashion of passing the time is taken by them quite seriously ; and they look on with surprise and disapproval when an English grass-widow has half-a-dozen men in her train, and an unmarried Englishman makes love to every pretty English girl he sees. Their social customs render such things impossible. Parents arrange marriages, and the contracting parties do not meet before the wedding-day, unless they happen to have been betrothed as children. 'The English have no heart', Indians say. And they ask how English people can leave their relations, homes and country to come to India? Flirting means want-of-heart, if nothing worse, they argue ; and an Englishwoman, armed with coquetry, seems to them a female devil.

An unmarried, middle-aged Indian is unknown in India ; and English bachelors, like the Commander-in-Chief, would not be flattered if they knew the construction that is put upon their celibacy by their Indian fellow-subjects. Younger English bachelors are pitied by Indians.

"Poor fellow! His father is stingy and wont let him share the paternal home and take a wife there" I was told, when I mentioned a well-known, gay young English bachelor in Bombay.

"But do not your womenfolk quarrel?" I asked a wealthy Hindu, who had described to me his home-life.

"O, we manage to run them all along together," he replied. "And then, you know, it is not very difficult, because a Hindu woman worships her husband and obeys him as if he were a god."

"But is n't it a nuisance to be worshipped?" I queried.

"O, its habit" he said. "We are accustomed to it. I know a man who wont let his wife worship him, so she gets up in the dark and walks round his bed, and having worshipped him, she goes to sleep again."

The lawyer who asked so many questions about English manners and customs, kindly took me to see another Hindu lawyer; and I sat for a time in a room that closely resembled the study of a professional man in London. But here and there I noticed little feminine touches that one does not find in the room of an Englishman. Dainty vases of flowers, pincushions, and bright antimacassars showed that the ladies of the house came into the room when no visitor was there. On the walls were pictures cut out of illustrated London papers—professional beauties and actresses—and these had been embellished with real hair and real eyebrows. And with these English ladies were Hindu goddesses, dressed in silks and satins and ornamented with pearls and spangles.

When the lawyer went to fetch a book, I caught a glimpse of his home, for he left the door half-open, and I could see into a large, empty hall, with a glass roof. Many doors opened into this hall, and I was told that the doors communicated with rooms occupied by the ladies of the house and the children. Not a sound was to be heard, and all the doors remained closed; but the lawyer told me that the hall was the *rendez-vous* of the family, and that there betrothals and marriages took place, and there the ladies passed the greater part of their secluded lives.

The lawyer did not smoke, or drink whisky; but he offered me the Hindu equivalent for these things—*pan*. The offer of *pan* is an introduction while travelling in India, and after *pan* has been handed round conversation becomes general. Cigars and cigarettes are now, however, very generally used in India, even little boys of five and six buying Swadeshi cigarettes in bazaars, and coolies, who earn only three or four rupees a month, buying cigarettes at half-an-anna the packet.

Indians are fond of sweet toddy, drawn from the flowers of the cocoanut; and Hindus of the lowest caste drink large quantities of fermented toddy, which goes by the name of arrack. The usual Anglo-Indian drink is whisky and soda; and it is a much disputed point whether whisky should be drunk in India. In a malarial district, whisky certainly keeps off fever; and a small quantity of whisky helps digestion in a country where little exercise can be taken by English people. Unfortunately many English people—both men and women—do not know when to stop taking whisky; and whisky is called, in consequence, by Hindus and Mahomedans 'the white man's curse'.

Mrs. Besant stated in one of her lectures a short time ago that the higher castes in India are now copying English people in the way of whisky-drinking; and that teachers should tell Indian children to abstain from every form of alcoholic liquor 'which is poison to all bodies, and more especially to Eastern.' I do not know on what foundation Mrs. Besant bases her statements. So far, at any rate, intoxication is not an Indian vice. The religion of Mahomed strictly forbids stimulants; but it does not forbid opium. Buddha made abstinence from intoxicating liquour one of his precepts; but he said nothing about *bhang*. And with Hindus it is difficult to draw a line between sweet toddy and arrack.

It has been found that after five years in India, an Englishman becomes irritable, or falls into the *laissez faire, laissez aller* habits of Indians. At such a time whisky is often a great temptation, for the constitution, in nine cases out of ten, has been undermined by fever or weakened through dysentery. History says that the Mahomedans were energetic and purposeful when they went to India nine hundred years ago. Now they are, if possible, less vigorous than the Hindus themselves.

"See how extravagantly England rules India!" Indians have said to me sometimes. "An Englishman is sent here for five years. The first year is spent in learning some Indian language. The next three years are passed in gaining sufficient knowledge of the country to carry on the work. And after one year of useful employment, the Englishman goes home."

But such extravagance is absolutely necessary as things are carried on in India to-day; and if Lord Curzon had not been made an exception to the rule, his reputation would not have suffered, perhaps. Ill-health spoilt Lord Curzon's last years in India; and made him give voice to words that still rankle in the Indian heart:—

"All Bengalis are liars!" for instance.

While writing about Hindu lawyers, I will briefly describe a missionary meeting that I attended in a large Indian city. I had often been to Exeter Hall, and I had attended many missionary meetings in England and given coin for 'the conversion of the heathen in India,' and when I walked up the steps of a hall to attend an Indian missionary meeting, I expected not-at-all to find tables so completely turned as was the case on that occasion, and I commend the account of that meeting to the English and American Missionary Societies that have spent and are spending vast sums of money in India.

I found the large hall closely packed with Hindu students. The principal speaker was a Sinhalese lawyer, who was returning to Ceylon after a year spent in America and in England. The Chair was taken by a Hindu Judge. Both the speaker and the Chairman were garlanded; and then the proceedings commenced.

The Sinhalese lawyer spoke in English, and his speech lasted for an hour. He told the students that in England, and in America, men had come to him, asking:—

"Can you tell us anything about God?"

"Can you tell us anything about the soul?"

"In the West," he said "religion has lost its hold on educated men. Some men there try to drown thought in pleasure, others seek to stifle it by mental work. But sickness comes to all and so does death. People in the West are turning to the East and asking for bread to feed their souls.

Shall we give them a stone?

No. Let young men in India study the great truths of the Vedanta, and stand forth as God-taught men. English missionaries have scoffed at the ancient religion of India; but now men in the West are finding out that Vedantism is the most scientific religion in the world."

Then he told the students how he had 'found God.'

The Judge spoke too; and he begged the students to remember that while modern science is a very useful thing to know, God—and only God—will satisfy the soul.

CHAPTER VII

A Native State

None can form true ideas concerning India without residing for a time in one of the Indian principalities—Hyderabad, by preference, because it is much the largest and most important of the native protected States.

In area Hyderabad is as large as Italy; and in order to understand the true position of Hyderabad to-day, let us imagine King Edward as ruler of Europe, with Russia left out, and having under his suzerainty the Kingdom of Italy.

"Of the varying degrees of sovereign power which the Native States in India possess, the maximum is held by his Highness the Nizam, who is in the enjoyment of the marked Sovereign rights of coinage, dating from the time of the Mutiny when his Highness' monies ceased to bear the inscription of the Delhi Emperors; of taxation; the infliction of Capital punishment; and the bestowal of honorific titles on his own subjects. In practice the vagueness that clouds the theoretical status of his Highness disappears. As in autonomous States generally, the administration is subject to, but not controlled by the Supreme Government, which possesses over the ruling prince powers of suspension and deposition. At Hyderabad these powers are represented by the Resident, acting as the channel of communication for the expression of the views of the Supreme Government, for Native States have not the right of exchanging embassies with the Suzerain or one another. Representing the Governor-General in Council, the Resident has jurisdiction over military Cantonments and the lines of communication. In Councils his voice is preponderant, but not predominant ; and in all internal legislation and administration the Nizam is independent. British Municipal law does not run in his dominions, although its enactments are respected as regulations ; provincial governors have no supervision over the State, nor their Courts any jurisdiction. So far is theory carried out that extradition treaties nominally exist between the two powers, seeing that to permit the introduction of British judicial systems would be tantamount to annexation. Yet practically the administration is coming to be, in the main, the same as that in the provinces, with the distinction that there are no European officials appointed by the Crown, as in Egypt, to administer the posts, for the Resident's powers are ex-territorial. In default of that privilege the British Government exercises the right of sanction and veto over all important proceedings in the State."

I happened to be in Hyderabad during a change of Residents; and it was conducted very simply. The out-going Resident met the new Resident at the railway station of Hyderabad City—it is a little unfortunate that the country and its capital have the same name—and they drove together to the Residency. A Salute of 13 guns was fired when they left the station, and a similar Salute announced that they had arrived at their destination. They drove in an open carriage, and were accompanied by a small mounted escort. Afterwards, the out-going Resident motored to Secunderabad and took train there for Calcutta. Hyderabad possesses no Anglo-Indian newspaper; so the arrival and the departure of the Residents was not announced in British India until some days later. The vernacular papers stated the changes; but English people in Hyderabad seldom look at a paper written in Urdu. The guns were heard only by a few persons; and the majority of English residents read the announcement in the Bombay papers two or three days after the changes had taken place.

At the entrance to the Residency are imposing stone towers, with loopholes, and it is a fortified building, large enough to hold all the Europeans and English people residing in Hyderabad in case of a disturbance. The Coat-of-Arms of the East India Company may still be seen on the portico of the massive house, and, of course, the Union Jack floats over the roof when the Resident is in Hyderabad City. A Visitors Book is kept in the hall, and in it names are written between the hours of 12 A.M., and 3 P.M.,—a terribly hot part of the day during the summer months!

At the Residency English people meet his Highness the Nizam on certain occasions. and he is then very gracious. English ladies are said to astonish him not a little by airing their Urdu in conversation and talking to him on domestic subjects.

The Resident occupies a very difficult position; and a Resident possessing both discretion and tact is needed at Hyderabad, for the Nizam is a shy person, and a poet. I was told by anti-English Hindus in Hyderabad. 'Most of the English Residents have been bad men; and if they have refused bribes, then their wives have taken them.' Such Hindus call the Nizam 'a mere puppet,' 'a man afraid to offend the English Resident,' 'an unfortunate prince with all the virtues and the talents of a great ruler, but one so overshadowed by the Government of India that he cannot act independently.'

Everyone who meets the Nizam is impressed with the fact that his Highness Asaf Jah, Muzader-ul-Mumalik, Nizam-ud-Dowla, Nawab Mir Mahabub Ali Khan Bahardur, Fatçh Jung is no ordinary person. He reminds people of Sultan Mahomed Ayde, to whom the Dekannees gave the title of Aristotle. Feristah says of this ruler: 'He was a prince of sweet disposition, humane, virtuous and just. He had a penetrating judgment in all affairs of the State. He spoke fluently Persian and Arabic. When prosperous events occurred, he was not intoxicated with joy, nor immersed in grief at the attacks of misfortune. In his reign the poets of Arabia and Persia resorted to Deccan and were benefited by the gracious flow of the stream of liberality. After his accession to the throne he would wear no other than plain white. He frequently observed that Kings are only the trustees of the divine riches, and that to expend more upon themselves than necessity requires is a breach of trust. He established schools for orphans, and gave monthly salaries to the blind in his dominions, and he gave alms to poor pilgrims.'

The present Nizam of Hyderabad is extremely wealthy and also extremely generous. Everyone has heard of his actions during the floods that washed away last year a large portion of his capital. The only fault found with him by Hyderabadis is that he does not show himself enough to his devoted subjects; but during the great tribulation of 1908, he gathered his people together like a father, sympathizing and weeping with them. He is very small, and very shy, but he has much princely dignity in public, and in private life he is said to be kind-hearted and sympathetic. He is fond of horses and dogs, and devoted to the royal sport of hunting wild animals. He writes poetry, and encourages poets and literary men in his dominions, and he makes no difference between Mahomedans, Hindus and Christians, giving large sums of money to mosques, temples and churches. His mutton-chop whiskers are copied by Hyderabadis, and every second man whom one sees in the streets of Hyderabad City resembles him in appearance. He has many palaces; but he lives generally in a palace that covers a square mile in the heart of his capital, and there he is said to have 500 wives and 5,000 servants.

It is well to bear in mind that many of the present princes of India date from the time when the French and the English were struggling to found an empire in Asia, that is to say, from the middle of the Eighteenth Century. The present Nizam is a direct descendant of Asaf Jah, the first Nizam of Hyderabad, a nobleman, statesman and general who held office at the Court of Delhi and went to Hyderabad as a Lieutenant of the Mogul Emperor and died there in 1748. His tomb may be seen at Roaza, where the Emperor Aurungzeb is buried.

I know of no more interesting place to visit in the picturesque dominions of the Premier Prince of India than Roaza,—especially at the present time when so many things that happened in Bengal during the reign of Aurungzeb are being repeated. The tomb of the great Emperor is not carved and has no inscription of any kind. It stands about half a foot from a stone platform, and is covered ordinarily with a white cloth, but richly draped on festival occasions. The simplicity of the tomb is said to be accounted for by the Emperor's request that his funeral expenses should be entirely defrayed by caps he had quilted and sold, and by the fact that the money received for these things did not exceed ten rupees. The proceeds of the copies of the Koran, made by himself, in leisure moments, were eighty rupees, and these monies were given to the poor, after his death. He died on the 4th of March 1707, in the fifty-fourth year of his reign and the eighty-ninth year of his life, after performing his morning prayers and repeating the Creed. His last words were, 'Carry this creature of dust to the nearest burial place and lay him in the earth with no needless coffin.'

From letters written to his sons before his death, I give the following brief extracts:—

"I came a stranger into this world and a stranger I depart. I know nothing of myself, what I am, or for what I am destined. The instant that passed in power has left only sorrow behind. . . . I had a patron in my own dwelling (conscience), but his glorious light was unseen by my dimmed sight. Life is not lasting, there is no vestige of departed breath, and all hopes from futurity are lost. I brought nothing into this world, and except the infirmities of man carry nothing out. Come what may, I have launched my vessel to the waves . . . . The Begum (a favourite daughter) seems afflicted, but God is the only Judge of hearts. The foolish thoughts of women produce nothing but discomfort. The domestics, and courtiers, however deceitful, must not yet be ill-treated. It is necessary to gain your views by gentleness and art. Extend your feet no longer than your skirt . . . . I am going. No man has seen the departure of his own soul, but I see that mine is departing. Farewell! Farewell! Farewell!"

It is impossible to be too enthusiastic about the scenery of Hyderabad; which reminds people of Italy, Hungary, and other parts of Southern Europe. The country is not overrun by western tourists, and one is not met at every turn by guides demanding '*back-sheesh*.' The caves of Ellora, Ajunta and Aurangabad are well known; but the greater part of Hyderabad is untouched by the globe-trotter, and the visitor may wander undisturbed among the ruins of Hindu dynasties that preceded Mahomedan and Christian conquerors in India.

Lady Burton gives a very interesting description of Hyderabad in 'The Life of Sir Richard Burton.' Things have not changed much in the Nizam's dominions since Sir Richard and Lady Burton were there in 1875, and the following description might have been written yesterday. Lady Burton says:—

" An hour before reaching Hyderabed (Deccan) all nature changes to a strange formation which reminded us of the Karso at Trieste, only on an exaggerated scale. An outcrop of huge granite boulders, which is wild nature, but looks as if arranged by art, forms shapes like an ancient town with battlements and castles, and covers a radius of thirty miles round the city like natural defences .... Early the following morning we went out on elephants to see the town. We went through the city unarmed and without guides. I mention this because everyone knows what a bad name Hyderabad has. Everything is on the feudal system. You meet brown nobles riding with troops of retainers, carrying the arms and wearing the uniform of their chief. The houses are flat, like those of Damascus, the town is clean, the streets are broad and spanned by arches whose bold simplicity is very startling. The

Nizam's City palace, at least a mile long, is carved with delicate tracery, and many a mosque, like lacework, rises here and there. But the cachet of all is size, boldness, simplicity .... There are two parties in India on a certain question—the treatment of the native. One is all for keeping him down and treating him harshly; the other condemns this and would place him on an equality. Neither party actually mixes freely with the native, and the native says:—

"The English are just, but they are not kind." Great Streets run north and south, and nearly bisect the City. Every respectable man is armed with a gun. 'Of course, you had a large escort,' friends said, when we returned to Bombay. We had nothing of the kind, nothing but a single mahaut. But it is not easy to dispose of prejudices. Murray has said that Hyderabad is one of the filthiest cities in India. I tell you it is one of the cleanest. All that I can say is, that so far from 'insult and personal injury,' we were most pleasantly received by what Bevar quotes as 'the most disorderly, turbulent and ferocious set of ruffians within the limits of India.' I can only say that of all the visits paid to various parts of India, it is the one that has left the most lasting, the most happy, and the most romantic impression on my memory."

Guide-books still give to Hyderabad a bad name, and advise tourists to stop at Secunderabad—the English military station in the Nizam's dominions, about six miles from his capital—and to drive over to Hyderabad or to go there on an elephant. Writers of Guide-books apparently do not care for beautiful scenery, and judge places by hotel comforts. The hotels in Hyderabad could be improved, no doubt; but long may they continue in their present condition, if by so doing they help to keep away western tourists. In no city in India do cultured English and Indian people meet so pleasantly as in Hyderabad; for the Private Secretary of the Prime Minister is 'at home' once a fortnight, and at his house English visitors and English residents are introduced to the nobility of the Nizam's dominions, men with eastern culture, learning and refinement, and manners that are now called 'old world' in Europe.

Everyone who visits Hyderabad goes to see the ruins of Golconda, about six miles away from the capital. Marco Polo wrote that the kings of Golconda possessed 'all the treasures of the world,' and 'all the wealth of Golconda' has been a conjuration ever since he made that extravagant statement. The Koh-i-noor was found in a Golconda mine in 1650; and history tells us that the Hindu Kings who built the first Golconda Fort were some of the wealthiest Kings that the world has ever seen. Golconda is now, however, a little hackneyed. The tombs of the Golconda Kings are used by well-to-do Hydrabadis as country residencies during the hot weather; and, consequently, brass pots and silver plates are very much in evidence. I was received at Golconda by an Arab gentleman, who offered me *pan* and spices; and while he was doing the honours of the tombs, I felt glad that Lord Curzon put a stop to tomb-dwelling in British India.

The view from the summit of the Fort is, of course, magnificent. Rocks and boulders seem to speak of some superhuman race that lived in the adjacent country before 'The Lion of God' (Hyderabad) was founded. In the clear, amber-colored air are seen royal palaces, shining lakes, graceful mosques, sombre tombs with bulbous roofs and the castellated dwellings of armed nobles. The eye travels over a wide, open country,—country yellow and orange during the hot weather, but green, blue and purple after the monsoon has broken. Mahomedans in bright-coloured coats and gay turbans, and little boys dressed in silk and tinsel move about ; and along the highways stroll lordly elephants, with gorgeous trappings.

I was not surprised to hear that H. R. H. the Princess of Wales enjoyed her visit to Hyderabad very much.

"She looked as happy and light-hearted as a young girl", I was told by a non-purdah Indian lady.

"And H. R. H. the Prince of Wales, what did you think of him? " I asked.

" He has a great sense of humour " the Indian lady replied, " and he has, at times, a smile that is positively wicked."

CHAPTER VIII

HYDERABAD (DECCAN)

In Hyderabad our thoughts turn to the condition of India when the Mahomedans went wealth-hunting all over the country in the name of the Prophet—when an old Mahomedan historian wrote, after a city had been set on fire by the invaders, 'Everyone threw himself with his wife and children upon the flames, and departed to hell. Those who escaped the flames were killed by the sword.'

India was at that time divided into many small kingdoms; and the Hindu rulers warred among themselves. To-day, Indians who talk about national life and call themselves 'nationalists,' often forget that such ideas were made possible by Mahomedan and Christian conquerors, who broke down and afterwards joined together the possessions of many small and insignificant Hindu kings. The Caste system tends towards the disintegration of a country, and by integration alone can a country become strong and independent. The Mahomedans worked in the direction of integration, and the English continued the work; and now some Hindus talk as if India had been a nation before Mahomedans and Christians set foot in the country. The cruelties perpetrated by Mahomedans, while they made their religion an excuse for robbing Hindus, are forgotten to-day; but we read that a

Mahomedan General put out the eyes of Hindu prisoners by 'cutting them from their sockets with a razor like slices of melon;' and that the shooting of Hindu prisoners into flames, in cages discharged by machinery, was a pastime for Mahomedan soldiers in the fifteenth and sixteenth centuries. At that time, however, it is only fair to remember, the Inquisition was doing just as bad, and perhaps worse things in Europe; and the Portuguese were perpetrating in India most cruel acts and introducing the Inquisition into Goa.

Of course, I know that Mahomedans would not do such terrible things in these enlightened days; but while speaking of the bomb outrages in Bengal, a Mahomedan in Hyderabad said to me:—

"Lord Minto is weak. He should cut off a hand and a foot of each man and boy connected with bombs. That would very quickly put a stop to outrages for the future."

In this book I speak only of the things I have seen and the words I have heard, unless I quote history; and I must repeat that, in my opinion, Mahomedans and Hindus have not mixed in India. They have come much closer together than English people and Indians have done; but more than one leading Mahomedan in India has said to me:—

"If the English left India, then we should be top dog again."

That Mahomedans and Hindus should become one nation is the pious desire of every Hindu reformer; but the ideals and aspirations of Mahomedans are of a different character. All over the world to-day Mahomedans are uniting; and—as I said before—India is for Mahomedans now a piece in a game of chess—a castle, a knight, a king, or a pawn.

Mahomedans are a comparatively small community in India, and it is to their advantage to 'keep in' with the English; but a Mahomedan in Hyderabad said to me, very frankly: 'If there were as many of us in India as there are Hindus, then we should give England, no doubt, quite as much trouble as Hindus are giving now.'

To set Mahomedans against Hindus, and *vice versa*, is said by Hindus to have been a part of Lord Curzon's ill-fated policy in India; but I prefer to believe that he meant to mark his administration by perfect justice and that he failed to do so because the climate was too much for his delicate constitution.

Hyderabad City is called 'the Constantinople of the East,' because the Nizam is the head of Islam in India. This fact gives him a unique position, and power apart from his princely influence. To Hyderabad City flock devout Mahomedans, for it is their Sacred city. The Nizam is for them the living representation of the Prophet. When, occasionally, he shows himself on a gigantic elephant, or in a yellow motor with a golden shield in front, they think of Allah and Mahomed. The enthusiasm, love and devotion inspired by the Nizam is largely due to the fact that if anything happened to the Sultan in Europe, then his Highness might become the head of Islam throughout the world.

The Nizam is said to attend to business 'when the spirit moves him' to do so. But his Government gives satisfaction to his subjects, for he is a Ruler who knows how to choose his Ministers and whom to place in authority. The ancestors of the present Prime Minister of Hyderabad, his Excellency Maharajah Kishen Prasad Bahadur, went from Delhi to Hyderabad with the first Nizam-ul-Mulk (Lord Regulator of the State);

and England has no firmer friend in India than the Hindu Prime Minister of Hyderabad. The man of paramount importance in Hyderabad is, no doubt, the Parsi Private Secretary of the Prime Minister, Nawab Faradoonji Jamshedji, who has lived through three changes of Government and cannot resign because the Nizam refuses to accept his resignation. He, too, is a lover of England, his heart having been won for Albion by an English lady in Hyderabad who was to him mother, friend and councillor, and to whose picture, hanging in his sanctum, he says still 'good night' and 'good morning.'

The Government of Hyderabad consists of two Councils—the Cabinet Council which is composed of the Prime Minister, the Minister in charge of the troops, and Departmental Ministers; and the Legislative Council, in which official and non-official Members are presided over by the Prime Minister, or his representative. There is a special Court dress for all Hyderabadis and all Hyderabadis wear a special turban. The Salutation for the Nizam is 21 Salaams, and for the Prime Minister (from this Salutation a few are exempted) 19 Salaams; and to see the nobles falling into line on a State occasion, and salaaming, all at once, is a pretty sight.

Mahomedans in the capital of Hyderabad and other cities in the Nizam's dominions are often highly educated; but Hindus, who make up the bulk of the population, are as ignorant in Hyderabad as they are in British India. Her Royal Highness the Princess of Wales interested herself in female education during her visit to Hyderabad; and the result is a very successful zenana school on modern lines, with an up-to-date head-mistress, who was educated in an English College.

Things move slowly in Hyderabad ; but fast enough to satisfy Hyderabadis, who are extremely Conservative. Their copper coinage would have puzzled Euclid ; and the Nizam's Post Office will open any letter with an Imperial stamp on the envelope and return it promptly through the Dead Letter Office!

English is spoken by all educated Mahomedans and Hindus in Hyderabad City; and the table arrangements in wealthy houses there are almost entirely English. Afternoon tea is a favourite meal ; and if the mistress of the house is out of purdah, she will then appear in the drawing-room and sit beside her husband while he fills the tea cups. I met in Hyderabad the first Mahomedan lady who broke purdah in Madras; and she told me that her carriage was then pelted with stones and sticks by Mahomedan men and boys. Things have not altered much in India as regards breaking purdah ; for the wife of a well-known Maharajah, who broke purdah two years ago, is still afraid of being poisoned by bigoted relations and makes her cook taste each dish in her presence before she touches it. In Hyderabad almost all Mahomedan ladies are purdah ; and the ambition of every working-man there is to shut up his wife and daughters and hang curtains before the windows of his house, for he thinks that by doing these things he will rise in the social scale, he will become 'a gentleman.'

In Hyderabad education is still a privilege ; and in Hyderabad there is no glut in the intellectual market. In Hyderabad peasants are slightly poorer than in British India. There enormous wealth is seen side by side with grinding poverty. Yet there is in Hyderabad little discontent. Why? In Hyderabad the Prime Minister is a Hindu, and the Private Secretary of the

Prime Minister is a Parsi. Mahomedans have from the time of Akbar placed Hindus in prominent positions; and history tells us that Hindus have served Mahomedans faithfully. Englishmen do not trust Indians; consequently the most important, and the best-paid billets are held by themselves. And the consequence is what? Jealousy. Discontent. Bitterness.

The Nizam's Army, which is the largest armed force in the service of an Indian Prince, includes Arabs, Rohillas, Afghans, Sikhs, Rajputs, Beluchis, Turks and other nationalities. The Arab Cavalry, the African Cavalry Guards and the Golconda Regiment have a strange and picturesque appearance; and none should leave Hyderabad without seeing the famous Myseram Regiment, named after Monsieur Raymond, the Frenchman who commanded the Nizam of Hyderabad's Army while the French and the English were struggling for supremacy in India. Myseram is a native corruption of 'Monsieur Raymond', and the Myseram Regiment still venerates the man of whom Colonel Malleson wrote. 'No European of mark who preceded him, no European who followed him in India ever succeeded in gaining to such an extent the love, the admiration and the esteem of the natives of the country.' A fair is held still at Monsieur Raymond's tomb on the anniversary of his death, salutes are then fired by the Irregular troops, and stories of the 15,000 soldiers he commanded are recited. Sir Khurshed Jah's Amazon Guards wear the uniform and carry the muskets of Monsieur Raymond's original troops, and are a quaint reminder of the days when the scales of power and influence in India dipped toward France.

Sad to relate, Hyderabad has suffered much from European adventurers, from the time when 'King

Palmer, arrived there with a Begum of Oude as his wife to the present day. I went to see the monument of 'King Palmer' in an old cemetery at the back of St. George's Church; and afterwards I attended the evening Service. It happened to be the Sunday following the Nizam's birthday; and I heard his Highness prayed for with the King Emperor, the Queen Empress, the Prince and Princess of Wales, and the Viceroy of India. And the clergyman said in his sermon:—

"Long live the Nizam whose birthday we have just been celebrating! We live under a Mahomedan Ruler; but he is just, good and generous. Long live the Nizam!"

Englishmen who are in the Nizam's Public Service speak enthusiastically of his justice, kindness and generosity; and an English lady, who has lived in Hyderabad for many years, said to me, while speaking about the troubles in Bengal:—

"English people from all over India must come here if there is any disturbance. They will be quite safe in Hyderabad."

"Our faithful ally" is a title the Nizam has inherited; for as everyone knows, the Governor of Bombay wrote to the English Resident in Hyderabad during the Mutiny:—

"If the Nizam goes, all goes."

The Nizam's Government kept the Mutiny from spreading to Southern India, and suffered much anxiety, for the Nizam was then an officer of the Court of Delhi. The fall of Delhi was known to Mahomedans in Hyderabad three days before the English there heard about it; and the documents of those days prove that by siding with the English, the Nizam and his

Government risked not only their positions, but also their lives.

I had an opportunity to talk with an important Member of the present Nizam's Government when I was at Hyderabad; and I told him that while English people in Hyderabad loudly praise the Nizam, Mahomedans and Hindus seem to think that England wants to encroach.

"The Nizam's Government have no such fear," he said. "But people here cannot forget and forgive Berar."

"Lord Curzon again!" I interrupted.

He smiled.

"Lord Minto is everything that can be desired," he went on to say. "Of course very much depends on the sort of man chosen to represent the Government of India here—I mean the British Resident. Some Residents have meant well, but have interfered too much."

I suggested that a visit to England from 'our faithful ally' would be a great event. But he was silent; and as I had been told why his Highness will not leave India, I said no more. We went on to speak of Lady Maud Warrender, who is very popular in India, Miss Violet Clarke, and Mrs. Sarojini Naidu, the Hyderabad poetess.

Many wealthy Hyderabad nobles have small armed forces, and these add not a little to the dangers and the intrigues that may surround a Nizam of less ability than the present very popular Ruler of Hyderabad. The Nizam's son and successor has not yet received from the Dominant Power the recognition that Hyderabadis consider to be his due; and they point out that while the sons of various petty Indian Princes are styled Princes, this title is denied to the Heir Apparent of Hyderabad.

"Only the sons of Kings can be Princes," Lord Curzon is reported to have said when he visited the Nizam.

His Highness has a private railway station, and he shows himself very rarely to his subjects. So mystery gathers round his movements. He is said to consult a woman who resembles the anchorites of by-gone days in England—many of the things one sees in Hyderabad savour of the Middle Ages—and this old, dirty, witch-like person can be seen by any visitor. She possesses rare powers of divinition and premonstration; and the wealthiest and most influential Hyderabad nobles go to her in times of perplexity and trouble.

It is generally believed that Hindus are greater mystics and wonder-workers than Mahomedans ; but among the Suffis will be found, I think, men who surpass Hindu yogis in some respects. Thus I was told in Hyderabad about a Suffi who could dissolve his body and put it together again. The story ran like this. A very old Suffi, who could not leave his room without assistance, promised to prove to some eminent men in Hyderabad that his body could disappear from the eyes of beholders and be found in quite another place. Several of these gentlemen arranged to remain in his room while others waited in the place where he said that his body would be found after he vanished from sight. His body grew faint and disappeared; and immediately afterwards he was seen in the place where he had promised to appear—and then he was found to be in a state of ecstasy.

Not long afterwards he died; and before passing away, he said to my friend :—

"After I am gone, you will notice a strange, strong scent in your house. You will not be able to see me ; but in this way I will make you aware of my presence."

A few days after the Suffi's death, the wife of my friend, to whom nothing had been said about the experiment, exclaimed :—

"What a strange scent there is in the house !"

Others noticed a peculiar odour, which lasted for a short time and then passed away.

My friend explained to me the processes used by the Suffi ; and these corresponded with the methods of Hindu yogis, namely, sealing the senses, controlling the breath, deep meditation, concentration of the mind, etc.

"Have you tried these things yourself ?" I asked.

"Yes" he replied. "But I found them too fascinating. I have a wife and a large family. I have duties to perform ; and people who practise these things find the life of the senses cumbersome and irksome and lose patience with it."

Another thing said about the Nizam is that he takes opium. To some extent this may be true, perhaps, for opium is given in small quantities as a medicine to people in Hyderabad when they reach the age of forty. Opium is said to strengthen the constitution and to prolong life. Mahomedan women take a great deal of opium, I am told ; and as they live longer than their sisters in the West, the effect of opium may be to lengthen the human span, as well as to make it pleasanter for people who never touch alcohol and have no other means than narcotics whereby to escape from the self-consciousness that is 'the glory and the scourge of the world' at present.

I chanced to be in Hyderabad during the month of weddings—May ; and even at Chudderghat, where English people live, marriage festivities went on both day and night. Sometimes a wedding in Hyderabad spreads over a fortnight ; and occasionally a Hyderabadi is ruined for the remainder of his days by the marriage of an only son, or a favourite daughter. A wedding took place in the house of my next-door neighbour, a Mahomedan holding a Government position; and I was told, 'O, its nothing much, only the wedding of a poor relation in the house !' The festivities lasted three days and three nights ; and one morning, at about four o'clock, I was suddenly awakened—English people generally sleep out of doors during the hot weather in northern India—by blazing torches and clashing music. I sprang up, and I saw the sky filled with many-coloured fireworks. The bridegroom, aged eighteen, was going to the house of his child-bride, wearing a red mantle ornamented with silver and gold spangles, and riding on a white horse.

The following evening, shortly after dark, he came back again, riding on the same horse, but dressed in a long red coat and a fez, and carrying a sword. Behind him, in a palanquin, covered with a crimson shawl, was the little bride ; and in the procession walked many friends of the family, also servants who whirled innumerable firesticks. On arriving at home, the bridegroom dismounted, and took a key from his pocket ; and I was told that he had carried the little bride to the palanquin, and had locked her in there, as a sign of marital authority, and that, owing to the great heat, she would probably be carried into the zenana at the back of the house in a state of semi-consciousness. During three days processions of gifts, accompanied by drums and flutes, took place, coolies bearing on their heads large trays, covered with gorgeous cloths. In British India such marriage ceremonies are now shorn of their former splendour; but in Hyderabad few changes have taken place since the Mahomedans settled there in the time of Aurungzeb.

The quaintest wedding that I saw in Hyderabad was a procession formed to take a Hindu bridegroom of six and a Hindu bride of four for an airing after the marriage ceremony. The married pair sat opposite one another on a large piece of coloured wood; and were carried on the shoulders of men with the help of large bamboo sticks. They looked like babes in the wood, being almost entirely hidden by flowers and leaves. They prattled merrily, and seemed to be delighted with their smart clothes. I was told that they were legally married, but would live in their own homes for many years to come, and only meet occasionally in order 'to get to know one another.' It was the prettiest sight in the world to see those gorgeously-dressed babies enjoying their honeymoon in the cool of the evening! Some dozens of men were in the marriage procession; and passers-by smiled and blessed the little husband and the tiny wife perched on the wooden tray.

CHAPTER IX.

THE MOST BEAUTIFUL VIEW IN INDIA

CONVENTION has made Indian seaside places of no account among Anglo-Indians; yet the Bay of Bengal offers health-giving breezes to all who will take advantage of them and many pale-faced English children might gather roses for their cheeks at Waltair, a seaside place half-way between Madras and Calcutta. Waltair was formerly a military station; but now the houses built for the officers of British regiments are the country residences of maharajahs, rajahs and their families. A very small English community resides at Waltair; and the English centre there is a pretty little Club, built on a hill. The solitary English hotel is some miles away from the sea; and the few English officials, whose duty it is to live in Waltair, have perched their white bungalows on hills far from sparkling waves and golden sand. Waltair is a very pretty place; yet English people do not visit it. No enterprising person would build a boarding-house at Waltair; and an English visitor must choose between the hotel, far from the sea, and Eurasian boarding-houses lying at the foot of the hills, at Vizinagapatam, two miles distant.

Waltair has a long sea-side drive, and a band-stand where in days gone-by military music enlivened the beach. Now a melancholy indifference characterises the English people whose duty it is to make Waltair a place of residence; and only at the Club, on the hill, can be found laughter and merriment. There the men have built for themselves a card-room in the garden, where, safe from the intrusion of wives and daughters, they can play bridge and grumble at the native and the climate. Ladies have the run of the Club, and meet there to gossip, read English papers, and arrange little dances. A store enables the memsahibs to their shopping on the premises; and a library is kept stocked with the latest novels. A little polo, a little dancing, a little tennis are indulged in by sahibs and memsahibs; and as railway travelling is cheap in India, sahibs and memsahibs run up to Calcutta at Christmas for balls and race meetings.

Surprisingly few English tourists go to the Chilka Lake, which lies just outside the Madras Presidency, in Orissa. Yet this inland sea is one of the beauty spots of India. A long, sandy ridge, in places not more than 200 yards wide, separates the Chilka Lake from the Bay of Bengal; and a single, narrow mouth, cut through the sandy ridge, connects it with the sea. The Rajah of Kalikota has a house on an island in the middle of the lake; and Lord Curzon was heard to exclaim, when he was there:—

"I think the view from this place is the most beautiful in India!"

The lake spreads over an expanse of water 44 miles long ; and the average depth is from 3 to 5 feet, and scarcely anywhere exceeds 6 feet. The narrow strip that connects the lake with the sea keeps the water salt from December to June; and during the rainy season, the sea-water is driven out and the Chilka becomes a fresh-water lake. It is pear-shaped, and bounded on the south and the west by hills that project into the water and not the surface with little rocky islands.

One of these places, called Breakfast Island, has a story little known in India and probably altogether forgotten in England.

In the palmy days of the Sahib Company, a Collector, named Mr. Snodgrass, built for himself on the banks of the Chilka Lake, at Rambha, a beautiful residence, which he furnished regardless of expense. Horses and elephants filled his stables and he lived like a Nawab. He had many visitors, although in those days people travelled by sea from Calcutta to Puri, and from Madras to Ganjam; and he lavished hospitality on every Englishman who found his way to Rambha. Opposite the residence of Mr. Snodgrass, two miles from the bank of the lake, lay a small island, about fifteen feet square. This place went by the name of Breakfast Island; and there Mr. Snodgrass built an office, consisting. of one room, with a conical pillar at the top, to which hung a lamp. He called the office 'the light-house,' and said it was necessary to have a place where he could work without fear of distraction, or interruption. To Breakfast Island the office books were removed ; and there Mr. Snodgrass carried on his business. Meanwhile the Sahib Company's representatives in Madras found out that the revenues collected from the Ganjam District were not at all satisfactory and heard of the princely style in which their representative was living ; and they informed Mr. Snodgrass, by letter, that the management of the Ganjam District was not at all satisfactory. Mr. Snodgrass put the letter in his waste-paper basket.

Afterwards came an order that he should send his books to Madras ; and to this he sent an evasive reply, knowing that the ports of Puri and Ganjam were inaccessible in the rainy weather, and that many miles lay between him and the representatives of the Sahib Company. So things went on for two years; and then the authorities decided to send a small body of soldiers to Rambha to take over the Collectorate and bring Mr. Snodgrass and his books to Madras. Mr. Snodgrass knew that it would take the soldiers six months to march along the Trunk Road to Rambha, and he had scouts out to warn him of their arrival, and when the detachment was about a week's journey from Breakfast Island, he ordered men to put all the office books and papers into a boat. Midway between Breakfast Island and the shore a plug came out, and the boat sank to the bottom of the lake. The boatmen swam ashore, but the books and papers were lost, or spoilt. When the soldiers arrived, Mr. Snodgrass explained the mysterious plug to the officer in command, and expressed regret for the accident; but he was taken to Madras, found guilty of employing the revenues of the Company for his own private use, and dismissed the service without a pension. That, however, was not the end of Mr. Snodgrass. He went to London; and there, in rags and bare-footed, he swept a crossing in front of the Sahib Company's Office in Leadenhall Street. Daily the pompous, wealthy Directors had to pass their former servant, who had been reduced by the Sahib Company to this humiliating position. Public opinion, or pity, made them call a meeting, at which it was decided that Mr. Snodgrass had been sufficiently punished, and that he should receive a pension for the rest of his days. The following morning, a carriage drove up to the Company's office; and a fashionably-dressed gentleman alighted. It was Mr. Snodgrass, who had called to thank the Company for giving him the trump card. Shortly afterwards he was run over by a cab and killed. His house at Rambha is now the property of the Rajah of Kalikota.

A few 'travellers-bungalows' are found along the shores of the Chilka Lake; and these places are fairly comfortable, because a good many European sportsmen use them during the shooting season, also a few Englishmen from Calcutta. Black buck and other varieties of deer are common on the shore, and larger game can be had among the hills. The lake abounds with all kinds of fish, prawns and crabs; and the angler can spend happy, peaceful days in a beautiful canal which connects the lake with Ganjam. But the man who cannot live on fish and game must take with him all else that he may require; for fishermen and ryots are the only people residing on the banks of the Chilka to-day. The enterprising Bengal Nagpur Railway is now doing its best to make the Chilka Lake a popular resort for tourists; and as yachting, shooting, fishing and swimming can be carried on there, no doubt before long hotels and boarding-houses will spoil this beautiful inland sea. Now, little girls wearing a single fig leaf, and little boys as nature made them, come to stare at English visitors; fish is caught in primitive canoes by men who think a waist cloth sufficient covering; and picturesque native sportsmen bring game to the 'travellers-bungalows,' where the Government charges a rupee a day for a room, without attendance.

All over India, the tourist finds 'travellers-bungalows' provided by the Government. These places vary very much in size and comfort. Sometimes the caretaker is a good cook, and will supply meals at an extra charge of two or three rupees a day; but it is wisest to take a servant who understands something about cooking while visiting places off the beaten track. Bedding is never provided in India, and a rezai, sheets, pillows and a blanket form an important part of a traveller's baggage. Only leathèr seats are found in first-class railway carriages; and the chief duty of a servant on a train is to make up and put away his master's bedding.

While writing about travelling in India, I will say something on the vexed question of English people and Indians occupying the same compartments. If the ordinary Englishman had his own way, carriages would be reserved for first and second-class English passengers only. As it is, unless a whole compartment is paid for, an Englishman cannot be sure that a Hindu, or a Mahomedan, will not occupy a neighbouring sleeping-berth. Of course, the habits and customs of Englishmen and Indians are very different. Some Englishmen say that the smell of sandal-wood makes them sick. Others abhor the chewing of betel ; and yet more have an objection to the gutteral noises that some Indians think natural and pleasant. I have never seen any rudeness on the part of English travellers towards Indians; probably because guards and station-masters do their best to sort people out and put English travellers together. But Indians have told me that they prefer to reserve a second-class compartment rather than to risk getting into a first-class carriage with a testy major or a haughty captain; and a rajah often takes a whole first-class compartment, not because he likes the expense, but on account of racial pride.

"My ladies are travelling by this train," a rajah said lately to two young Englishmen, who were sitting in a first-class compartment. "I will double your fares, if you will let me have this carriage."

"Get out!" was the British remonstrance.

An Indian train is made up of first-class carriages, to which are attached small compartments for servants; second-class carriages; third-class carriages; and intermediate compartments, which are reserved for English and Eurasian passengers only. In the second-class carriages English and Indian people travel much together; and from a Calcutta platform I witnessed a struggle between the wife of 'a chartered hand' and an Indian gentleman. The Indian, who wore European evening dress (the train was timed to leave at 9. p m.), held an official position; and he had secured all the lower sleeping-berths for his wife and daughters by booking them the previous day. The English woman had engaged no berth at-all; but she refused to occupy an upper berth. For quite ten minutes the arguing continued, the Indian saying that his wife and daughters could not climb to upper sleeping-berths, and the English woman insisting on having the berth she wanted. Finally, the guard removed the family of the Indian gentleman to an empty intermediate compartment; and the Englishwoman established herself in the otherwise empty second-class carriage.

Missionary ladies have told me that they prefer to travel in intermediate compartments, especially when they are going a long distance. The intermediate fare is half the second-class fare; and the carriages are generally clean and well-lighted. Some missionaries say that the smell of Indian food makes them feel sick while travelling. But Hindus take for a journey only dry food, or some preparation called 'trash'. They cannot have rice and curry without washing and removing some of their clothes; and, occasionally, a very strict old Hindu woman will eat nothing on the train, but will break her journey in order to cook food, bathe and have a meal. At all hours of the day, and night, men run up and down platforms selling fruit and various kinds of sweetmeats; but boiled rice, dal, or cakes baked with ghee are never offered to Indian passengers. In drinking, while travelling, the Hindu is most particular. He alights from the train, and sits on his haunches while water is poured down his throat; or he goes to some place on the platform where 'Water for Hindus' is written up, and there fills his *lota*. At Benares Cantonment Station, Mrs. Besant may sometimes be seen drinking water in Hindu style. A servant dips a *lota* in a well close by and draws up fresh water. She removes her shoes, walks to a little distance from these obnoxious leather objects, and sits down in Hindu fashion. She takes the water in a glass and pours it down her throat, while Hindus look on and worship, and English passengers are very much perplexed, amused and astonished.

It is curious to see, while travelling in India, purdah ladies brought to the train. Sometimes a native lady is carried in a palanquin to the door of a compartment, and a sheet is held over her while she climbs the steps. Occasionally half-a-dozen purdah ladies walk up the platform under a sheet, which is held over their heads and falls to their feet. Often, in the north of India, I have seen two ladies neatly balanced on the shoulders of a man in baskets. Sheets are fastened to the yoke on the man's neck, and the ladies curl up in the baskets and wrap themselves round with white linen. Not seldom, bright eyes may be seen peeping out of a little opening, eyes that quickly disappear when a husband, or a father, approaches. The latest style of purdah travelling is to drive to the station in a closed motor ; and in the case of an Indian Princess, a short time ago, I saw the motor proceed along the platform to the door of the compartment reserved for her Highness. A sheet was then held over the Princess, and she disappeared into a carriage with closed windows, followed by her female attendants.

CHAPTER X

A Sacred City

If any Englishman desires to see Hindus as they really are, let him spend a month at Puri, in Orissa. Puri is said to be an unhealthy place; and this is true at the season of the year when Jagan-nath is taken from the temple to a garden a mile away for his yearly holiday. After that little jaunt, the god is ill for a month; that is to say, he and his wife are receiving a new coating of paint. When Jagan-nath is at the temple, Puri is not an unhealthy place; and, at all seasons of the year, the beach is free from infection, and on the beach are the few houses inhabited by English people. The Magistrate was good enough to let me stay at the Circuit-House; and there I was given the room occupied by Lord Curzon when he visited Puri and went to see the Black Pagoda—the ancient home of Jagan-nath.

The Circuit House—a large rambling bungalow with a tower used as a light-house—stands on the sandy beach, not far from the Court-House, where the Magistrate, who is also the Collector, transacts his business.

"Halt! Who goes there?" piped a small native sentinel, if I came in after eight o'clock; and the answer 'Friend' sent him back to his box quite happy and contented.

On a moonlight night, the Puri beach is a scene of peace and loveliness; for the wide sea and the long line of sand are then bathed in a soft yellow light, and glittering waves break on a golden shore. Then an amber light melts into rosy dawn, and the crimson sun, rising in a ball from the ocean, says that it is time to get up, have chota, bathe, and go for a walk.

Lazily the days passed at Puri !

Lying in a lounge chair, surrounded by ruins taken from neighbouring temples, watching little black imps playing in the sea, and talking to fishermen who offered their wares for a few annas, hours passed unnoticed. The Magistrate, the doctor, half-a-dozen invalids at a Sanitorium and a few visitors at a Rest-House formed the white population of Puri when I was there ; and these people passed one another on the beach, or met at the Club, if eligible, and every Sunday evening gathered in a tiny Church beside the sea, where (so said a little 'chartered hand' at the Sanitorium) the Magistrate read the Church of England Service 'in order to show the supremacy of England.'

There was a curious pathos about that short service; for the few people in the Church were strangers in a strange land, and while the Magistrate read the psalms and the lessons, the thoughts of his hearers wandered to England, and the breaking of the waves on the shore reminded the congregation of homes beyond the seas. A breeze came through the open windows and blew out the candles ; and then familiar hymns were sung in a dim, uncertain light, and the Magistrate gave the Benediction in the dark. None thought of shutting out the sound of the sea ; and all stood up while the Magistrate walked slowly out of the little building. He threatened to read a sermon ; but nobody believed that he would ever do anything so prosaic ! The Hindus called the Church 'the

Magistrate's private puja place'; and looked on him as a sort of priest, because if any English person died in Puri, he ordered the coffin and read the Burial Service. He was popular with the Hindus, although he collected rents for the Government : for during Jagannath's brief yearly holiday, he was constantly on horseback, supervising the proceedings, and he did not shrink from visiting the Pilgrims' Hospital when natives died there like flies from cholera and small-pox.

No native went to the part of the beach where the English people bathed and walked about; and no English person visited the place where the Hindus took their ceremonial baths, and burnt their dead. Red flames could be seen on dark nights by those who looked westward; and there jackals and hyaenas assembled and made hideous music. Sometimes a jackal went mad, and ran through the town, spreading terror broadcast until it was shot; more often a dead hyaena was seen, slung over the shoulders of a low-caste man who wanted to earn a rupee from the Government.

Sometimes I saw the Magistrate riding through the town; but he, and the English doctor who had charge of a jail at some little distance, were the only Englishmen who went there. English visitors drove to look at the walls of the temple, and at the garden to which Jagan-nath goes for his yearly holiday; but few, if any, cared about the religion and the lives of the Hindus, and many said that to go into the town was dangerous, because the pilgrims were poor and dirty, and brought diseases and catching complaints to Puri. Yet the town was a very fascinating place; and, in the main street, I liked to stand on the doorstep of a shop and watch the men and women swarming up and down the steps of the temple, carrying flowers and other offerings to the god, and bringing away food that he had enjoyed (so it was said) in essence.

No Englishman—not even Lord Curzon—has been allowed to enter the temple ; but Hindus in Puri told me much about the things that go on inside it. Six hundred Brahmin priests wait on Jagan-nath; and as the priesthood is an hereditary office, the morality of some of these priests does not seem to be of a very high order. Many of the priests are reported to be very wealthy ; and a rajah, who lives opposite the temple, makes a good deal of money, it is said, by selling food offered to the god. The right to do this has come down to him from his ancestors ; and when Jagan-nath goes for a drive, he sweeps the road before the car with a golden broom. This rajah has a carriage ; but he does not use it, and I was told that many men of his position in that part of India will not use English carriages, because by so doing they must occupy a seat lower than the coachman. This raja, like other Hindus in Puri, desires to have nothing to do with the *feringhi*, but if English people do not interfere with him, then he is quite willing to live under the rule of England.

Sometimes little girls, covered with ornaments—daughters of the priests, I was told—were carried in and out of the temple on the shoulders of servants. Sometimes a palanquin brought a woman of high caste to worship—perhaps a pious Princess who had built a house in Puri and hoped to die on sacred soil. Women of the lower castes came and went, also men and children. Bells and drums announced when the god rose in the morning, and took his meals ; also when he retired with his wife for the night. The bed-room door was closed, with many salams; and then every living being left the temple, which was guarded until daybreak by sentinels at the entrance. The walls were too high to be scaled; so the jewels of Jagan-nath, which are said to be of enormous value, remained safe until the priests came early in the morning to wake the god, dress him, carry him to the audience chamber, and offer him food. Quite a little army of cooks lived in Puri; and the food, after having been placed before the god, was eaten by the priests and the temple women, or sold to pious pilgrims, more especially to widows.

The great idol Jagan-nath at Puri is said to contain the bones of Krishna—the god who is more popular than all the other gods in modern India. I was shewn a picture of Jagan-nath, taken by a Brahmin who visited the temple for the purpose of sketching the god; and this showed a short, broad, wooden image, with goggle eyes and no hands. Hooks are fastened to the wrists; and by this means silver hands are added to the idol when he wears full dress. His wife is as ugly as himself; but the pair are said to be very fond of one another, and during the yearly holiday, when they are separated, Mrs. Jagan-nath makes great preparations to receive her lord again, and does so, at last, with much rejoicing. Once a year, a huge car, with enormous wheels, is taken to the gates of the temple; and Jagan-nath is put into it with much ceremony. Men and women vie with one another for places inside the iron chains by means of which the car is dragged for a mile; and sometimes, in the excitement, pilgrims faint, and are trodden upon and killed, or are badly hurt. But I was told that pilgrims never throw themselves under the wheels of the car, and have never done so, and that stories to this effect are fabrications. For one month the god remains at his country residence; and then he returns, with the same ceremonies, to the temple, where his faithful wife receives him. Afterwards he retires for a month from public view; and then—being repainted—he once more receives pilgrims and accepts their offerings.

I asked a young Brahmin in Puri, who had been educated in a Christian College, his opinion on the Hindu religion; and he said that God has made different religions for different parts of the world; and that each man will be judged according to the use he has made of the religion given to him by Brahman. God can be found in all religions, he said. All religions meet in Brahman. But for a man to leave his own religion is displeasing to God, for if God had wished a man to belong to another religion than the one professed by his parents, then He would have placed the man in a country where that religion is practised. 'Idols are nothing to me' he said; 'but I reverence Brahman, whom they represent, and they are a great help to uneducated and undeveloped persons who can know God only in some form or substance. I may be reborn a Christian perhaps, and if so I will not become a Hindu; but being born a Hindu, I will stick to the religion given to me by God, because He knows which religion is best for my present state of development.'

Thousands of pilgrims flocked daily to Puri while I was there, singing as they walked in groups from the railway station to the town; and these people were quiet and orderly, for they were in Holy Puri, and if they died there, then their souls would go straight to heaven. Holy cows wandered about the town, and when an irreverent Englishman stood in the way of a holy cow, the holy cow pushed him aside and walked on. Holy monkeys ran along the walls of the temple and on the roofs of the houses, and the Hindus treated these mischievous little animals as if they were divine creatures. Pariah dogs lay on the roads, covered with sores and reduced to skin and bones; and none put them out of their misery. To kill is a crime; but to starve an animal to death is no sin. Thus I was told about two young tigers found in a country district. They were shut up, and a letter was sent to the nearest Magistrate, asking what was to be done with them. The answer was: 'Kill them.' So the Hindus let them slowly die of starvation.

The pilgrims, who were nearly all very poor people, wore gay cloths. Red was the prevailing colour ; but brown, green, violet and orange were mixed with the red, and sometimes a girl wore over her head and face a muslin veil ornamented with much tinsel. Widows were distinguished by a single white garment ; and such girls and women had no jewels. But most of the women had two or three ornaments ; and, if too poor to have a silver bangle, or an imitation gold necklace, then an amulet enclosed in a small leather case was hung from the neck. Each little girl had a single silver fig leaf, an heirloom handed down from mother to daughter ; and each little boy had a charm round neck or waist, and no other covering than matted, curly hair.

Outside the temple, under umbrella-shaped tents, sat Sanyasins, smeared with ashes and wearing only a rag at the waist. Some of these holy personages had long hair, mixed with hemp, coiled round their heads; and, in the distance, the coils looked like snakes. Others had matted hair falling to the ground—their only covering. I saw strange and forbidding sights in the streets of Puri. For instance, a man walking on four stumps, his arms ending at the elbow and his legs at the knee, and carrying on his back a pot into which pice were thrown by pilgrims. Still worse was the condition of a young man with the face and the head of a baby, the result, I was told, of pressure. I shall never forget the weary, agonised expression on that young man's face, as he walked along the road, smeared with ashes, and wearing the apricot-coloured robe of a saint. I saw, also, two boys with small heads, dwarfed features and slanting foreheads, who could not speak. These idiots were garlanded, and smeared with ashes, and made to fight for pice by the man who had charge of them. Children with twisted limbs were there, blind and diseased persons sat in the dusty road, and pice were given to beggars by pilgrims who had only a little rice or grain to live upon themselves.

Fish is eaten largely by the richer natives in Puri, and one of the amusements of the place is to watch the canoes coming in with the nets. The fishermen go out before daybreak, and return at about nine o'clock, dragging their nets after them. The canoes, made of logs of wood, fastened together with rope, come leaping over the waves, upsetting the fishermen, who then wade through the water, pulling the nets after them. The fish are sorted, packed in ice, and sent to Calcutta.

From the main street of the town many little narrow lanes lead to the sea, and the houses in these streets are small and whitewashed A slanting roof of dark, red brick stretches further than the house, and is supported by pillars, thus forming a verandah. There the men of the house pass their spare time, talking, eating betel, and reading in sing-song fashion. Seldom a woman is seen there, for the interior of the house is the women's province. Boys and girls play about, and children sit on the shoulders of fond fathers and grandfathers. In the early morning, little girls make designs with chalk outside the doors, and stick flowers in mud or some kindred substance, and the streets are carefully swept and made clean before the heat of the day begins. In schools, kept by Hindu widows, the girls look quaintly busy. The boys attend schools conducted by Brahmins; and it is no uncommon thing to see a stout Hindu sitting with a stick on his knee, watching his small sons learning their lessons. Many little boutiques line the principal street in Puri, and the articles offered for sale are arranged on the ground, and the salesmen squat beside their wares, talking to customers and chewing betel. Brass *lotas*, plates, and boxes are sold by weight, also images of gods and goddesses. Cloths made in Manchester and Birmingham are offered to pilgrims whose homes lie in the jungle; and paper fans and cheap walking-sticks are carried home by men and women as reminiscences of a pilgrimage that exhausts, in many cases, the savings of a life-time.

Shops selling sweets and cakes are open to the street; and hornets and wasps gather on the sweet things, and nobody drives them away. To kill a fly, or an insect, would be considered a sin in Holy Puri; and I was told that in some parts of India beggars are paid by pious persons to let vermin feed on their bodies.

There is only one wine and beer shop in Puri, and this place shows half-a-dozen bottles in a glass case. At the Club, English people can buy what they want; but whisky agents do a very small business among the natives in Holy Puri. A board advertises

'The Municipal Market,' and there a few natives deal in country vegetables, fish and goat-flesh. Chickens and eggs are difficult to obtain, because only the lowest castes will break eggs and kill chickens. So English people send to Calcutta for provisions, and live largely on game during the shooting season. Sea-fish English people are advised not to touch, probably because human bones and other things are thrown into the sea at Puri. Goats are relied upon to a great extent, a cow being too holy an animal to be milked.

Missionaries make no head-way in Puri. No Salvation Army officer lives there; and no clergyman is seen in the Church. Puri is a stronghold of the Brahmins; and they teach there the essence of Hinduism. If a missionary attempts to preach in Puri, the Brahmins gather round him, and argue, and talk, until he gives up his hopeless task and goes away. Politics the people of Puri care little about, although the babus have a Club and read newspapers. So long as the pilgrims are allowed to do as they please, and prejudices concerning cows and monkeys are respected, Hindus in Puri will give no trouble to the Government.

CHAPTER XI

MODERN CALCUTTA

HOWRA, the principal railway station in Calcutta, might, with a little imagination, be mistaken for Waterloo, although Indian porters are on the platforms and the carriages for hire have native drivers. The river Hooghly, that divides Howrah railway station from the city, has a decided look of the Thames about it, in spite of Hindu men taking ceremonial baths and Hindu women washing bright-coloured cloths in its waters; and, crossing the bridge, one comes to tall, dirty-looking buildings that are not at-all unlike houses at Westminster.

Calcutta was made by the English about 200 years ago; and it is, in my opinion, a bad imitation of the metropolis of England. The business hours kept in Calcutta are English, for offices open at 10 and 11 A.M., and public places, such as the Museum and the Imperial Library, admit no visitors before 10 A.M.,—an hour at which the sun is already scorchingly hot during the summer months. When Calcutta first became the head-quarters of the English in British India, very few English people lived there, and nearly all the English residents could follow the Governor-General and the Government to the hills when the hot weather set in; but now Calcutta is the home of many Englishmen and their families, and if work could be done there early in the morning, during the summer months, then it would be better for all concerned, I think. In Madras public institutions open much earlier than in Calcutta and Bombay—but then Madras is still called 'the benighted Presidency!'

The hours for English meals in India are much the same as in France—tea or coffee soon after daybreak, breakfast at eleven, afternoon-tea at four or five, and dinner at eight or nine o'clock. Some English people add a two o'clock tiffin; but the Englishman who desires to keep his health in India does not eat in the middle of the day—at any rate not during the hot weather. Moreover, servants often live at a distance from the house and go home for their rice and the siesta that all Indians need during the extreme heat of noon; so tiffin must be dispensed with by many English people who live in cities.

I have found that the closer an Englishman keeps to the hours and the food of Indians, the less likely he is to suffer from the complaints that make invalids of so many strong English persons in India. Indian medicines, it seems to me, suit the climate better than the prescriptions of English doctors. Omum water, made from a native seed, is the best cure that I know of for cholera and dysentery; and Chareta, the dried wood of an Indian shrub, will, if taken daily in small quantities, ward off boils and prickly heat. Only English people suffer from prickly heat in India, and an Indian doctor told me that the fine texture of the English skin is the cause of this unpleasant irruption. Prickly heat attacks nearly all English children who cannot go to the hills in the hot weather, and when it suppurates, the face and the body become a mass of sores. English doctors give one medicine after another for prickly heat; and when I asked an English doctor why he did not recommend Chareta, he took me into his garden and showed me the shrub growing there.

"I use it" he said, "but I lose by it."

Well-boiled rice is the best food to live on in India, not the pretty, white table-rice from which the greater part of the nourishment has been withdrawn, but the large-grained, brown rice used in the mofussil. Such rice contains a great deal of oil and is very nourishing; but as it makes people stout, English people will not use it in a climate that tends to obesity. Nearly all English people in India eat too much meat; and some of them buy beef, which is about half the price of mutton. Formerly chickens and ducks were plentiful in the mofussil; but now poultry in country places is bought up by agents to supply city markets. Fish is cheap in the capitals of British India; and eggs, although very small, can be had almost everywhere.

Let us visit the Calcutta market, which is by far the largest and the best market in India. It stands in the Maiden—the large open space called 'the lungs of Calcutta.' Many private carriages and vehicles for hire are at the entrance, and coolies with badges and baskets surround visitors, begging to carry home purchases for a few pice or an anna. The fruit stalls attract attention first, for they are laid out invitingly and made gay with festoons of coloured paper. Indians love gay colours and show considerable taste in decorating dinner tables, fruit stalls and baskets of flowers. So the fruit stalls that face the entrance to the market are charming to look at. But the fruit is expensive. Bananas are always plentiful; and so are mangoes, oranges, pomelos and melons at certain seasons of the year. Imported apples and grapes are shown in small quantities, and plaintive cries of 'Sab' and 'Mem' follow English people who glance at these things and pass on. Nuts and dried fruits are sold by Mahomedans, and the English visitor looks with astonishment at the beards of these salesmen, for a man with dark hair may have a beard dyed a bright shade of orange, and a grey-haired man will have, very likely, blotches of deep yellow on a white beard. The explanation of these beards is said to be that the owners have visited Mecca. How devout—at any rate in outward appearance—the Mahomedan salesmen are! If a visitor goes to the market at sunrise, or sunset, they will be found kneeling on their stalls, facing Mecca; and the most urgent demands will not induce them to attend to business before their prayers are finished. Passing on, the visitor comes to the stalls where English vegetables are arranged with care, carrots and radishes giving touches of vivid colour to light green lettuce and dark green cabbage. Indian vegetables are there, too, ladies-fingers, brinjals, and dozens of others with curious names.

In this part of the market English and Eurasian ladies meet together and gossip. Some of these ladies are keepers of boarding-houses, and they ask why things in the Calcutta market become daily more expensive? One says that high prices are due to the Swadeshi movement; another puts high prices down to the Famine. All agree that year by year it becomes more difficult to live in Calcutta. Then these ladies pass on, followed by coolies who carry on their heads the purchases of the morning. English Society ladies send their cooks to do the marketing; and such mistresses are at a premium, because salesmen allow one anna on each rupee spent at a stall, and annas soon accumulate when a mistress does not know the ups and downs of trade. To go to the market means 'to lose caste' among English Society ladies in Calcutta; and the people who benefit most by English caste ideas are native servants. The meat market is a necessary nuisance. There first, second and third class beef and mutton are sold amid noise and confusion, and the visitor gladly leaves the smell of the shambles and passes into the fish market, where, however, things are only a little less noxious. The fish—cheap and plentiful—is sold by shrieking women, and prawns, crabs and other sea-things sprawl among glassy-eyed, drab-coloured fishes. The poultry market shows the smallest of chickens and eggs no larger than those of guinea-fowls in England; and lying on the stone slabs are snipe and other wild birds, dead or dying. Few Hindus are seen in these markets; but Mahomedans mix with the servants of English people, or sit on door-steps, smoking the small hucca that is so popular in northern India.

The brightest part of the market is the centre, where Japanese dealers are found, also Indian merchants who exhibit native silks and embroideries. There Eurasian boys and girls walk up and down, smoking, laughing and flirting wealthy Hindus and Mahomedans buy English ribbons and dress materials for their wives; and European and American tourists run in and out of shops, asking the prices of embroideries made in India, of pineapple, tinsel, Kasi silk and other things that cannot be bought at home. At the back of the market is a miniature Petticoat Lane, low caste Hindus and poor Mahomedans congregating there to buy goods displayed on barrows—a curious assortment of books, broken china, gods and goddesses made in England Manchester cloths and native muslins. And last, but, not least, is John Chinaman, who makes boots and shoes at ridiculously low prices and will supply a customer with a pair of leather shoes for a rupee. He is one of the sights of Calcutta, shuffling along the streets, in baggy white trousers and loose blue coat, and wearing a small sailor hat over his pigtail. He enjoys listening to the band in the Eden Gardens, and may be seen there in the evening, near the band-stand, with hands in pockets and cigarette between teeth. Shoe-making is John Chinaman's chief occupation in Calcutta; and it is said that the Swadeshi movement has given an impetus to his trade, for Indians do not boycott shoes and boots made by Chinamen, while they will no longer buy English leather articles, if they can help it.

Southern India was scarcely touched by the Mahomedan Conquest, and there the fez is lost among turbans ; but in Calcutta one sees in the streets many Mahomedans, and at sunrise, and sunset, these people spread their mats in the Maidan and say their prayers. A Mahomedan is never ashamed to acknowledge Allah in public; and the Amir of Afghanistan turned aside to pray when the cry 'I bear witness that there is no God but God' came to him from the mosques. It is the same with all Mahomedans—from prince to peasant they stand silent when that ringing cry is heard. They pray anywhere and everywhere ; and on one occasion I was put to much inconvenience in Calcutta, for all traffic was stopped for half-an-hour by the police in order to permit Mahomedans to carry out their religious programme. They knelt across the streets, one hundred deep, and no carriage could pass through them. At last they stood up, touched lightly first one cheek and then the other of friends and acquaintances and gave their blessings to little boys who bent down and touched their feet.

Friday is very strictly kept by Mahomedans in India, and for one month of the year they fast, neither eating nor drinking from sunrise until sunset. To touch no water for twelve hours in the heat of an Indian summer is indeed a penance; and I have seen Mahomedans with lips like parchment after a day spent without water and have heard them say that their tongues felt like burning coals. Among Mahomedans, Christian missionaries make very few converts. I was told that the Church of England Zenana Mission in Calcutta has not not made two converts in a quarter of a century. Mahomedans say that Mahomed came after Christ, and that his revelation is, consequently, the latest that God has vouchsafed to men. They are great students of the Bible and they confront Christian missionaries with arguments that those good people find difficult to confute. They say that, on the Day of Judgment, God will ask Jesus Christ if He ever claimed to be more than a great and good man; and that Jesus will say that no claim to more than human goodness has ever been made by Him, or by His Mother. Mahomedans rank Jesus Christ next to the Prophet; and have for Him and His Mother the greatest respect and reverence. Those of us who have studied Sunna know how hard it is to introduce changes among Mahomedans, more especially as a Mahomedan boy is taught the Koran before he learns to read and write, and Mahomedan women visit zenanas in order to instruct little girls in the forms of the Mahomedan religion as soon as babyhood is passed.

A Mahomedan may have four wives, if he is able to keep them in comfort; but only the first is married with any ceremony and her eldest son is the lawful heir. The first wife takes precedence in the zenana;

and, if she is a lady of rank, the other wives bow to the ground in her presence. Some Mahomedans in India have one wife only; but most Mahomedans there avail themselves of the Prophet's permission to introduce several wives into the zenana; and even Princes educated in England take advantage of the conjugal licence permitted by Mahomed after they return to their own people. As it is a breach of etiquette to speak to a Mahomedan about the ladies of his house, very little is known concerning domestic life in Mahomedan homes; and I am told that to-day Christian missionaries, who work among Mahomedan women, find the doors of rich houses closed and have to content themselves with visiting the wives and daughters of poor Mahomedans who pay a rupee a month, or nothing at-all, for the education of their female children. By introducing scholarships into Mahomedan schools for girls, the Government has bribed some Mahomedans to let their daughters and wives be educated; but the ordinary Mahomedan man still thinks that the less women know about reading, writing and arithmetic, the better it will be for home life and the family.

A wealthy Mahomedan merchant invited me to his house, where his brother met me and took me to a room on the roof—a room built entirely of large panes of glass and furnished with luxurious arm-chairs and sofas. Half-a-dozen Mahomedans, dressed almost like Englishmen, but wearing the fez, were there, and tea was served in small, Egyptian, glass cups with a golden edge. Oriental cakes and sweets were handed round, also cigarettes made in Egypt; and, after some conversation, we went out on the roof, where fruit-trees and vines made a pretty picture. Birds sang in cages and doves cooed in avories, and we sat under small, shady trees. As far as I could see stretched houses and courtyards, and the merchant told me that his brothers and cousins lived in these places and that he was the head of the family. Children played in some of the courtyards; but the windows were screened and no woman, or girl, could be seen. I doubt not, however, that bright eyes peeped out of crevices and the *feringhi* on the roof was criticised and discussed.

The merchant talked to me about the Koran ; and I found that he believed in a Day of Resurrection. He would rise again in his body, he said.

"And will Mahomedan women share in this resurrection?" I asked.

"Yes" he replied, "but I am puzzled what will happen to them then."

"Why ?" I queried.

"The Prophet has promised a wife to each man, but he has not said that each woman shall have a husband" replied the merchant.

The Mohurrum is celebrated all over India and the ceremonies connected with it vary very much. Thus at one place, in Bengal, a camel is speared to death, a sight few English people care to witness. 'Cages'—glistening white structures—are carried through the streets at midnight and afterwards are thrown into the nearest river. All through the Mohurrum one sees processions in the streets, sometimes men marching in rows and beating their bare breasts. Hindus of the lower castes join with poor Mahomedans in these processions and I have seen, during the Mohurrum, Hindus dressed like Englishwomen and dancing, and Mahomedans personating English soldiers, plague officers, policemen and others. Order and good humour generally prevail now during the Mohurrum ; but in former years rival Mahomedan sects gave a good deal of trouble to the Government. English people are often invited by rich Mahomedans to witness the sights of the Mohurrum ; just as Indians are occasionally asked to see a Christmas tree, or a Father Christmas.

The usual out-door dress of a Mahomedan gentleman in summer-time is a long coat, shaped at the waist and made of silk, trousers of the same material, a fez, and English shoes and socks. In the winter, the same things are worn, only then warmer materials are used. In-doors, loose trousers of flowered-silk are worn, and over these a silkshirt, and then a little muslin garment, edged with lace. A round, embroidered muslin cap covers the top of the head, and on the feet are gorgeous slippers with pointed toes. The hair of a Mahomedan gentleman is closely cut, and he is very particular about his eyebrows, eyelashes and moustache, carrying in his pocket a little mirror so that he may arrange each hair with care. The eyes of Mahomedans are large, clear and full, and unspoilt by alcohol of any sort. In them we see often more feeling than intelligence. The teeth and nails of a Mahomedan gentleman are always immaculately clean, and his whole person shows careful attention. Chess is his favourite game; and the gramaphone is his pet musical instrument. I visited a Mahomedan house where sixty gramaphones were kept constantly going, and the noise—although softened by distance—made me wonder why religious teachers have not added a gramaphone to the tortures of hell ? I had heard a Tamil song on a gramaphone, also a Buddhist sermon ; but never before a dance and a funeral march mixed together, a coon ditty with the

Glory Song as a chorus, Madame Melba and half-a-dozen more great singers trying to shout one another down, and a medley of Christian hymns and Music Hall melodies. Mahomed did not approve of music ; and it will be remembered that the great iconoclast Aurungzeb looked out of his palace one day and saw a funeral procession passing by.

"Who is dead ?" he asked.

"Music," answered one of the mourners.

"Pray bury her deep," said Aurungzeb.

Mahomedans in India have, as a rule, a good physique, and are well-proportioned ; but they lack muscle and have a tendency to grow fleshy. I am told that a Mahomedan gentleman treats his wives with firmness and kindness, and that the docility of ladies in Mahomedan zenanas would teach a lesson to suffragettes. It has sometimes amused me, while talking with a complacent Mahomedan, to fancy him the husband of three or four of the English ladies who now-a-days attack the houses of Statesmen and scream down Members of Parliament. However, it is whispered that sulkiness wears out more than one Mahomedan husband, that purdah ladies will not take his 'no' for an answer, that he is forced to yield under pressure of coaxing and temper, that he is, in fact, only a limited despot.

A strong contrast to the well-to-do Mahomedan may be found in the wealthy Armenian, who hails from Mount Ararat and who never forgets his home and ancestry. The oldest Christian Church in Calcutta was built by Armenians ; and they carried on business in India before the East India Company went there. Armenians are among the wealthiest and most respected people in Calcutta to-day. I met a member of the Apcar family, and he took me to see the Armenian College, where I found light-eyed, dark-haired, fair-faced Armenian boys being educated. Each year wealthy Armenians in Calcutta send to Armenia for poor boys and educate them in the Armenian College. These boys take naturally to business and do very well in the jute trade. It is generally believed in Calcutta that Thackeray was born in the large house that is now the Armenian College ; but no tablet marks the place, and I am inclined to think that Lord Curzon was not satisfied as to the accuracy of this commonly-received statement. I saw the register of Thackeray's christening at St. John's Church—formerly the Anglican Cathedral of Calcutta—and I was 'minded to cut it out,' for I was alone in the Vestry. A Calcutta journalist, to whom I spoke of the temptation, said, laughing:—

"Do you imagine that anyone here is interested in Thackeray ? The last polo match and Lady Minto's latest dress are the only things that English people here care about."

In Southern India many Indians speak English and in Madras every little street boy can answer a question in that language ; but, in the north of India, English is not so much learned, and there a knowledge of Hindustani, or Hindi, becomes necessary. As everyone knows, Hindustani is a polyglot, made up of Arabic, Persian, Sanskrit and local dialects. Hindustani means 'the Camp language ;' and Persian was used at Court, and for business purposes, until the English took possession of India. Yearly more and more Indians speak English ; consequently very few English people now take the trouble to learn an Indian language. However, anyone who desires to travel in India must know Hindustani ; and Indians appreciate the attempts that are made by some English people to master one of the numerous languages of the country. And Hindustani is not at-all difficult. A year is allowed to officers and missionaries for the acquirement of Hindustani, and this time is quite sufficient. A story is told about a Christian Brotherhood in India that was visited at noon by an English friend. The visitor found the Mission House very quiet; and in six rooms he discovered six sleeping missionaries, and beside each missionary was a sleeping munshi.

CHAPTER XII

Calcutta Past and Present

The Calcutta G. P. O. has been built on the site of the old Fort William; and, thanks to Lord Curzon, the historical buildings of that fortified factory can now be traced by means of brass rods that have been carefully laid down. The so-called Black Hole is marked by flat marble slabs and a tablet on an adjacent wall gives a brief account of the events that called Clive to Calcutta in 1756. In front of the Post Office is a marble pillar on which the names of the people who are said to have perished in a cell only 18 feet square are inscribed. Hindus and Mahomedans say that when Lord Curzon was challenged to prove by historical documents that the tragedy of the Black Hole really happened, he did not accept the challenge; and that to thrust 146 persons into a room only 18 feet square is not possible. But letters written after Suraja Dowla took Fort William prove that the atrocity recorded on the monument actually occurred.

A letter from Mr. Holwell, who was Governor of Fort William at that time, dated February 28, 1757, is still in existence. He says that 146 prisoners were 'smothered' in the Black Hole prison on the night of June 20, 1756, by 'the Moors'. The size of the room was unknown by the prisoners when the guards, with drawn swords and scimitars, drove them into it. If the Englishmen had guessed that the prison was a cube of about 18 feet, with walls on three sides and two barred windows on the other, they would have fought for their lives ; but before they realized the size of the place, resistance was made impossible by confusion, wounds and noise. Mr. Holwell went in first, and he climbed to a widow, hence his escape from suffocation. Only one woman went into the cell—an Indian woman—and she was carried to a window. But her English husband was killed; and, the following day, the Moors decided that she was too young and too good-looking to be set at liberty. Perspiration streamed from the Englishmen like water, and they stripped naked. They begged the Moors to fire on them; they offered bribes. Some died of wounds; some went mad. The Moors brought water and laughed to see the poor wretches fighting for it and to hear them cursing, screaming, praying and crying. Before midnight the noise grew less, for many had become unconscious. An awful smell of decomposition set in ; and, at daybreak, when the Nawab ordered the door to be opened, the few survivors staggered into the open air like drunken men. Only 23 emerged alive from the Black Hole. The dead bodies of the others were thrown into a ditch ; and over this spot Mr. Holwell erected a monument, which was replaced during the administration of Lord Curzon by a plain marble column.

It will be remembered that on the 20th of June 1756, Fort William surrendered to the Nawab of Bengal without a blow. That young man had been warned by his predecessor that ' the English traders are like bees. Left to themselves they produce honey, but they violently attack those who interfere with them. ' And the mother of the young Soubahdar had tried to deter him from marching on Calcutta by the jeer:—

"Will you make war on mere traders?"

But he was avaricious, and reports of treasure to be found in Fort William allured him to Calcutta. Moreover, he was justly alarmed to see the English and the French traders fortifying their factories. The garison of Fort William numbered at that time only 200 regulars, the militia were badly armed and inexperienced, and no commander was available. When Suraja Dowla and his troops appeared, the Council, with the exception of Mr. Holwell, slunk off on board ship, and the soldiers, gaining possession of the liquor stores, became drunk. Mr. Holwell was forced to throw a letter of capitulation over the ramparts; and afterwards he and his companions were bound and carried into Suraja Dowla's presence. The Nawab ordered their chains to be removed, and promised them his protection, and then he retired to bed. Later on the Nawab's soldiers forced Mr. Holwell and 145 people into the Black Hole, a small cell used for condemned criminals.

When news of the capture of Fort William reached Madras (Fort St. George was at that time the head-quarters of the Saib Company in India), a force of 900 Europeans and 1,500 Sepoys, commanded by Colonel Clive, and five of His Majesty's ships, under Admiral Watson, set out for Bengal. Fort William was re-taken, on the 2nd of January, 1757; and the Hindu Governor, through whose turban a bullet passed, sent word to Suraja Dowla that the soldiers from Madras were quite unlike the English soldiers in Bengal, and that it was impossible to resist them. In the centre of Fort William a mosque had been built, some of the adjacent buildings having been demolished to provide materials for that purpose; otherwise Fort William had not been altered, and one of the first things that Clive demanded of the Nawab was permission to finish the ramparts that had been a prime cause of the attack made six months previously. Clive's opinion of the gentlemen who ran away when Suraja Dowla surrounded Fort William is still on record. He wrote privately to the Governor of Madras, and advised him not to believe a word they might say, 'for they are bad subjects, and rotten at heart, and their conduct finds no excuse, even among themselves.'

The English inhabitants of Calcutta are said to have received after the battle of Plassey 5,000,000 rupees for damages sustained during the time Suraja Dowla's soldiers were at Fort William, the Armenian residents 2,000,000, and the Saib Company 10,000,000. Much of this money arrived in specie by boat when the treasury of Moorshedabad was at the mercy of the English; and the people of Calcutta then 'went mad with excitement, rushing out into the streets, dancing and singing, and congratulating one another'. A mint was established, with the consent of Mir Jaffir; and from that day Calcutta shot ahead. The Saib Company then made Calcutta the centre of their possessions in India; and before long Warren Hastings took up his residence there as Governor-General.

Look at Calcutta to-day!

The Viceroy has a lordly, if not regal residence, with the mouths of cannon pointed toward the town, and whitewashed lions on the gateways. Wide streets show European shops in which everything that the heart of man, or woman, can desire may be obtained. Army and Navy Stores make English people feel 'quite at home.'

Hotels are numerous,—expensive, it is true, but at the command of all who can afford to pay for luxury, or comfort. Clubs, in which, according to Indian ideas, every member lives like a prince, face the Maidan. The Viceroy's brilliantly-clad Body-guard dashes through the streets during the Calcutta Season, and bands clash out the National Anthem when the representative of the King-Emperor puts in an appearance. Large, white houses, surrounded by entrancing gardens, are the homes of English Civil Servants. Roads are crowded with carriages, and each memsahib aspires to clothe her servants in a livery that will out-do in brilliancy of colour, if not in taste, the liveries of other people's servants. Occasionally a wealthy Indian drives rapidly through the crowd, his horses going faster than the horses of English people, his liveries eclipsing in lightness and brightness the trappings of English-paid coachmen, his glittering turban and gilded coat adding to the theatrical appearance of the scene. The result is a certain, or, rather, uncertain gaudiness ; for in India servants and carriages are cheap, and love of display is not an English quality. Races, polo, golf, Viceregal balls and State functions are made into pageants ; and military parades bring all this ostentatious splash to a climax. Many English people—most, nearly all, in fact—are caught in the mesh of oriental pageantry that for 150 years has been considered by England to be a necessary part of her rule in India.

Let us pass from the English part of Calcutta to the crowded, narrow streets in which the people of India congregate. A funeral is approaching. Only the lowest castes will touch a dead body, so the corpse is borne on the shoulders of coolies. Dressed in a clean cloth, and with face uncovered, the dead man seems to be sleeping. At the ghat the body will be burnt, and relations will sit by until the flames die out. Then they will bathe, wash their cloths, and go home, believing that already, or after a rest in some place that is neither earth nor heaven, the dead man will live again. Endless lives are before him. Endless lives lie behind him. The life he has just left is but a bead on a string. To-morrow, or afterwards, he will enter another body; and so it will go on, and on, until he attains Liberation.

Now comes a man carrying in his arms the little, stiff body of a dead child, covered with a cloth. The relations, who follow, do not cry, do not show sorrow. The child has gone to sleep, and will wake up later in another body. In and out, in and out, the soul goes, these people say, until it finds the path to the highest happiness and realises that it is one with Brahman.

" Think thus on me
Have faith in me, adore and worship me ;
Thus shalt thou come to me, Arjuna ;
Thus shalt thou rise to my supreme abode.
Where neither sun nor moon hath need to shine
For know that all the lustre they possess is mine."

The ordinary missionary in India is a conundrum. He puzzles not only the natives, but also many of his compatriots, for he puts down so much to 'the climate'. The climate necessitates a large house, servants, punkahs, carriages, ice and other things ; and, in consequence, he lives in India sometimes very much more comfortably than an English clergymen can live at home. An enormous amount of money has been spent on the conversion of India to Christianity, yet only the lowest and most ignorant castes have listened, and will listen to missionaries. Roman Catholic priests and nuns live very self-denying lives in India ; but missionaries of the Church of England and of undenominational bodies are, in many cases, as I said before, conundrums. Sometimes these people blame the Government for their want of success ; and I was asked by a missionary to put myself in his place. 'I am paid to come here and make converts to Christianity' he said, 'and the steamer that brought me to India conveyed at the same time cheap idols made in England. If I tell Hindus not to worship idols, they turn round and ask :—

"Then why do English people make idols for us ?"

The Government prides itself on its impartiality. Hindus, Mahomedans and Christians are treated alike in India. Hindus and Mahomedans do not try to make converts; but Christian missionaries are paid to do so, and these people seem to me to be strangely sanguine.

"Will you have an idol made in England, or made in Germany ?" I was asked in a Calcutta bazaar.

"Thank you" I replied, " I will have a Swadeshi bronze image of Krishna."

Calcutta is supposed to be named after the goddess Kali, who has a temple about two miles from the Viceroy's residence. There one hundred goats are sacrificed every morning; and if a missionary calls the custom 'cruel', Hindus say:—

"Thousands of cows and sheep are daily killed to provide food for you and other Christians. We sacrifice goats to please our goddess, not to satisfy our appetites."

One evening I went to see Kali's temple. A horrible smell of blood seemed to fill the air and I was asked to buy images of a blood-thirsty looking goddess whose tongue hung out of her mouth, and I was shewn a stone on which 100 goats are daily sacrificed. Many palm trees surround the temple of Kali, and as a storm was coming on, they waved their heavy heads in an ominous fashion. Native policemen followed me, for at that time riots were taking place in Calcutta and the policemen were not sure how a *feringhi* would be received by the worshippers of Kali The temple itself I was not allowed to enter; but I walked round it and listened to priests reciting prayers. Many women lay prostrate on stone slabs, or prayed under a tree that is supposed to have supernatural powers when a child is desired. Little shops for the sale of flowers and other offerings were there, and images of Kali were offered to me.

"Ten rupees for seeing Kali's temple" demanded a man who walked with me in the temple's precincts.

I can understand why missionaries shudder and sigh when they go to Kali's temple. But to do the goddess justice, she has many forms, and as a malignant being, delighting in blood, she does not appeal to many Hindus. They prefer to think of her as the mother of the universe, as a female aesthetic, or as the reproducer and type of beauty and the wife of Kala, Time, the great Dissolver, who is carved as the skeleton figure of Death on the caves of Ellora.

If Christian missionaries could lift the veil and see the meaning of Hindu symbols, we should hear less denunciation of 'the heathen' and 'heathenish ways'. But the missionaries whom I met in India, with a few notable exceptions, were men and women with crude intellects and narrow minds, people who repelled and disgusted learned Hindus and cultivated Mahomedans, and who showed by words and deeds that they thought a white skin superior to a black one. Yet, in India, a white man, who is exposed to the sun, soon becomes so dark that his nationality puzzles a passer-by ; and Eurasians, who are pressing into missionary circles, cannot in many cases be distinguished in appearance from the Hindus with whom they refuse to associate.

I passed a Hindu wedding party on my way back from Kali's temple, and, in the subdued light of evening, the little procession seemed like a scene in an English pantomine. The bridegroom, who looked exceedingly shy and nervous, sat alone in a motor, and the motor was festooned with flowers. His empty carriage, drawn by a pair of fine horses, followed. Finally came his relations, in carriages. Such processions now take place after dark in British India, and are, consequently, little noticed by English people.

I had brought with me to Calcutta an introduction to a wealthy Hindu zemindar and at his house I met many educated Hindus and heard their opinions on the present state of affairs in India Accompany me, if you will, to the house of this Indian gentleman, situated in the native part of Calcutta, a tall, roomy building, standing in a square that was at one time a fashionable quarter of the city. Two rooms are in front of the house, and a door shuts off the real dwelling, to which the ladies and children of the family have free access. The banker told me that his most intimate friend has never seen his wife ; and that she may speak to his male relations on rare occasions only. He receives visitors in an office, or in a room furnished with a large, flat, wooden platform, about a foot from the floor. A white sheet is stretched over this chauki, and there men lounge, smoke and talk. The banker wears spotless white muslin from the waist to the knees, and a long piece of the same muslin is thrown over his right shoulder when a visitor comes into the room. The muslin is caught between his legs, and in that way makes loose trousers. His arms and feet are bare. He is tall, stout, and well-proportioned. His face has a good-humoured expression ; his hair is thick, black and curly. He is a pleasant person to look at ; but, at times, while talking about England, his eyes flash, and he becomes sullen and silent. A strict Hindu, eating only vegetables, rice, ghee and sweetmeats, a worshipper of idols is this banker ; and he said to me, scornfully:— "An Englishman sneers at a Hindu who does not wear pants ; and when a Hindu puts on pants, the Englishman laughs."

"England is trying us to the utmost", he told me. "Our meetings are suppressed, our leaders are transported, our newspapers are confiscated. This state of things can't go on. Even men like myself are looking about for a means to put a stop to the tyranny of England."

"You are silent" a Brahmin said, turning to me.

"I am thinking about something that happened this morning" I replied. "I left the Museum at about 11 o'clock, the time when business men go to their offices, and I waited for a tram, at a stopping-place. Several Englishmen were there, too, and when the tram arrived, we all mounted the platform. There we stood still, for inside the first-class compartment were many Hindus, and each Hindu had seated himself on a bench made to hold two persons and had stretched out his arms over the second seat. None of us would ask for a place, and the conductor did not volunteer to make room for us. Presently an English lady mounted the platform.

She looked into the tram, and hesitated; and an Englishman, with white hair and a pleasant face, told the conductor to clear a bench on the platform and make room for the lady to sit down there. I went on to the Imperial Library, and shortly afterwards, while I was talking to the Superintendent of the reading-room, the gentleman who had helped the lady came down the passage.

" Excuse me," said the Superintendent. "I must go. That is one of the highest officials in Calcutta. I must see what he wants."

" In that case, at any rate, Englishmen were willing to take a back place," I said.

The Hindus agreed that the 'bara sahib' is generally a polite person; but regretted that the 'bara sahib' is so 'stand-off' and unapproachable.

" Why did not you ask a Hindu to make room for you?" I was asked.

" I can't tell you" I answered. " In England, room would have been made for me without my having to ask for it".

" It is simply astonishing to an Englishman to see how rude Hindus are to women" I continued. " They seldom, if ever, offer a seat in a tram or a train to a lady, and they will let a woman struggle down steps, with a child on one arm and a bundle in the other, without offering to help her. They smoke in the face of a woman without any apology. Only yesterday I spoke to a Hindu boy, who had lighted a cigarette and was blowing the smoke in the faces of two ladies, and he said :—' If I were an Englishman, you would not speak to me like that'.

" Our ladies do not travel alone" said a Hindu.

" But you know that Englishwomen go about by themselves, and you know, too, that it is considered polite in England to give a woman precedence and to offer her a seat in a crowded tramcar or on a train." I told him.

" I tried to treat an English lady in the English way once" said a young Hindu, " and she was very much offended. I got into a first-class carriage, and seeing an English lady alone there, I went to sit in front of her, and I asked her where she was going to ? Immediately she went to the further end of the carriage; and, at the next station, she moved into another compartment."

"You had not been introduced" I said, laughing. "But if you had opened the door of the carriage for the lady, when she left the train, she would have thanked you. And it is not necessary to push before a lady into a railway carriage, as so many Hindus do to-day".

I rose to go away; and the banker slipped his feet into sandals, and walked with me a little distance. Then I suggested :—

" You Hindus say that there is but one Spirit, and that that Spirit is in all men."

" The Spirit is atrophied in most Englishmen" he replied. " The only spirit we recognise in the English to-day is the whisky spirit".

" Perhaps, if you knew English people you would not talk like that," I said.

"Perhaps not," he replied.

He put his hands palm to palm—the Hindu salutation, meaning ' God in you, and God in me '—and he walked away.

CHAPTER XIII

THE HINDU STUDENT

THE Hindu Student is to-day the most discussed person in the country. Many and conflicting opinions are expressed concerning him; for he is 'the coming man', and people naturally see in him the immediate future of India. Englishmen, in nine cases out of ten, assert that he is the result of a Government education —a cheap education when compared with the education given to boys and young men in England. In a little book, called *How India is Governed*, published in 1882, Mr. Alexander Mackenzie, a Member of the Legislative Council of Madras, said :—

"In no country of the world are such facilities for the attainment of knowledge provided for the masses of the population at such small expense to those immediately benefited as in India. The paternal care of the Government has covered the country with a network of village, primary, normal, low, middle and high schools, besides colleges in the presidency and other large towns, and many special training schools for those who wish to study engineering, medicine, law, industries, etc. ; and these are available for students on a scale of fees so low as to be almost nominal. It is often said that it is not the duty of the State to provide at great cost to the public an expensive university education for all comers, the majority of whom cannot possibly find opportunity for turning such a high standard of acquirements to account, while they are, in fact, morally unfitted by it for the ordinary avocations of the class in life to which they belong. There can be no doubt that these high schools and colleges are annually turning out a large body of young men who cannot find employment in the various offices or departments of the Government, or in private offices (the supply of candidates for such work being enormously in excess of the demand), and who are practically unsuited for, as they are unwilling to undertake, work of any other character. And it is feared the presence of a large body of intelligent, well-educated, unemployed and needy men, widely scattered throughout the country, must carry with it some elements of possible mischief. In connection with this, the necessity for stringent measures to repress the growing audacity and licence of writers in the vernacular papers, as shewn by the introduction by the Government of the 'Vernacular Press Acts,' is of considerable significance."

These words, written twenty-seven years ago, are very true to-day; and people who demand that the millions of India shall receive a western education, without religious teaching and moral training, take upon themselves a great responsibility. The missionaries began a cheap western education in India by means of pennies collected from poor people in England. The Government of India has carried on a cheap western education with the help of taxes that fall heavily on 'the patient, toiling millions' of India. If Indians of the middle classes had had to pay more for their western education, then they would have imbibed it more slowly. In India, men write M. A. and B. A. after their names who, if they lived in England, would have had no chance whatsoever of going to College ; and if all the billets held by Englishmen in India to-day were divided among educated, needy Hindus, only a few of the people who now clamour for promotion could be made happy, contented men.

As regards education in India, none can speak at the present time with more unction than the Parsi, because his community—80,000 strong in India—is prepared to spend to-day Rs. 25,000,000 on a Parsi Central College. An intelligent Parsi explained to me that the last generation sat at the feet of Spencer, Huxley, Tyndal and Morley ; and the result was a hard-and-fast materialism.

"We wrote God with a little 'g'" he said "and although we kept to the Parsi head-dress, and other outward marks of our ancient religion, we were, at heart, materialists. But of late years materialism has lost ground in India. The Theosophical Society has taught people here to reverence the ancient religions of the world, and has shewn them that such religions have a scientific basis. Men like Sir Oliver Lodge and Professor James have replaced Huxley and Spencer ; and now we want our children to receive religious instruction and moral training. Besides, the English system of education does not suit the Oriental mind. Cramming and examinations may be all right for the West, but in the East they make boys like parrots. We want our boys to think; not to shine in the examination hall, and then to forget all that they have learnt. We don't blame the Government of India. All the great religions of the world have adherents here ; and the Government must treat all alike. So the Government cannot give a religious education. It is the bounden duty of Parsis to follow the example set by the Mahomedans at Aligarh, and the Hindus at the Central

Hindu College at Benares. A western education without religion is fatal to Indians. You have but to look around and see the consequences of such an education to-day."

A Parsi, who is the headmaster of a large Government school for boys in Bombay, kindly gave me the following figures concerning the average cost of a boy's education in India. He said that very few young Indians become M. A.'s, most of them are satisfied to be F. A.'s and B. A.'s ; but that the charges made for the M. A. examinations correspond with the figures given below.

The average monthly fee for a schoolboy in India, at a Government school, is 2½ rupees. The school course takes eleven years; so his total school fees would amount to 330 rupees. During that time about 70 rupees would be spent on books. The average monthly fee for a college student is 8 rupees. He has to attend college for four years, in order to complete the B. A. course. So his total college fees would be 384 rupees. The cost of books at college would be about 100 rupees. Railway or carriage fare for 15 years would be about 2 rupees a month, amounting to 360 rupees for 15 years. The fees for the different college examinations amount to 72 rupees. So the cost of a Government education, at school and college, extending over 15 years, would be as below:—

School fees for 11 years	Rs. 330
Books while at school	70
College fees for 4 years	384
Books at college	100
Railway or carriage fare for 15 years	360
University examination fees	72
Total.	Rs. 1,316 (£ 87:14:8)

For £ 87:14:8 the Government of India will educate a boy and give him a B. A. degree; and for about £100, it will do the same things and make a young man an M.A.. Consequently, thousands of young men in India yearly take degrees, who, if they were in England, would have no chance of writing F. A. or B. A. after their names. It is no uncommon thing for such young men to become postmen, porters on railways, and typists; and then to abuse the Government of India and the English nation because they are 'crowded out' of the intellectual circles to which they belong, if not by birth, then by education.

In many directions to-day we see indications that a Government education in India is to be made more difficult; and Indians are, in consequence, beginning to understand that they must bestir themselves. 'The education of the masses and of women must now be taken in hand by ourselves', they say.

Discontent and unrest among students is a feature of the rising generation, it is true; but I believe that the Rev. W. S. Urquhart, Principal of the Duff College, is right when he says, 'I take it upon me to say, without fear of serious contradiction, that the prominence of the students in recent political troubles has been greatly exaggerated. It seems to be the theory of certain newspapers that whenever a group of young men get together and conduct themselves in a somewhat excited manner, they are bound to be students. But the constitution of such groups should be carefully examined before such sweeping statements are made. In the crowds that frequented Beadon Square (Beadon Square takes in Calcutta the place of Trafalgar Square, London, when a public meeting or demonstration is to be held) some months ago, students seemed to me to be conspicuous by their absence. Undoubtedly a few scatter-brained youths are allured by the fervour of demagogues into ways that lead to riot and tragedy, but they are the exceptions.' The 'scatter-brained youths' that Mr. Urquhart refers to, have been, in most cases, decadents—boys and young men made of the stuff that runs into anarchism. *The Antiseptic*, an Indian Medical Journal, edited by a Hindu doctor, said in December 1908: "The outbreak of anarchical outrages in India is almost as great a calamity as the establishment of bubonic plague and endemic disease in this country. The official mind sums up the causes of anarchism in India in one word 'UNREST.' And 'UNREST' according to the official, is synonymous with SEDITION. That may be the official way of looking at anarchism. It certainly is not the scientific way. The growth of anarchism on this continent of Asia is a comparatively recent growth. We are inclined to think that the modern anarchist is the product of present-day civilization. One striking feature of modern civilized life is the rapid increase in the number of insane people. And in this essentially neuropathic age anarchism has shewn itself as one variety of mental derangement. As a rule anarchists are men of acute sensibility, and disordered imagination. They have been influenced to an enormous degree by the sophisms spread by the writers on property, religion, government and capital. One of the most noticeable features of the anarchist's mind is its general exaltation. The anarchist considers that the avenging of offences and the preventing of iniquitous acts are his special province, and he acts on the insane idea that the citizen is entitled to substitute himself for the State, the dispenser of justice and the avenger of the oppressed. But it is a mistake to suppose that his insane actions have any foundation in altruistic ideas. The dominant desires in the anarchist mind are the longing for absolute equality and the thirst for material satisfaction. The desire for absolute equality has been noticed in anarchists of all countries. And the Bengal anarchists appear to be no exception to the rule. Political equality seems to be their object too. But with them political equality is inextricably mixed up with racial equality. And the not infrequent public assertion of racial superiority by the less thoughtful among the European residents in this country over their Indian fellow-citizens may not unnaturally have fanned into flame the dormant desire for absolute equality lurking in the minds of the potential anarchists of Bengal."

Bombs are an excresence of the great and universal movement now going on in India. They have been thrown by students in some cases ; but that students are an unruly set of boys and young men is not true, and that a Government education is responsible for bombs is also false. Everything points to the fact that the anarchist movement in India is a decadent movement—a poisonous fungus of native growth. In Europe and in America young Indians can talk freely; and no doubt they have done so. Very likely they have met anarchists in their travels and have made enquiries and borrowed books. But if the anarchist movement in India had been engineered from outside, then the bombs would have been better. The bombs used in India have been very crude. Empty cocoanut shells—cheap and plentiful—filled with nails and the latest chemicals have been used in most cases ; and many of the bombs have closely resembled the fireworks that are so generally manufactured locally for holiday entertainments and religious ceremonies.

It might be expected that Bengal would become the centre of the new movement, because Bengalis are the brains of India, and Calcutta is the centre of modern India. There Lord Curzon's whip brought out a complaint that has been growing in India ever since the Mutiny, and more especially from the time that Lord Ripon was Governor-General of India. Let me take a homely illustration. A child has internal measles. It coughs, and its mother plunges it into a hot bath. Suddenly the rash comes out, and the doctor is fetched.

What are Indians really fighting for ?

Racial equality.

Racial equality throughout the British Empire is the problem of the future—and the greatest problem that the British Empire has ever yet had to solve. In the solution of that problem lies the fate of the British Empire, for Asia has taken on a new lease of life.

India comes to England to-day, saying :—

"Trust me. Make me a part of the British Empire, in deed as well as in name."

At the Indian National Congress, held in Madras, in December 1908, a delegate said :—

"Let England trust us, and we will make her independent of the British self-governing Colonies. Let England trust us, and then she need no longer be afraid of Germany."

One of the greatest needs of India to-day is a good history from the time of the Mutiny to the end of the reign of Queen Victoria. I shall give in another chapter a short account of the Viceroys since the time of Lord Canning—a summary that was not easy to write, because, although many histories and biographies have been written, there is no book that gives a full and accurate account of the affairs of India from the time of the Mutiny until the death of the great Queen-Empress—Victoria the Good. I asked an English professor of history in one of the largest colleges in India to give me the name of a history of India from 1858 to 1900, and he said:—

"There is no such history—only text-books for the use of schools. I recommend to students Thompson's history; and I tell them to read the '*Rulers of India*' series."

The histories now available tell us that, before the time of Lord Ripon, Indians were not critical, or inclined to be discontented. They saw that the Government of India passed beneficent measures; and they said:—

"What matter if Rana rules, or Ravana rules, so long as peace, prosperity and justice are ensured?"

But when English people opposed Lord Ripon's proposals—proposals that would give to Indians a larger share in the management of their own affairs—then Indians began to doubt the justice of English people and to attribute to them selfish and self-interested motives. By that time English had become the common tongue of India; and Indians from all parts of the country could meet and discuss matters. Many Indians had been to Europe and to America, and had formed opinions on western manners and habits. Some Indians had set themselves to study the character and the history of the English nation. Mill, Spencer, Morley—these writers had formed new ideals in India. Not seldom have I been told by Indians:—

"The present Secretary of State for India has done more by his writings to bring about the present state of affairs in India than any other man."

Meanwhile more, and yet more, English people

had gone to India, and these people held aloof from Indians, and behaved as though the Indians were not British subjects like themselves. Eurasians increased in number, and pressed at the heels of English residents, just as Indians press at the heels of Eurasians to-day. Hindu lawyers filled the Law Courts—the Hindu mind is subtle and the Hindu tongue is glib—and these lawyers saw that while English people are always tried in India by English juries, Indians are tried by mixed juries, and by special juries which are chiefly composed of Englishmen. I was present in Bombay during the long trial of Mr. Tilak—the most important of all the trials for seditious writing held in India during last year—and I must say that I could not understand why the Parsi Judge challenged every Hindu who could have acted on the jury, and allowed the jury to be composed solely of men who did not know the language in which the article on which the prosecution was based was written. I watched the attitude of the jury very closely ; and I came to the conclusion that most of the jurymen had made up their minds before the trial commenced. No doubt to be tried in a foreign language is a great hardship, no matter how able and trustworthy the Court translator may be ; and to be found 'guilty' or 'not guilty' by men from across the seas is one of the greatest misfortunes that a man can be called upon to bear. I shall have more to say on this subject while writing about Hindu editors and newspapers.

In the time of Lord Ripon, Indians began to ask why they might not carry firearms; and why the highest posts in the Army and the Civil Service are reserved for Englishmen ? Of late years the attitude of England toward the great self-governing Colonies has been much discussed in India.

"Is the mother afraid of her daughters?" Indians ask.

"Why cannot the King-Emperor insist on our being treated as British subjects in the British Colonies?" they want to know.

Now they are waiting for the Charter that England will before long be asked to give to the South African Colonies.

"Will that Charter have a colour line?" they ask.

Those of them who have studied the constitution of England, and who understand what a constitutional Monarch can, and what he cannot do, say, proudly :—

"When that Charter is given, then let England choose between the British Colonies and India. The consequences of the choice must fall on her own head."

Students hear these things talked about, and a handful of them have become anarchists. They have nothing to lose but their lives ; for they are not earning money, and their wives and children are supported by their fathers. One has but to look at the faces of the Bengal anarchists in order to see what they are. Decadent was written large on the face of Kudi Ram Bose, who was executed on the 11th of July, 1908, for helping to throw the bomb that killed Mrs. and Miss Kennedy. Profulla Chandra Chake, the man who threw the bomb and shot himself when he was arrested, was an older and stronger man. Many of the Bengal anarchists are only boys ; and, if the Government of India were to make known the bill that will have to be paid to Mr. Eardley Norton—1,000 Rupees a day is said to be his fee in ordinary cases—then Indians, who are a thrifty people, and who know that the money will have to come out of their own pockets in the form of taxes, then Indians would look upon anarchism in quite a different way. Many of the youthful anarchists have been encouraged and influenced by the rash conversation of their elders, no doubt. I myself heard a babu in Calcutta, whose house is not far from the garden where the bombs were prepared, relate that his little son had said to him :—

" Father, when I am a man, I will blow up all the bridges made by the English."

These words were repeated as a joke less than three months before the first bomb outrage occurred; and the babu looked astonished when I rose up and left the house.

That the unrest and discontent of 1908 culminated in the death of two innocent and defenceless Englishwomen will be recorded by history ; and at whose door a tragedy that all Indians deplore should be placed, history alone can decide.

CHAPTER XIV

MARRIAGE AND WOMEN

IT is a common thing to read in books and articles, written by English persons, denunciations of the system of early marriage that has been in vogue in Hindustan from time immemorial. But the more we study the question, the more clearly we see how scientific the system is from an Indian standpoint. India is a tropical country and young people mature there very quickly. Indian boys and girls become men and women at a time when English boys and girls are still children. A betrothal has in India all the sanctity of marriage ; and the reason commonly given for this is that, after the Mahomedans went to India, it became a criminal act to touch a married woman but it was not considered a criminal act to touch an unmarried girl—the penalty for so doing being merely to marry the girl or to maintain her. So Hindu girls were betrothed at a very early age and the betrothal was to all legal intents and purposes a marriage, although the girl did not become a wife in the real sense of the word before she reached maturity. The usual age for a husband in India has been, and is still, nineteen or twenty, and for a wife thirteen or fourteen. At the age of thirteen many Indian girls are already mothers.

English zenana missionaries, who are nearly all middle-aged, unmarried women, have found in Indian homes little married girls of tender years, and have flown to the conclusion that such children were really wives. These English ladies have won for Zenana Missions large sums of money by writing and lecturing about 'child marriage in India'. Mrs. Besant very pertinently remarked at a public meeting, not long ago, that in all probability unmarried women in England have suffered quite as much from want of marriage as child-wives in India have suffered from early marriage. Be that as it may be, it is certain that English missionaries have greatly misunderstood the Indian system of early marriage. They have not taken into consideration the climate of India; and have ignored or been ignorant of the fact that betrothed boys and girls formerly obeyed their parents, and that the mother of the young husband controlled the movements of the young couple and took care of the health of the boy-husband and the girl-wife. Only now is the control of parents, which was formerly considered a religious duty, giving way before western ideas of independence; and how much of the so-called 'unrest' in India is due to attempts made by young Indians to copy English ways, and set up a separate establishment after marriage, will be known one day, perhaps. Formerly a young Indian took his wife to his father's house. He had no rent to pay, no separate kitchen to think about, no doctor's bills to consider. Whatever he earned went to the head of the home—the father, or eldest brother—and he and his wife and children shared with the rest of the family. Formerly the young Indian wife had no need to study domestic-economy, physiology, sanitation and the management of children. Now she stands in great need of such knowledge; and English zenana missionaries must look to their laurels and write text-books on these subjects. The days for teaching fancy-needle-work in the zenana have gone by. Indian girls owe a great deal to English lady missionaries, no doubt; but Hindu girls formerly learnt their deepest and most lasting lessons from the old Shastry, or old Brahmin who read to them the Bharata, Ramayana, or Bhagavata in their leasure hours. These three books have been read to Hindu women from generation to generation; and in this way they have imbibed the higher thoughts of Hinduism. I am told that this habit is growing less and less among Hindu women and that now, very rarely do they gather together—mother, daughters, daughters-in-law, and women servants—to listen to the old Shastry or the old Brahmin, and that simplified editions of the Bharata, Ramayana and Bhagavata for the use of Hindu girls are much wanted at present.

In a country where boys soon become men, early marriage is a necessity, if the purity of family life is to be preserved. Until lately the boy-husband obeyed his mother in domestic matters and the girl-wife was controlled by her mother-in-law. The mother said when the young pair were to meet; and, at other times, the girl-wife did not speak to her boy-husband; in fact, it was considered immodest for her even to look at her lord and master when others were in the room. For three months before the birth of a child and for three months afterwards the young wife remained with her own mother; and her husband was not allowed to see her. Perhaps this humane regulation had something to do with an institution that is much misunderstood by English people, I mean the dancing girl, commonly called the nautch woman.

The position of Indian women is slowly changing, but still it resembles very closely that of women in

Greece during the days of Pericles. We know that the Greeks took many of their habits and customs from Asia, so it is possible that they copied eastern ideas about women, and that women are in India to-day in much the same position as they were in the days of Buddha and Confucius. Still, for the sake of comparison, I will not go further back than the time when art in Greece reached its climax, the glorious days when the Parthenon was built. It was an age of great men and mighty achievements ; but the only women in Greece who shared in the glories of that time were the *Helaerae*, a class of women that corresponded very closely with the present dancing girls of India.

Mr. Arthur T. Grant, says in his book, "*Greece in the Age of Pericles*" Women were in the age of Pericles surrounded by restrictions of the closest kind. They lived in separate apartments, usually in the upper part of the house. They very rarely went out of the house. In the streets of Athens very few, if any women were seen, probably none of free citizen origin. No education seems to have been given to them. It is probable that the wife of Sophocles or Phidias could neither read nor write. The philosophical movement of the time did not touch them. The theatre was so intimately connected with religion that its doors could not be entirely closed to them ; but they were only allowed to be present at the tragedies. The comedies were performed before an exclusively male audience. The women who had an influence on Athenian history were not married women. The wives and mothers of the great men of Athens are, for the most part, names only, to which we can attach no importance at-all. The whole life of the wife after marriage was within doors. Beyond the threshold indeed she was rarely seen.

To rear up children and attend to the house was the whole duty of women, and however lax the ideas of Greece may have been about the conduct of men, they were always sufficiently strict when they referred to wives and daughters. The idea of intellectual companionship was excluded from the Athenian marriage. The matter was arranged by the parents, and the married couple often had not seen one another before the ceremony of betrothal. In all the utterances of practical men of the day concerning marriage, we never hear of mutual affection as the main condition of success. Marriage was a duty to the State, and a duty to the family, an affair of religion and of patriotism, but not of individual happiness. A pleader of the day said 'We have wives in order that we may beget legitimate children, and have a faithful guardian of our household.'

Mr. Grant goes on to say, "If we would complete our picture of Athenian life, we must remember the large number of courtesans (*Hetaerae*) who enjoyed a better education than citizen women, and were more skilled in the arts of pleasing, and whose position, though not regarded as respectable, was at any rate fully accepted by the morality and convention of the time. The partial recognition which was given to them in Athens allowed the *Hetaerae* to escape the debasement that is their lot in modern society. There were doubtless many in Greece who had the character and ability of Aspasia."

We all know how Pericles wept at the trial of Aspasia, and that his fall from power and influence in Athens began after her acquittal was won by his tears. This wonderful woman has made the *Hetaerae* famous; and, according to Hindu ideas, she might have been born again in a famous Sanskrit poetess, Maduravani.

It is a common thing for English people to confuse the dancing girl with the ordinary prostitute ; so I note the following differences between them. The dancing girl is admitted into the temple. The prostitute may not go there. The dancing girl would shudder at the approach of an English soldier. The sons of dancing girls have risen to high positions, and have been honoured by the Government of India on various occasions. Lord Ampthill shook hands with a dancing girl after witnessing her theatrical performance. Dancing girls have given large sums to charities ; and some of them have been celebrated as actresses and Sanskrit poetesses.

It has been, and is still, a criminal act under the law of India to touch a woman unless she is a lawful wife, or a dancing girl. In order that men may not infringe the law of the land, dancing girls have been well educated and made attractive. The dancing girl is looked upon as a physical necessity in India ; and when I come to speak of unlegalized prostitution in India, then I think readers will agree with me that the dancing girl is a more merciful solution of certain social evils than the outbursts of Mrs. Josephine Butler and Mr. Stead. When the mind is trained from infancy to a profession, then doubtless less degradation, shame and sorrow will be felt than when poverty, or temptation, or love, throws a girl into the great, unorganised army of western prostitutes. Thanks to sanitary regulations, and an early education in matters connected with the health of the sexes, the dancing girl is a healthy, happy person. Whoever challenges this statement has but to consult Indian doctors and obtain statistics. We all know how prostitutes are treated in England and in the self-governing Colonies; and I have no hesitation in saying that the regulations of India are more scientific and humane as regards prostitution than in any other part of the British Empire, and that Christians might with advantage learn lessons in morality and charity as regards prostitutes from Mahomedans and Hindus.

Judging by the Social Conference held in Madras in December 1908, I should say that Indian women are changing. Half-a-dozen Indian ladies then made speeches on female education; and they spoke very well indeed. The audience was a large one, and the men—many of whom were delegates to the Indian National Congress—listened to the women with careful and sympathetic attention. Some of the speakers were Caste ladies; and I believe I am right in saying that Caste ladies have seldom, if ever, spoken in public before.

Evidently Hindu women are no longer satisfied with the life led by Athenian women in the days of Pericles; and some of them echo to-day the words put into the mouth of Medea by Euripedes :—

"Of all things that have life
And sense, we women are most wretched. First
With all our dearest treasures we must buy
A husband, and in him receive a lord.
A hardship this. A greater hardship yet
Awaits us. Here's the question, if the lord
Prove gentle or a tyrant? If the worst,
To disunite our nuptials hurts our fame,
Nor from the husband may our sex withdraw
The plighted hand . . . .
If all our care
Gives us a gentle husband, one that binds
No galling yoke, happy our life indeed.
If not, death were more welcome . . . .
Yet will they say

We live an easy life, secure from danger
Whilst they hold the spear in battle.
Misjudging men ! Thrice would I stand in arms
On the rough edge of battle, ere once bear
The pangs of child birth."

But lest Suffragettes in England should imagine that their Indian sisters are rebelling against 'that rude creature man,' I append a paper read by an Indian lady in Madras, last Christmas, at the time of the Indian National Congress.

"The important duties of ladies are (1) Bhakti towards their husbands ; (2) Bhakti towards their priests and elders ; (3) Devotion to God ; (4) Staunch attention towards domestic affairs (*i. e.*, to act as good housewife). In order to attain the above objects and for the execution of such duties, education is necessary to an extent. But generally our women misunderstand this and think that looking after domestic affairs alone forms their chief duty and not education, which is quite wrong from a sastric point of view. They generally spend the most part of their time in discussing about various useless topics. Is it not better to utilise this time in educating themselves ? I don't mean by education of females studying the various branches of literature as philosophy and others, or securing degrees in any English University; but to attain such knowledge in literature of their own languages that would prove sufficient to understand our sastras and the lectures on our religion by various Pundits and to help their husbands by looking after minor domestic accounts, if they do not find time, and to understand any strange news if brought home by their husbands. This is the education I mean, necessary to Indian ladies. I do not mean that you should not learn more than this, you are at liberty to do it. Every task the ladies set in to do, must be done with the permission of their husbands or elders, as this is one of the bye-laws of our Sastrias (Dharma Sastra). They can easily reap the fruitful consequences of performing such duties as were mentioned hitherto and educating themselves. This education will render them helpful in leading their husbands to good paths if they are likely to get into bad ways. Our ladies have a blind idea that ladies of older days have never been educated, but this is not so as by consulting various sastras we learn the following instances.

In Mahabharata, Savitri discussed about Dharma Sastra with Yama and got her husband alive again who was dead. (2) In the same Mahabharata a lady has given a lecture on Chastity to a Brahman, named Kousika. (3) In the same Mahabharata, Draupadi explained Dharma Sastra to Yudhishtra while he was put into great difficulties by his cousins Duryodana and others.

If the above ladies were not educated they would not have been in the least able to suggest such helping plans.

So I request you, gentlewomen, not to entertain the idea, *viz.*, female education is not necessary, in your mind and I request you again to try to encourage female education as much as possible."

CHAPTER XV

MOORSHEDABAD AND PLASSEY

SURPRISINGLY few English people have been to Moorshedabad—the ruined city that was before the battle of Plassey the capital of Bengal. Yet a train that leaves Calcutta at 11 P. M. reaches Moorshedabad at 7 A. M.; and one wakes up then in an old-world atmosphere that is very refreshing after a month spent in Calcutta.

The Nawab Bahadur, commonly known as Prince Wasif, is a lineal descendant of Mir Jaffir. He was educated in an English Public School, and he wears English clothes and eats English food. He is fond of England and spent much time there before his father's death. Now he lives among his own people, and interests himself in education and things of that sort, besides looking after his large estates. In a palace built for his father by the Government, he receives English visitors; but he lives in a palace at a little distance from this modern structure, a much older palace into which no Englishman may enter. His mother, brothers and other members of his family have apartments there; and a high wall surrounds a place that is said to resemble a small oriental town.

Lord Kitchener and Lord Curzon visited Moorshedabad, and were very much interested in the historical monuments that the Nawab guards with great care; also in the library, which contains a collection of copies of the Koran that is of immense value. These books, illustrated with rich colours and bound in covers ornamented with gold and jewels, resemble the missals used by European Kings during the Middle Ages.

The palace grounds are entered through a tall gateway, above which the Nawab's band plays as sunrise and sunset on silver trumpets, hautboys and other sweet-sounding instruments. A short drive leads to the palace—a large building with a broad flight of steps on which 5,000 spectators can witness the ceremonies of the Muharram, which are yearly carried out at Moorshedabad with care and exactness. One hundred horses are in the stables, also many elephants; and on entering the palace one sees the polo prizes won by the Nawab and his brothers, and the beasts that have fallen to their guns in the jungle. Massive ivory furniture gives to the drawing-room an oriental appearance; but the palace is furnished throughout in English style, and in the galleries are pictures by famous British artists. In the Nawab's study, the latest English novel lies beside *The Pioneer*; and only by looking out of the windows does the visitor realise that the palace belongs to an Indian prince, and not to an English nobleman.

Looking through the windows, one sees a winding river, glittering like gold in the sunlight, and on it barges and sailing boats. Lordly elephants walk leisurely along the banks, and women, wearing gay cloths, draw water and poise on their heads brass *lotas* and red, earthen pots. Gorgeous flowers are in the gardens—yellow jasmine and red hibiscus—and, as far as the eye can see, are tall palms with glistening green leaves and fruit shining like burnished gold.

And in front of the English palace is a relic that carries one's mind at once to the time when the English had not thought of making Calcutta the capital of British India—the remains of a mosque for the building of which Suraja Dowla carried on his head the first basketful of bricks.

One morning, before the sun was up, I went to see the tomb of this unhappy Nawab, which is carefully preserved by the Government. At the feet of the murdered man lies the faithful Begum—his favourite wife—who fled with him from Moorshedabad after the battle of Plassey. History tells us that Suraja Dowla was weak, self-willed, cruel and avaricious; but that, nevertheless, two women loved him devotedly,—his mother, who broke from her purdah and rushed out into the street when his dead body was paraded through Moorshedabad, and the wife who has been given a place in his tomb by the Government. It is related that he fled from the battlefield on a swift camel, and returned to one of his palaces at Moorshedabad. Night had fallen, and, in the dark, he sent away the ladies of his harem, and the eunuchs, and with them the greater part of his gold and jewels. Afterwards he disguised himself, and left the palace with his favourite wife, hoping to join Mr. Law, who, with 100 French soldiers, was marching to his assistance. A fakir, whose ears he had cut off as a punishment for some trifling offence, found him cooking food in a garden, and informed Mir Jaffir of his whereabouts. Soldiers were sent to seize him and convey him to Moorshedabad; and there, at the instigation of Mir Jaffir's son, Miriam (Miriam was killed by a flash of lightning a year afterwards), he was murdered. He asked for time to say his prayers, and water for ceremonial ablutions; and, while on his knees, he was stabbed by hired assassins. A gnarled, twisted tree now marks the spot where the murder took place, and a wall encloses the ground on which 150 years ago the man 'who opened the door of Bengal for England' was done to death.

Only a few stones are left to-day of the palace from which Suraja Dowla fled, the palace Clive entered after the battle of Plassey, and of which he said, when describing to the Select Committee of the House of Commons in 1772 the gold and jewels in the vaults:—

"I stand amazed at my own moderation."

It is not easy to visit the historical remains of the former capital of Bengal, for jungle now covers most of the city; but, mounted on an elephant, I went from place to place, thinking, while I was carried through sweet-scented flowers and thick foliage, of the time when Clive entered Moorshedabad at the head of a small band of tired soldiers. Thousands of natives had gathered to see him march through the streets; and, as he said afterwards, he and his handful of soldiers might easily have been killed with stones and sticks. But it was not to be so. Silently, quietly, the masses watched the hero of Plassey while he and his soldiers marched to the house of the Jugget Sett, the bankers who had lent much money to French and English traders in Bengal and who held in thrall the representatives of the Saib Company at Fort William. A few ruined walls mark now the houses of these men, who have been called 'the Rothschilds of India'; but, at the time of the battle of Plassey, the bullion stored in their cellars would have dammed up the river that is now fast washing away the records of their power and wealth.

I wandered among the ruins of the place where Omichund was undeceived about the white and the red treaties, thinking how the reputation of Clive has suffered at the hands of a man whose passion for phrases surpassed his love of truth, and remembering that Admiral Watson—he sleeps in St. John's Churchyard, Calcutta,—was not a Member of the Council of Calcutta, and for that reason refused to put his name to the false document, and that Clive said, in the House of Commons:—

"If I had forged Watson's name, I would have said so."

The hero of Plassey was no coward, no hypocrite. He had, it is true, vast ideas of Empire, and proposed to the British Government of his day that all India should be divided into Presidencies, as is the case at present ; that the Presidencies should be ruled by English Governors, under the control of a Governor-General; and that the whole of the National Debt of England should be paid off by the gold and jewels of India and Ceylon. Morose, some say opium-drugged, fond of cards and women, vain and extravagant Clive is said to have been ; but the man who cut his throat after the House of Commons decided that he had 'rendered great and meritorious services to his country,' had no need of Macaulay's blushes.

There is in the Public Library at Pondicherry a very interesting collection of French books and documents dealing with the time when the French were in India. I visited the old capital of the French trading settlements before I went to Calcutta, and found there, among other things, the autobiography that La Bourdonnais wrote while in prison, using pocket-handkerchiefs for paper, coffee for ink, and a piece of pointed wood as a pen. Never was a book written under sadder circumstances than that record of a noble-minded Frenchman who refused to break his word given to the English, and who, on his return to France, was, in consequence, thrown into prison. That biography and other books of the same sort, should be read by those who desire to understand the conquest of India by the English ; for in English works there is a natural tendency to add to facts a national varnish. The Memoirs of Mr. Law, who was the only friend Suraja Dowla had at the time of the battle of Plassey, are in the British Museum. Mr. Law was the Governor of the little French settlement at Kossimbazaar (a suburb of Moorshedabad) when Clive insisted upon the colony being dispersed, and Admiral Watson threatened 'to raise such a conflagration as all the waters of the Ganges could not extinguish,' if the French soldiers were not sent away from Moorshedabad and its precincts. Mr. Law gives an interesting account of Suraja Dowla, and a very fair estimate of the behaviour of the English in 1755—7.

It is impossible, while visiting the ruins of Moorshedabad, not to wonder what Calcutta will be like in years to come. In India, extremes of draught and rain, and fierce heat, undermine foundations and attack mortar, and only stone walls seem to be able to withstand the elements. There have been many Delhis, and the Benares of to-day is built on cities of the same name that stretch back further than memory.

It the English left India to-day, what great architectural works would mark their conquest of the country? The Bombay railway station is, perhaps, their greatest structural achievement. They have copied the architecture of the country to a great extent, and by a few forts only have they added to the durable buildings of the Mahomedans. No great Cathedral points out that a Christian nation has ruled over India for 150 years. Churches are plentiful, but they show no particular style of architecture, and comfort seems to be more thought about than pillars, windows and aisles. Now-a-days English people go to India for a short time only, and many of them regard the country as a dangerous but important national ornament. Picture galleries are non-existent in India, for collections of portraits in the residencies of Governors cannot be called picture galleries. The Theatrical Companies that visit India are third, and fourth rate, and the country possesses no theatre that can compare with the theatres in Melbourne, for instance, Viceroys and Governors of Presidencies come and go, and there is no connecting link between them. The Mahomedan rulers lived in India and built palaces and mosques there that are now visited by tourists from all parts of the world; but the English in India have been called a caravan, and the Government has been compared with caravansary.

Some people say that if an English Prince of the Royal Blood held his Court in Calcutta, the loyalty of Indians would be stirred, because formerly Hindus looked upon their rulers as divine beings. But such people forget that the Mogul Emperors were never worshipped by Hindus, and that while Hindus will do homage to princes of their own blood and religion, they remain without a salam in the presence of a Royal *feringhi*.

Nothing amuses me more than to hear English people talk, of ' our great dependency,' 'our Empire in India,' 'our Indian subjects'. Such people never speak of ' our Commonwealth of Australia,' ' our Dominion of Canada', ' our New Zealand subjects'. These expressions show how wide apart England and India really are ; and make me think of a collection of Hindu pictures, in which I saw a very pale, youthful-looking, ascetic Virgin Mary, with a crown on her head and the title 'Victoria, Queen-Empress of Great Britain and India.'

On my way back to Calcutta, I went to see the battlefield of Plassey.

A minute station, without a waiting-room, bears the historical name of Plassey; and the only vehicle at the Plassey railway station was a small bullock wagon. 'Muck! muck!' cried the driver; and he twisted the tail of the poor little bull and prodded it with a stick while it trotted over a sandy desert. A good Rest-house is now, thanks to Lord Curzon, in course of construction, where books, beds and food will be provided—also a guide. But I think a guide in India is a nuisance; and I advise anyone who is really interested in the battlefield of Plassey to visit the place as I did that morning.

Several times the driver took the wrong track, and we had to go back again; but, at last, he stopped beside a clump of trees and said:—

"This is the battlefield."

Then half-a-dozen natives rushed out of some huts, and one of them, who could speak Hindustani, led the way to a small and very plain marble monument on which Clive's name and the date of the battle are engraved.

I was told, after my return to Calcutta, by the Government Architect, that a monument to Clive was then on its way from Italy; but when I was at Plassey, only a small and very insignificant marble pillar bore the name of Clive.

My guide had much to say about the visit of Lord Curzon, who arrived at Plassey on 'the Nawab's own elephant'; and he showed me a place, unknown to history, where a spear, dropped by Suraja Dowla, is said to be buried. I made him happy with a rupee, and sent him to fetch fresh milk; and he hurried away, followed by a little herd of men and children.

Then I was able to picture the battlefield of 150 years ago. I saw, in imagination, the grove of mangoes (Clive's sketch of these trees can still be seen at Fort St. George, Madras) under which the tired English soldiers lay down to rest. I pictured the hunting-box of the Nawab, in which Clive and his officers spent a sleepless night, listening to the music in Suraja Dowla's Camp. I followed Clive onto the roof at daybreak, and watched the grey mist lifting from the river and the trees; and I saw the vast, unwieldy army of the Nawab advancing in the dim light of dawn. On it came—cannon on flat, low carriages, drawn by white oxen; hordes of men armed with bows and arrows; leaders mounted on gaily-caparisoned elephants; and a little band of fifty Frenchmen, with a modern gun. I heard Clive give the order for the disposal of his small force, and—with the help of miniature cannon placed by Lord Curzon on the spots occupied by the few guns Clive had at his disposal—I traced the ccmmencement of the famous battle.

Clive's men fell fast, and he ordered the English soldiers and the sepoys to retire behind a natural embankment and lie down. Shouts and jeers from the enemy greeted this rearrangement. But the stars in their courses fought for Clive that day. Rain fell: the ammunition of the enemy became damp and useless.

Then (so history tells us) Suraja Dowla sent for Mir Jaffir, who had kept his men out of action; and this friend of the English came reluctantly into his nephew's presence.

"Mir Jaffir," said the Nawab, throwing his turban before his uncle, "that turban you must defend."

Sullenly Mir Jaffir went away. Afterwards there was a panic, reports being spread among the Nawab's soldiers that the English were advancing upon their Camp. The order was given to retire; and to the astonishment of Clive and his handful of officers and men, the huge army of Suraja Dowla turned and went slowly back to the village of Plassey. Only the gallant little band of Frenchmen stuck to their gun; and the place from whence they were dislodged by the Englishmen, with so much trouble, may be seen to-day.

The Nawab's shooting-box is gone. Not a single mango tree remains. A short portion of the embankment that protected Clive's little force can be traced, and the river still winds along the plain. In imagination one can see the vast, disorganised Camp of Suraja Dowla entered by Clive and his soldiers after the battle, and picture the strange influence exercised by Clive over his men, for history says that only a few strong oxen were taken to drag the guns to Moorshedabad, and the medley of provisions, baggage and animals was not touched. Clive promised his soldiers a reward later on; and that evening the tired little English force set out for the capital of Bengal, about thirty miles distant.

CHAPTER XVI

THE GANGA-JI

ON the way to Benares, I stayed at Buddha-Gaya, where, it is said, Buddha became 'enlightened', or, in the words of Hindus, obtained 'liberation.' The name Buddha is an epithet meaning 'the perfectly enlightened one,' or rather, the one who by perfect knowledge of the truth is liberated from all existence, and who, before his attainment of Nirvana, or extinction of worldly existence, reveals to the world the method of obtaining it.

Sir Edwin Arnold has made Buddha-Gaya beautiful and sacred by 'The Light of Asia'; and, although quarrels and law suits are going on there to-day, I found the temple and its precincts very interesting.

Buddha has had more followers than any other religious teacher; his religion has led to no bloodshed, has had no martyrs; and the swords of Mahomedans, the bloody sacrifices of Hindus, and the Holy Inquisition of Christians, make one turn with a sane, strong affection to the man who, 2,500 years ago, gave to the world the Five Precepts that are kept to-day by all good Buddhists; namely: "Do not kill. Do not steal. Do not love any woman but your lawful wife. Do not tell a lie, in other words, do not bear false witness. Do not touch intoxicating liquor." The carved stone railing at Buddha-Gaya is among the oldest of the architectural remains yet found in India. Such things are of later date than Stonehenge, later—much later—than the Pyramids of Egypt, later even than the temples of Greece and Rome; in fact, one of the surprises and disappointments of India is the modern date of its architecture. St. Paul's Cathedral and Westminster Abbey are ancient buildings when compared with the mosques and palaces of the Mahomedan Emperors; and, as I have already mentioned, Delhi and Benares are built on decayed and buried cities.

Buddhism flourished in India from about 400 B. C. to 600 A. D.; and was then driven out of the country by the Brahmins. At the time when St. Thomas, the Apostle, is supposed to have gone to India, namely after the death of the Virgin Mary, the country was to a large extent Buddhistic. The people who killed St. Thomas are thought to have been Nature worshippers. Very interesting relics of St. Thomas are preserved in a Roman Catholic Cathedral, at Mylapore, near Madras. These were found while the Portuguese were in India. At St. Thomas' Mount, about ten miles from Madras, the place where the Apostle was killed is shewn; also a cleft in a rock which holds, always, beautifully-clear water. As no spring can be discovered, and St. Thomas is said to have struck the rock with his staff when he wanted water to drink, pious Roman Catholics believe that some supernatural power presides over the water. At the date of the Feast of St. Thomas, the water rises. A 'Weeping Stone' is shewn, namely a stone that was said to weep on the anniversary of the Apostle's death. And above the altar, in the Church, at the top of the Mount, is a picture said to have been painted by Saint Luke. A Brahmin artist, who has visited Rome, tells me that a similar picture is to be seen in the Vatican. We have to thank Lord Curzon for the preservation of some of these very interesting things.

While Buddhism was the dominant religion of the country, Chrsitians suffered no hardships and were allowed to live quietly in India; but after the Brahmins regained their hold on the country, then Christians had to live in caves and on the tops of mountains. When the Portuguese became powerful on the West Coast, Christianity revived; and the greatest of the Mahomedan Emperors—Akbar—married a Christian wife. This lady was beautiful and young when the Portuguese missionaries sent her to Akbar, hoping that she would be able to convert the Mahomedan Emperor to Christianity. She failed in her efforts; but, later on, she became the wife of Akbar, and he gave her a separate palace, and allowed her to carry on there the rites of the Roman Catholic religion. At that time, religious persecution was rife in Europe; and when I saw the tomb of this Portuguese lady, many thoughts concerning Mahomedans and Christians passed through my mind.

Budda, after he came 'enlightened,' went to Sarnath, which is about four miles from Benares; and there he first 'turned the Wheel of the Law,' that is to say, he preached his first sermon. Sarnath was at that time known as 'the Deer Park'; and some Budhists think that he lived in the monastery that is now being unearthed by the Government. But the excavations show no earlier date than the time of Asoka—250 B.C.—and an enormous, upright, stone pillar, that has lately been uncovered, is inscribed with rules for the conduct of monks in the days of that wise and enlightened Emperor.

Sir Monier Monier-Williams says :—

"Asoka did for Buddhism what Constantine did for Christianity,—gave an impetus to its progress by adopting it as his own creed. Buddhism then became the state religion of Magadha, and therefore of a great portion of India."

Sarnath is now set in a plain; and only a few children and beggars wander among its ruins. A Jain temple is at a little distance; and the monks there told me that Jainism is older than Buddhism. However, I think there is very little difference between the two religions; and Buddha was a reformer, and a philosopher, he claimed to make old things new, not to give to the world a fresh theory of existence. Jains are even more particular than Buddhists about not taking sentient life. The Jain monk drinks through a strainer, for he hesitates to kill the smallest animalcule. But he walks on the earth; so he must crush insects at every footstep!

Among the interesting things lately unearthed at Sarnath, is a gigantic figure of Buddha, with an enormous chatta, or umbrella. This is of bright, red stone, and looks as fresh to-day as when it was carved and erected 2,200 years ago.

A Buddhist monk, who happened to be visiting the ruins, showed me the bath used in the monastery, also the refectory and the chapel; and he explained that the many small, round, flat slabs, stamped with images of Buddha, that have been discovered, contain probably the ashes of monks who lived and died in the monastery. It was usual in those days, he said, to burn the body of a dead monk, mix his ashes with soft clay, stamp the surface with the image of Buddha, and then put the slab away on a shelf in the chapel. The Government is now carrying on the work of excavation at Sarnath in a dilatory fashion ; and tourists take little interest in the buried monastery. A shed has been erected to hold the images and other things excavated ; and in this rude museum I saw the money used in those days—cowries, also earthen pots and drinking vessels. People who have read Buddha's instructions and rules, given to his Brethren—two large volumes—can form a good idea of the lives led by the monks in the time of Asoka—a daily routine of study and meditation, charity and detachment, varied by sermons, and monastic ceremonies at which Kings assisted. Robes were dyed by the monks with jak fruit, as is the case to-day; rice was stored in granaries, or begged from door to door; and the end held in view was the escape from a round of births and deaths, sorrow and pain, by the attainment of Nirvana, which the Hindu calls Liberation, and modern science knows by the name of 'cosmic consciousness.'

The great stupa of Asoka, which is supposed to be the oldest ruin in India, is at a little distance from the monastery ; and it closely resembles the dagobas in Ceylon, built by Buddhists about 300 B. C.

The sun had set before I left Sarnath, for the Buddhist priest had much to tell me about the past, present and future of his religion. He believed that Buddhism will before long revive in India; and he spoke of the progress it is now making in Europe. He took from his leather belt a Sinhalese newspaper and read a message sent by a dying Buddhist monk to his Brethren a few days previously:—

"You must not regret my departure; it is but for a time, and you see that I have no regret—nay, I am triumphant. During my life, my motives have been pure.

I have devoted myself to the cause of truth, and I have been unswervingly faithful to my teachers. Therefore I have overcome difficulties, therefore I have triumphed, therefore I triumph even now. And now listen to what I, who am dying, have to say to you about death. As your life, so will be your death. There have been priests, who, not having lived the true life, have lost hope and died as if they had been unordained. Let not this be so with you. Live dispassionately, observe the Precepts of our Lord, be ever ready to sacrifice your lives for the cause of truth ; and then you will triumph in the hour of death. Take courage, and work; my influence will be with you. In ten or fifteen years there will be a great re-action in favour of Buddhism; and then you will observe a certain person working for the advancement of the cause. Now my time is near. I make my salutations to my elders. Remember—always—association with the righteous is good, is a thousand times good. May my company be with the righteous."

Benares can be seen best by hiring a little house-boat, for a few days, and living on the river. Such a boat is clean and fairly comfortable, and on its flat roof the ever-changing scenes can be watched from dawn—when Hindus bathe, pray and meditate, and the burning ghats send lurid flames to meet the rising sun—until dusk—the time of tinkling temple bells, evening baths, and devotions.

Come and watch with me the sun rising on the Ganga-ji, at Holy Kasi!

One side of the river is flat, and almost without houses; the other springs abruptly from the water, and has temples and dwelling-places clinging to it, as ivy clings to a wall. Almost every Hindu prince has a palace beside the Ganga-ji ('ji' means 'master', 'soul'), and around these tall, many-storied buildings are clusters of small houses and here—there—everywhere is a shrine, or a temple. Before a crimson glow spreads over the eastern sky, the pilgrims begin their ablutions; and dawn shows the ghats covered with men and women, while at the edge of the river, on planks and rafters, sit Sons of the Ganges (Brahmins), engaged in meditation. Bathing, washing their brass *lotas*, praying, or meditating, the pilgrims take little notice of a tourist in a boat or walking on the ghats. Many have come from a long distance; some have vows to perform; others are ill, or dying. Hindus believe that the first Kasi, and the Ganga-ji, descended from heaven, and that anyone who dies beside the river will return at once to Brahman.

So many pilgrims die on the ghats, and are carried to the burning places, and their ashes are afterwards thrown into the river—a river that nothing pollutes, the water of which can be kept for years in bottles by pious pilgrims who carry it home, a river that has a strange, magnetic influence and draws to its banks not only Hindus, but also Christians and Mahomedans. The mosque of Aurungzeb, rising tall and graceful amid temples and shrines, reminds those who have eyes to see and ears to hear that Allah is Brahman, and Brahman is God.

" By faith ye are healed ", said Jesus, the Christ ; and that faith has a great deal to do with the wonders worked by the Ganges is shewn in the following Hindu parable.

One day, Siva and his consort Parvathi were strolling by the river at Kasi ; and Parvathi said to the Lord :—

" It is said that if anyone bathes in the Ganges, his sins will be washed away and he will reach heaven."

And Siva asked, laughing :—

"How many do you think believe in the efficacy of the river ? Faith alone can make it efficacious."

"But they must have faith" argued Parvathi, "for otherwise they would not come here to bathe."

"That is not so" said Siva ; and, in order to convince her, he took the form of an old man and transformed her into an old woman; and then, apparently, he died.

Parvathi cried to the people : 'If there is one sinless man among you, he can bring my husband to life again by pouring water over him.' But every man thought himself impure, and went away. At last a man who had not even washed his teeth that morning and who had just left a home of ill-fame, heard her ; and he asked 'Is it really true mother?' And when she said 'It is really true,' he plunged into the river, and poured water over the old man ; and the old man revived.

Then Siva pointed to the man and said 'Faith did it.'

Faith, says the parable, is stronger than will ; faith is the strongest thing in the world, for faith is the realization that I am I.

Many Sanyasins live beside the Ganges ; and a saint has built for himself there a hut on the peak of a hillock. He has lived in that place for seven years, and goes out of it only to bathe in the river at sunrise and sunset. The hut is so small that he cannot stand up, lie down, or stretch out his arms. It has shutters; and these are drawn-back in the morning, and then he touches with a bit of stick the heads of the pilgrims who prostrate themselves before him, and he accepts their offerings. He eats only a few grains of rice daily ; and the poorest pilgrims go to him for food and money.

Sitting motionless beside the river may be seen clean-shaven Brahmins, wearing only a waist-cloth, with arms and legs crossed, and eyes fixed on the ground. Such men might easily be mistaken for statues in the soft light of the rising sun. Holy Kasi is a stronghold of Brahminism. To Holy Kasi travel young Hindus from all parts of India, in order to receive religious teaching from the men who in days gone-by were the only Hindu schoolmasters. Each year eager boys beg their way to Kasi and ask the Sons of the Ganges for instruction. Such students live on the verandahs of pious residents, and rise long before daybreak to chant prayers, and to study by the light of a hurricane lamp. They carry back to their distant homes the essence of Hinduism; and in this way the Brahmins spread their doctrines among the masses.

Christian missionaries make little headway in Kasi; and the million idols of Hindus there sadden the hearts of those who cannot see that idols are images of Brahman. Once a year all the idols are thrown into the river, and new idols are bought, thus signifying that the symbols have served their purpose.

But let us return to the river and watch hundreds and thousands of men, women and children climbing the steep banks, making offerings in temples and shrines, and asking the blessings of Sanyasins. The women wear over their heads muslin veils, dyed crimson, green, orange, and red; dyed locally, for in Europe such brilliant colors are never seen. Widows, dressed in white, mix with the crowd; and the moving masses remind one of windows in European Cathedrals, when the sunshine pours through them and colored lights fall on marble floors. The pilgrims carry flowers in little brass bowls or brass baskets, and make offerings in temples and shrines; and many enter the temple of the goddess of smallpox, for that fell disease is often found in places where pilgrims congregate.

The boat drifts down the river, to the burning ghats, where coolies are seen, carrying dead bodies fastened to bamboo sticks and wrapt in gay-colored cloths. Sometimes relations and friends are at the ghats; but often the pilgrim has come alone to die at Holy Kasi. After death, the body is burnt, and the ashes and the bones are thrown into the Ganga-ji. The coolies wash their cloths and lay them out to dry, bathe, and go away. Relations and friends do the same things; and, although, no doubt, at home are weeping mothers and sorrowing wives and children, the dead body is treated as a polluted thing, a thing to be got rid of as quickly as possible, a thing that has nothing to do with the soul that used it.

Benares is an Indian city. In the Cantonment—a civil and military station—one general store provides for Europeans; and shopping must be done by memsahibs at Allahabad. Benares City is made up of narrow streets, tall houses and bazaars. I went to see a Hindu banker there; and found my way to his house with the help of a servant, for the city is a labyrinth. Silk manufacturers and brass manufacturers sit at open doors, and drawn-up shutters show the interiors of low-built, dark shops. The houses lean forward, and the roofs almost touch; and, looking up, I saw, in the dazzling, yellow glare of the sun, bright-colored verandahs and gay shutters. Dazed, bewildered by noise and heat, I reached, at last, the banker's house; and the servant, who had met my carriage and conducted me on foot (the streets in the heart of Benares City are too narrow to admit carriages), led the way into a baronial hall that reminded me of a Tennysonian ballad.

A retainer presented arms at the entrance, and I passed into an open square with raised, stone corridors. The banker met me in a passage leading to his own apartments; and he said that his brothers and cousins lived with their families in various parts of the building. On the walls of his drawing-room were pictures of rajahs (rajahs are as common in India as counts and barons are in Germany), and from the high ceiling chandeliers were suspended. The room was darkened by shutters, and punkahs moved lazily over luxurious armchairs and sofas covered with dark satin and velvet. The banker wore the white muslin costume of a Hindu gentleman and his airy attire contrasted strangely with his sombre surroundings. He offered to show me the most famous temples in Kasi, familiarly called by English tourists the 'Golden Temple' and the 'Monkey Temple'; and when the sun had gone down, he took me in his motor-car to the Durg-kund, and there, at the entrance, I fed the sacred monkeys and gave to their attendants *backsheesk*. Then we went to see the holy cows fed by pious widows with flowers; and 'the well of knowledge,' into which pilgrims throw flowers; and the Bisheshwar Temple, which has a dome and spire covered with gilded copper. The precincts of this temple were crowded with pilgrims, who were washing feet and hands before entering the inner courts, arranging flowers and saying prayers. No policeman was there—no policeman was needed, for the pilgrims came to pray and worship, and so long as none interfered with them, they cared little about the *feringhi* and the Government. Under Mahomedan rule it was different. Then the Hindus saw their temples destroyed—1,000 in Benares during the reign of the Emperor Aurungzeb—and the ruins of their sacred places used to build Mahomedan houses. I looked with special interest at a building, half-mosque, half-temple, in which to-day Mahomedans worship on the one side and Hindus on the other; and I thought of the 1,500 temples that flourish in Benares under British rule, to say nothing of countless little shrines at street corners. The Mahomedans allowed the Hindus to build temples large enough to hold one idol only; and for hundreds of years such temples were constructed; and so strong is habit, that after the Mutiny, when a great impetus was given to temple-building, the Hindus continued to build very small and very ornate temples. In Southern India, where the Mahomedans had little power, Hindu temples are large, tall and gaily-painted; but in Northern India, they are small, and white, and in simplicity of architecture and color they copy, to a certain extent, the mosques of the Mahomedans.

In Holy Kasi, the stronghold of Hinduism, Mrs. Besant and some of her followers, have taken up their headquarters.

"Mrs. Besant is our greatest enemy", a missionary told me.

Missionaries must not forget, however, that since the time of St. Thomas, the Apostle, Christians have been in India; and that although Roman Catholics, Protestants, Methodists, Wesleyans, Baptists and Salvationists have for many centuries tried to convert India, the country is to-day wedded to the most ancient religion in the world—the religion of the Vedanta.

Theosophists claim that when Colonel Olcott and Madame Blavatsky went to India, the whole country was drifting into atheism. The Christian missionaries had undermined the faith of Hindus, but had failed to establish Christianity on the crumbling foundations of

Hinduism. The Government of India was giving a western education without any religious teaching whatsoever. Theosophy restored to India the Upanishads and the Vedanta. Mrs. Besant followed Madame Blavatsky; and, with the help of some wealthy Hindus, she started the Central Hindu College at Benares, where a western education is given and the religion of Hindus is practised.

The C. H. C., is affiliated with the University at Allahabad, and the English tutors and masters are University men, who give their services for a small stipend, or for nothing, at-all. In the college are 400 young men, and in a school attached to the college are 400 boys. I went to see the C. H. C., and I found myself in an old palace—the Maharajah of Benares having sold to Mrs. Besant one of his palaces for her experiment. In the grounds, I noticed a stone erected to a widow who had done *suttee* there; also a temple to the Goddess of Learning, given by a wealthy Hindu lady, whose only son died before manhood. Hundreds of bright-eyed, intelligent Hindu boys were walking about, talking, laughing and playing; and presently a bell called them to a large hall for morning prayers. The English masters and mistresses were present, a pundit gave a short discourse, and all joined in a Hindu form of worship. Then the work of the day began, and the classes were conducted in exactly the same way as in any other college and school in India. Many of the boys are boarders, and live in large houses attached to the central building. There the castes mess separately, the lowest castes being excluded altogether. In each boarding-house I saw a *puja* room, and a room for recreation, and many servants flitting about the corridors. I was told that the princes of India intend to open a college before long for their own class only; but I imagine that such people will always prefer to have private tutors for their sons. Mrs. Besant's students belong almost entirely to the professional and merchant classes, or, as we should say in England, to the upper middle classes. English is the language spoken in the college, for the boys come from all parts of India, and speak many tongues; and the task of learning English is made easy and pleasant by ladies who live with Mrs. Besant. The college has a fine library, most of the books having been presented; and there the boys can read the newspapers and the magazines of India and England. In the library is a signed photograph of the King-Emperor, sent after the visit of their Royal Highnesses the Prince and Princess of Wales to the Central Hindu College, and signed photographs of the future King and Queen of England are on either side of the British Raj. The tone of the College is loyal; and, although in the debating club discussions on all subjects are encouraged, politics in any active shape are forbidden. Many of the students are married and higher fees are taken from married boys, in order to discourage early marriages.

'A young man cannot study when he has a wife and children to think about', remarked Mrs. Besant, in one of her addresses to the students. Every Sunday afternoon, Mrs. Besant (when she is at Benares) lectures in the large hall, taking for her subject some Hindu hero or saint; and a college magazine is published, also a quaint little boarding-house paper called 'Brains.' The C. H. C. is nine years old, and wants only eleven lacs to be placed on an independent footing. Now maharajahs and rajahs give it financial support, especially in the Sanskrit department, to which only Brahmin boys are admitted. Such boys went formerly to the Sons of the Ganges for instruction, and at the C. H. C. they receive a modern education as well as a special training in Sanskrit.

With the most orthodox Brahmins in Holy Kasi Mrs. Besant is not a favourite ; but many enlightened Hindus are much interested in the Central Hindu College and contribute generously to its support. As much building has still to be done, the place is not yet self-supporting ; and in the vacations, the boys go out to beg for their *Alma Mater*, and Mrs. Besant, who is sometimes called in India 'the grand old beggar,' lectures, and appeals to Hindu princes. Indians in South Africa send their boys sometimes to the C. H. C.; and such boys cannot be refused. Often an earnest student begs his way on foot from Southern India. Many boys, however, have to be kept waiting ; and the C. H. C. could have 1,000 boys and young men on its books to-day, if the boarding-houses were larger and more numerous.

I was invited to Mrs. Besant's bungalow, which she has named 'The Abode of Peace' ; and I noticed a Hindu god over the entrance. The bungalow stands in a garden, near a tank ; and I was told that this tank is Mrs. Besant's place of meditation and that she spends many hours alone there. Rishis once lived in holes cut in the steps ; and the place is very quiet, very picturesque. Horses and cows are kept by Mrs. Besant, and she indulges in riding and driving. Moreover she supplies her associates with milk—a very necessary article of diet in a place where Brahmin cooks are employed. I was honoured by a meal cooked by a Brahmin ; and I did not enjoy it. He brought several little dishes, and, with his holy fingers, he laid before me vegetable curry, fried potatoes, chapattis and a lump of boiled rice. I was told that it is difficult to find a Brahmin who will condescend to cook for English people ; and that food cooked by a man who is not a Brahmin lacks sanctity in the eyes of Theosophists. Mrs. Besant has her own Brahmin kitchen, and a Brahmin cook who travels with her in India. Theosophists attach enormous importance to the food they eat. A Theosophist lady at Benares told me that she ate 'gnostic food'; and this she described as bread and butter, tea and milk, vegetables and fruit. It is a little difficult to argue with Theosophists, because when history is quoted, they sometimes say : 'O, but So-and-So got it (the information) on the astral'. Also, Theosophists are convinced (like Brahmins) that they are the salt of a wicked world ; and some of them lose their temper when they are not taken at their own estimation. I have heard Hindus call western Theosophists 'a grotesque imitation of ourselves'; but I agree with a Servant of India who says that Theosophy mixes people together and has done much to help modern Hindus. An Englishman was pointed out to me at Benares, by a Hindu gentleman, who said:—

"Mr. Blank is one of us now."

"How so?" I asked.

"O, he dresses as we do, he eats our food, he sits and smokes like us—he is quite a Hindu."

The headquarters of the Theosophists at Benares resemble a small village, having a post-office, shops, and many large and small houses. Boys from the college and the school play about the grounds, and seem quite at home there. The buildings show no particular style of architecture, and are painted white and green. Mrs. Besant's house, which is the centre of everything, has a large chauki in the front room—a chauki covered with white linen—and from that place she delivers to her followers the latest bulletins from the 'Masters.'

To one thing, however, I strongly object, and that is the way in which Mrs. Besant, at the present time, tries to wrap up the Christian religion in Hindu swaddling clothes. This she does before public audiences. Her disciples imitate her; and I have come across in India very painful cases of English Christians whose faith has been upset by Mrs. Besant and by her ardent followers. Hindu audiences understand what she is aiming at when she places Jesus Christ among the 'Masters'; but some English Christians say that such ideas 'rob them of their Saviour.' Mrs. Besant does not love the missionaries; and they look upon her as the enemy and not the friend of India; and recognising, as I do, how much she has done and is doing for Hindus, I feel sorry that she should tread on Christian ground. Mahomedans laugh at Theosophists. Theosophy does not appeal to them at-all. But a few western Christians join the Theosophical Society, and try to spread a sort of Hindu Christianity; and the result is to-day a good deal of mental unhappiness.

CHAPTER XVII

ALIGARH AND AGRA

ANOTHER very interesting educational undertaking is the well-known Mahomedan College at Aligarh, founded by Sir Syed Ahmed Khan. This first attempt of Mahomedans in India to give to their sons a modern, western education in conjunction with their own religion, is sometimes held up to Hindus as an example.

"You could not found a college without the help of Mrs. Besant", is said.

But it is only fair to remember that the Mahomedans are a comparatively small and compact body in India, with a common language, while the millions of Hindus speak many tongues. The Central Hindu College compares very favourably with the Mahomedan Anglo-Oriental College, although the latter is much the oldest place, and is by far the richest of the two institutions. In both, 800 boys and young men are being educated; and both are affiliated with the University at Allahabad.

The English Principal of the M. A. O. C. received me most kindly, when I visited Aligarh, and conducted me over the extensive premises. As far as possible, the English Public School house-system is copied, each English Master having charge of a House and being responsible for the health and conduct of its inmates. Religious instruction in given by Maulvis, and the English Masters merely see that the boys go regularly and punctually to the mosque in the college precincts, and to the Koran classes held in the school and the college.

When the Amir of Afghanistan visited the M. A. O. C., a Koran class happened to be in progress, and he examined the boys in his own religion at considerable length ; and, afterwards, turning to his suite, he said, with tears running down his cheeks, 'I have been told lies about this place;' and now he takes an active interest in the college and subscribes to its funds.

Six English Masters lecture in the college and they are assisted by a large staff of Mahomedan teachers, and the annual reports show excellent educational results. Most of the boys belong to the zemindary class (corresponding with English Squires) and have wealthy parents. It is amusing to notice that zemindars to-day like to have their letters addressed 'Esq.', and even Nawabs prefer that little English title of courtesy to their own high titles. An Indian Prince, who shall be nameless, has every title that India can give him ; but he is unhappy because he has not been made a Knight.

The favourite games at the Mahomedan college are cricket and tennis, and the riding-school is well patronised. I met a party of boys out with the riding master ; and I thought how an English boy hangs onto a bare-backed pony by the mane and thus gains a good seat without any instruction. Then I remembered that an Indian boy remains a baby until he is five or six. An Englishman, sent from England to take charge of the son and heir of a Maharaja, told me that on arriving at the Palace, he looked into a court-yard, and he saw there his future pupil, driving a goat-cart, and surrounded by servants. Two horses, a black one and a white one, were led behind the goat-cart, in case the little boy, aged eight, should desire to ride one or the other. That little boy had never fed himself. Food was put into his mouth by zenana women. He had never walked half-a-dozen yards out-of-doors ; and when he was made to take a short walk by his English tutor, for the first time, he cried. Every morning his father's courtiers came to see him, and he took no notice of them, but played on until, at last, it pleased him to say 'Jao!' and then they rose and went away.

Indian mothers keep their little sons in zenanas as long as possible, knowing that when the days of babyhood are passed, an out-door life will absorb both thought and time, and boys will quickly develop into men. Mahomedans, however, marry later than Hindus do, and in the M. A. O. C., I did not find any married students. The physique of the boys in the M. A. O. C. is better than that of the students in the C. H. C., for Mahomedan boys eat eggs, chickens, fish and meat, and such a diet makes stronger men than rice, curries, fruit and vegetables can possibly do. In dress, Mahomedan boys resemble boys in England, only they wear a coat that reaches to the knees and fits at the waist, and a fez instead of a hat or a cap. I was shewn a house where little Mahomedan boys are brought up in entirely English fashion, under the care of a Matron ; and I was told that most of these little fellows will be sent to England to finish their education there.

The Principal of the College is 'at home' to the boys in his bungalow every afternoon from five to six ; and he told me that they ask him many questions about English poetry and English literature. Their favourite novelist is George Eliot, and Tennyson is their pet poet. Tennyson's heroines take their fancy, and they are anxious to know whether such women can still be found in England ? The boys are docile, and easy to manage, timid until the English masters win their confidence, but afterwards more affectionate and demonstrative than English boys are wont to be. They are not afraid of being laughed at, and do not suffer from *mauvais honte*, and they are easily moulded and influenced.

The English Masters are on excellent terms with the many rich Mahomedans who live at Aligarh ; and intellectual work keeps them from becoming narrow and bigoted. I was introduced to some of the Mahomedan teachers, and I found them intelligent, broad-minded men, interested in all that is going on in India, and also in Europe. So far, the boys have not been mixed up in any political matters, and have shewn no disloyal tendencies, and their feeling toward England is distinctly friendly and pleasant. Music and singing are not taught at the M. A. O. C.; for Mahomedans do not approve of such accomplishments ; in fact, art appeals to them very little. Simplicity is the key-note of their architecture ; chaste, cold, white or grey marble is the only material they care for in building palaces and mosques. Fortunately for the Mahomedan Emperors, marble was plentiful in India during the seventeenth and eighteenth centuries ; and they were able to make marble halls that Tennyson would have revelled in, had he been able to visit Agra and Delhi.

Mahomedans confuse dancing with nautch girls and temple orgies; and they look with grave disapproval on the balls given by Viceroys and Governors, although Mahomedan Princes, educated in England, take part in the State Lancers at Viceregal functions.

Some Mahomedan gentlemen had arranged to show me Agra; and we arrived there one night, by train, after the moon had risen. Never shall I forget the first sight of the Taj Mahal, while the train slowly entered the station. Set on a hill, above the river, it seemed to belong to the new earth and the new heaven promised by St. John—its unearthly beauty, enhanced by the soft light of the moon, reminded me of nothing that I had ever seen before. The white dome and white pillars seemed to fade away, and then to come back again, as if saying:—

"We are here to speak of beauty, and peace, and eternal love."

My Mahomedan friends laughed at my silence; for it is well known that Shah Jehan was by no means inconsolable after the death of the wife who asked for, and received, the most beautiful tomb in the world. But I was thinking of the Italian artist who conceived and carried out the Taj Mahal, the man whose eyes were put out (so tradition says) by the Mahomedan Emperor, for fear some other Eastern potentate should benefit by his services. That artist saw and reproduced lines and curves in which beauty finds an earthly resting-place.

We drove to the gateway of the Taj, and walked through the garden and between the cyprus trees to the marble tomb. Wide marble steps lead to a marble platform, with a marble minaret at each corner; and there, under a white marble dome, lies the Emperor Shah Jehan, beside his favourite wife—the Begum Arjnand Banu. Flowers made of precious stones relieve walls and floor; and when I admired the jasmine made of jasper, which seems to have been the Emperor's favourite flower, I heard a scoffing whisper. 'To-morrow' said a voice in my ear 'you shall see the Jasmine Tower built by Shah Jehan for a Court favourite after the death of Arjnand Banu'. Narrow, tapering layers of marble outline the bodies of the royal pair; and above and around is white marble, exquisitely carved and softened by inlaid, coloured flowers.

We returned to the garden, and watched the shadows made by the cyprus trees in the running water. Neither guide nor tourist disturbed us ; but frogs, who are no respecters of dead or even living kings, croaked to one another in the stillness and seemed to speak of the brevity of life and the vanity of earthly greatness. I would advise the English visitor to see the Taj Mahal, if possible, by moonlight; for although it is always a joy to the eye, by reason of its form and white loveliness, many visitors—chiefly Mahomedans—wander up and down the steps and in the garden during the daytime, and the bright sunshine seems to give a tawdry tone to the artist's white masterpiece.

Early the following morning we went to the tomb of Akbar, the greatest of the Mahomedan Emperors, the man who, while religious persecution was raging in Europe, treated Mahomedans, Hindus and Christians alike in India. At Fatehpur Sikri, his recreation ground was pointed out to us, the Ank Michauli where he played at hide-and-seek with his wives, and the *Pachisi* board, on which he used slave girls as pieces. His bedroom in 'the house of dreams' (the Khwabgah) was shewn to us, and, also, a stone stool used by a Court jester. 'Here' suggested a Hindu member of the party 'sat Mr. Bernard Shaw in a former incarnation'; and someone else asked whether in those days newspapers helped to keep Court jesters before the public? However, the only seat of a Court jester vouched for by historians is in the palace of Shah Jehan, at Agra, and opposite the throne occupied by the Emperor when he watched wild beasts fighting in the arena.

Agra was scarcely touched by the Mutiny; consequently no painful note is struck when that place is visited in the company of Hindus and Mahomedans. I would be sorry to go with such people into the Palace at Delhi, or the Residency at Lucknow. In India, by common consent, the Mutiny is never spoken about. In 1907, the Anglo-Indian papers let the fiftieth anniversary of the Mutiny pass by without comment. I notice, however, in magazines edited by Hindus, a tendency to lay at the door of Mahomedans the worst acts done during the Mutiny; and the fact remains that a Hindu, and not a Mahomedan, was responsible for the tragedies that English people find hardest to forgive and forget, that Nana Sahib ordered the Cawnpore massacres.

For Americans, the palace at Agra is a source of perennial delight. Such people seldom go to Cawnpore and Lucknow, but they want to see everything that tells of past greatness in India. So, in the cool season, they wander through the empty marble rooms of Shah Jehan's palace, followed by obsequious guides, who offer information that cannot be found in books. In the Moti Musjid, or Pearl Mosque, made of white, blue and veined marble, we came upon a little group of enthusiastic American ladies, short-skirted, bloused, and wearing topis and blue spectacles. Each lady had a guide-book, and read aloud bits of information about the time when Mahomedan courtiers worshipped Allah in marble surroundings; and all agreed that the Pearl mosque is 'just lovely', 'just cunning.' The Gem mosque, built for the ladies of the harem, in which Aurungzeb imprisoned his father Shah Jehan, excited their admiration, for the river flows under the walls of the palace, and the Taj Mahal can be seen on a hill opposite.

"Guess he had not much room to move about" one American lady remarked, the mcsque being little larger than a cell in Newgate.

"Guess he was cold at night" said another American tourist.

The guides assured the ladies, however, that in the days of Shah Jehan costly silks and satins covered the apertures and that Persian rugs and carpets were then spread on the marble floors.

We were shewn the Jasmine Tower, built for a Court favourite ; the room in which the Queen worked with her ladies, and a chamber where the Queen saw herself reflected in a thousand little mirrors. Fountains played at that time in marble courts, peacocks spread their tails in the sunlight, gay parrots were fed by royal children, and gold fishes swam between marble paths. Everything around us was of pure white marble ; we walked in a white marble palace ; and most beautiful of all, perhaps, was Shah Jehan's private mosque of plain white marble, without carving or ornamentation of any sort.

In the courtyard we tried to picture the time when nobles and courtiers, ministers and generals came on elephants and horses, and in palanquins to do homage to the great Mogul. We saw in imagination the retinues of these people, we heard the music, and we pictured the gorgeous coloring of the scene, the cloth of gold, and the jewels.

My Mahomedan friends spoke of the attempts made by some English Viceroys to revive the pageantry and magnificence of the Mahomedan Emperors ; the Durbars held at which Indian Princes have been made to play humiliating parts.

"Such shows are out-of-date and cannot be revived," they remarked.

The Fort and the Palace at Agra speak of the time when the power of the Mahomedans in India reached its climax. With Aurungzeb came the first indications of disintegration. In the time of that iconoclast the Hindus grew discontented. The Bengalis asked for more power and influence; and their requests were curtly refused. Things that happened at that time strangely resemble things that are going on to-day in India; and my Mahomedan friends seemed to think that the English would never have conquered India if Aurungzeb had been a different man. After the death of Aurungzeb, the power of the Mahomedan Emperors waned; and at Delhi, luxury and display replaced strength and good Government. Then too much power was delegated to Satraps; and these Viceroys tried to become independent rulers. So England was able to step in, and oust the Mahomedans who, for 700 years, had ruled over the greater part of India.

In the palace at Agra no traces of decay and effeminacy have been discovered. There the English have not been obliged to whitewash indecent pictures and obscene designs. In the Fort of Agra (the Palace is inside the Fort) 6,000 persons took refuge during the Mutiny. All Christians who did not go into the Fort at that time were murdered. The Fort was relieved after the fall of Delhi by Col. Greathed; and, although hard-pressed, the people who had taken refuge within its strong walls suffered little from privation, bullets and sickness.

CHAPTER XVIII

DELHI

I HAPPENED to be in Delhi during the fiftieth anniversary of the Mutiny, and there is no denying that many English people in the capital of the Mahomedan Emperors were at that time extremely nervous, although troops could havebeen brought in two hours from Meerut to reinforce the English soldiers at the Fort. At each turn I met one or two English soldiers, carrying only a little cane and apparently out for a stroll, and there was no nook or corner in the city where a disturbance could have gone on without their knowledge. A report had been circulated that a gun would be fired in case of danger ; and then all English persons were to go to the Fort ; and preparations were actually made in some houses for a sudden flight. Many natives from country places arrived in Delhi before daybreak, carrying the long sticks that such men use while walking ; but after a bath in the holy Jumna, they went quietly home.

Delhi is an Indian city. Not a single European shop provides for the wants of the little English community living in the Cantonment. A club, exactly like all other English clubs in India, and two or three English hotels remind visitors that there is such a place as England ; but the city is Indian throughout, and its ivories and silks are the joy of American tourists.

I have, however, never seen so many English soldiers out in the heat of the day as in Delhi ; and Hindu Rao's house, on the Ridge, which has been converted into a Convalescent Home for soldiers, is crowded in the hot weather, bullock carts, with the Red Cross on the roof, going up and down the hill, filled with pale-faced Englishmen.

I was introduced to two Australian ladies who have established a school for Brahmin girls in Delhi; and they told me that their educational efforts are a success, over 100 little girls being taught to read and write in Hindi, also to sew and take an interest in other things likely to make their home-life bright and pleasant. These ladies were in bad odour with the missionaries, for they lived without ice, punkahs and other things that most missionaries consider necessities in a hot climate.

"They live like natives," a missionary said, with a sneer.

On the other hand, the Australians assured me that high caste Hindus in Delhi will have nothing to do with English missionaries, and only the lower castes go to the schools established by missionary societies. I visited the schools for girls (these are not purdah) opened by the Church of England Zenana Mission in Delhi; and in them I found the lower castes only, and chiefly the daughters of native Christians, sent from various parts of India. However, the college established by the Cambridge Mission is a great success ; and the Cambridge Brothers have made a Hindu gentleman Principal of this place—a broad-minded act that has proved very beneficial to the college, an Indian Principal being much stricter than an Englishman could possibly be without losing popularity.

Caste is unpleasantly strong in Delhi. Thus, at the post office, one very hot day, I was offered a glass of water by the Brahmin post-master; and, not wishing to offend him, I took a seat on a raised platform beside his chair, and waited. The water did not come, and I grew tired of waiting; but the post-master would not hear of my going away, and kept saying, 'Its coming; its coming directly.' At last a man appeared with a glass of water; and then I was told that the neighbourhood had been scoured to find a native Christian, as no high caste Hindu would give a glass of water to a *feringhi*.

Many English missionaries are in Delhi, and Christian hospitals there try to show to the natives charity and benevolence; but the missionaries have made only a handful of converts in that great Indian city. Funds for missionary work are not falling off, I am told, but the enlarged area of missionary effort among 'the heathen,' in India makes the money now sent from England insufficient. Statistics alone can prove the truth of these statements; but I notice that English people, who reside in India, help the missionaries very little, and globe-trotters put few rupees into missionary-boxes. American ladies give largely to the various zenana missions, hoping thereby, perhaps, to help on the emancipation of their eastern sisters; but the funds raised in India for missionaries would scarcely pay for their carriages. The type of Christianity that I came across in India was crude and stereotyped; and I was not astonished to hear that the Hon. Emily Kennaird had, during a visit to India, expressed a desire that all the missionaries there would lock up their Bibles for a fortnight!

The uneducated native missionary is too ardent. Thus I was told of one such Christian missionary who went from village to village, saying: 'Christ died for your sins, and if you don't take Him for your Saviour, you wont go to heaven. Now I have told you the truth, and if you don't accept it, you will go to hell'.

With the educated native clergyman, one must, however, feel a certain degree of sympathy. A young Hindu clergyman said to me: 'English people can form no idea of the sacrifices an educated Hindu makes when he becomes a Christian. All means of support are cut off from him; he joins the Christians with the clothes he has on and nothing more. He has given up home, relations, prospects and friends. The Burial Service has been read over him by his own people; and, if Christians cannot give him work, or food, he must starve. Occasionally an English missionary understands how it is with him, but often he meets with rebuffs. 'I can't support you, you must find work', is said to him. Take my own case. I was a Brahmin. I became a Christian. I found friends among Christians; and I was able to become a clergyman. But I am not treated as an equal by English missionaries. They expect me to salam and take off my shoes when I go to see them. I offered to shake hands with an English clergyman the other day, and he looked very much astonished. I mentioned that I had dined with the Bishop.

"What!" he exclaimed. "You have sat down at the same table as his lordship, the Bishop!"

"Indeed, yes," I said. "My ancestors would not eat with some Princes. Why should not I dine with a Bishop?"

This young man went on to tell me about his first visit home after he became a Christian. He was not allowed to go inside the house. Food was brought to him in the garden; and his female relations stood inside the house, weeping to see him treated as an outcast. After the meal was over, the place where he had been sitting was washed with pails of water and all the things he had touched were broken or thrown away. Very bitterly did this young man speak about English missionaries. 'They expect us to do all the drudgery,' he said. 'They drive in carriages, but they think the sun can't hurt 'a native.' They receive large sums of money from the missionary societies for horses and out-fit; and out of these things they make a profit. They have an allowance for each child, and money from the missionary societies to pay for each accouchment; but we native clergymen must pay for our own families and all family expenses. Some English missionaries make money by snap-shots, and run after every starving child they see to snap a harrowing 'famine picture.' I don't wonder they make few converts, for they go to villages in the day-time, while the villagers are at work. We native missionaries go to the villages at night, and sit up till the early hours of the morning discussing and teaching; but the English clergyman in India must have his 'beauty sleep.'

A Mahomedan convert told me, 'I am the only Christian in my part of India.'

"Have you relations?" I asked.

"Yes, I have thirteen brothers and sisters," he answered.

"What is their religion?" I enquired.

"Atheism," he replied.

He told me that an English lady, who went to the Holy Land from India, brought back Jordan water for the baptism of the first Mahomedan in her district. The water was kept for twenty-two years; and when the bottle was opened, the water turned from white to crimson.

Roman Catholics do not work so hard at making converts as Protestants think it their duty to do ; but images, flowers and incense in their Churches appeal to low caste Hindus, being like some native religious customs. Moreover, Roman Catholicism is looked upon as a ' caste ' by natives who want to rise in the social scale. ' What is your caste ? ' a lady of my acquaintance asked a cook; and he answered, ' Roman Catholic.' The strict purdah of nuns appeals to Hindus, who find it difficult to understand Protestant missionaries of the gentler sex—ladies on bycicles, going about in tram-cars and on trains, taking snapshots, and associating freely with men. A Protestant female missionary in Northern India told me that, on one occasion, when she was driving through the city, a Hindu called her by a name that is applied to nautch dancers and women of that sort. ' He thought, no doubt, that I did not understand Hindi,' she said. 'But I jumped out of the carriage and thrashed him with my umbrella. Since the Swadeshi movement started, we have had to be careful', she added.

In Delhi, an Englishman is treated with more respect than in places further south. Policemen salute when he passes and natives salam and move off the foot-path. The horrors of the Mutiny are not forgotten in Delhi; and the common people there are very much afraid of an Englishman. I met several persons who had witnessed the struggle; and an old English lady showed me a garment dropped by the Emperor Bahardur Shah, when he fled from the Palace. She escaped from Delhi in a covered cart, with her children; but many of her friends were killed, and to this day she carries a pistol and lives in fear of an outbreak.

American tourists, as I mentioned before, care very little about the Mutiny. Their great desire is to see the Palace of the Mahomedan Emperors ; to walk in the marble rooms where Queens once sat with their ladies and worked with the needle, or played games ; to visit the Hall of Private Audience, in which the Peacock Throne is said to have stood, the marble baths, and the Pearl Mosque built by Aurungzeb. I confess that the empty, marble Palace, from which the silver doors, gilded ceilings and jewels have been stolen, did not interest me ; and when a guide pointed to the words on the wall: 'If ever there was a paradise upon earth, it is here, it is here, it is here,' and declared that Lady Minto had pointed to himself and had said : 'If ever there was a guide upon earth, it is he, it is he, it is he,' I was glad to go away. *Backsheesh*, *backsheesh* is the demand everywhere, from the man who claims to have been an eye-witness of historical scenes to the gardener from whom American ladies buy flowers for keepsakes.

In the Moti Musjid (the Pearl Mosque), imitation flowers in precious stones on walls and floors are being repaired ; and I was told that Lord Curzon still takes an interest in this place. An Italian, engaged on restorative work in the Delhi Palace, amused me, for I found that in five years he had taught the Indian workmen his own language. 'Learn Hindustani!' he exclaimed. 'Not me. Me take stick, tell native Italian name for thing, and give native stick if he forget.' A good deal of money is now being spent by the Government on the restoration of the Palace at Delhi; and, as its marble halls are now a show, and guides are allowed to demand *backsheesh*, I cannot see why a rupee should not be charged as an entrance fee. Plague and famine are in the land; and tourists should surely pay to see places kept up by taxes levied upon the people of India? To restore the whole Palace would cost too much, so only here and there a spot has been selected for restoration; and the stones used are modern and inexpensive and cannot compare with the stolen jewels they replace. The Italian, imported by Lord Curzon, does business on his own account, and sells jewels and trinkets copied from the jewelry worn in the days of the Mogul Emperors. These things, made in Delhi, and sent to Italy to be set, or mounted in gold, are largely bought by tourists; and I doubt not that some globe-trotters would, if they could, carry away bits of the Palace itself and write their names on its marble walls and pillars.

In the Fort that encloses the Palace, the first horrors of the Mutiny were perpetrated; when, in the words of Sir Evelyn Wood, 'Mahomedan soldiers hastened from Meerut to Delhi and proclaimed there the restoration of the Mogul Empire.' Then the Chaplain of the Fort, and his daughter, and English people who had hurried over the bridge on hearing that a native force was marching upon the city, were cruelly murdered. Standing on the spot where the Mutiny commenced, I realized something of the horrors of those days. Books leave many gaps to be filled in by readers, people who, perhaps, have never pieced together the actual facts of the Mutiny and have only vague ideas about Delhi, Lucknow and Cawnpore, and feel for Nicholson, Lawrence, Outram, Campbell and others a great deal of national pride and hero worship. But in these days, when so many Indian problems have come up for reconsideration, it is our duty to form a just and true idea of the Mutiny; and, standing on the spot where the first victims fell, I thought of the old Mahomedan Emperor, who, with his sons and grandson, looked out of the Palace that morning and saw the awful attempt that was being made to restore power and dignity to the former rulers of India. For fifty years Delhi had been in the hands of the English; and the Emperor Bahardur Shah and his family had been prisoners in the Palace. The sons and one of the grandsons of the Emperor, were shot by Lieutenant Hodson, after the fall of Delhi, their only sin being a desire to regain the Empire of their forefathers. Lieutenant Hodson was a brilliant soldier, we are told, but had previously been relieved of his duties as a Magistrate owing to 'an excitable temperament'; and at the tomb of the Emperor Humayun, where the old Emperor Bahardur Shah surrendered to the English, Lieutenant Hodson shot with his own hand the two sons and the grandson of the last of the Mahomedan Emperors. Sir Evelyn Wood says that this act was generally approved in India at the time, 'when quarter was seldom asked, and still more rarely given'; and Sir Colin Campbell followed the body of Hodson to the grave the following year, 'to mark my regret and esteem for the most brilliant soldier under my command and one I was proud to call my friend.' Sir Evelyn Wood adds that the conduct of Hodson has since been reprobated; and in his view justly. The Tomb of the Emperor Humayun is one of the landmarks of Delhi; and from its dome, where the visitor seems to be far from earth, among the clouds of heaven, it is not difficult to picture the surrender of the aged Emperor, in the garden below, the order given by Hodson that the three Princes should get into the cart, and then the murder of the defenceless men with a pistol.

It will be remembered that on the 10th of May, 1857, the 3rd Native Cavalry, and the 11th and 20th Native Infantry regiments at Meerut mutinied, and marched to Delhi, killing every European whom they met on the way. Neither in the Fort, nor in the Cantonment were any British troops at the time; and the 5th Native Infantry, under Colonel Ripley, and the 74th Native Infantry, under Major Abbot, shot their officers and went over to the mutineers. Delhi was in the hands of the enemy when Sir H. Barnard, on the 8th of June, took up his position on the Ridge, outside the ramparts. This low-lying line of hills shows to-day the graves of many English officers; and from the Mutiny Memorial—a red sand-stone building covered with the names of officers and soldiers—both Englishmen and Indians—who fell in the siege of Delhi—a view of the whole British position during those memorable days can be obtained. Delhi was the key of India in the eyes of Colonel Nicholson, the hero of the siege ; and he insisted on the capital of the Mogul Emperors being retaken, at any cost. General Nicholson reached the Ridge on 7th of August; and found there about 6,600 troops—English and native—and 26 guns. Many attacks had been made by the enemy, and near Hindu Rao's house two engagements had taken place. The enemy had received reinforcements, and besieged the Ridge; and sickness, sunstroke, a perpetual fall of bullets, disease, and death tried the courage and endurance of the British force, which was commanded by Brigadier-General Archdale Wilson. General Nicholson's first engagement took place on the 25th, when he defeated the Neemuch Brigade and blew up the Najefgarh Bridge, thus allowing siege guns to reach the Ridge. On the 25th of September, the Rifles from Meerut arrived, and the Jummoo Contingent followed soon afterwards; but the English force was still too small to attempt an investment, and it was decided to breach a portion of the wall running round Delhi and make a direct attack. From the 7th to the 11th of September, the wall between the Mori, Cashmere and Water bastions was pounded; and, on the morning of the 14th, the assault took place. Nicholson is said to have been the first to mount the wall; and he was shot at the Lahore Gate, and taken to the rear to die. Afterwards the Kashmir Gate was blown up, and the city was entered; and, after six days of street fighting, Delhi was once more in the hands of the British. The gates of the city show still the assaults that took place on the 14th of September, 1857; and in the Cemetery, near the beautiful Kudsiya Garden, is Nicholson's tomb. Every inch of the Ridge is sacred ground for the English; and to-day English soldiers wander there, glad to talk to anyone from home. Flat slabs, enclosed by iron railings, bear the names of officers who died on the Ridge; and, at the Mutiny Memorial, none asks for, or would accept, *backsheesh*. It is the same at Cawnpore, where an English soldier is in charge; and I venture to suggest that as English soldiers are plentiful in India, and have little to do there, all English Memorials and English places of historical interest should be committed to their care.

On Sunday, I went to St. John's Memorial Church in Delhi; and on the walls, which are covered with memorial tablets, I read, 'cruelly murdered', 'cruelly murdered,' 'cruelly murdered.' Civilians—men, women and children—are memorialized in that way; and the English Service seemed to have a peculiar sadness in that little Church that weathered the Mutiny. Afterwards,

I went into the graveyard, and looked at the iron dome and spire, riddled with bullets, that in the time of the Mutiny stood on the tower. Monuments to fallen soldiers, and tombs of civilians, who fell during the Mutiny, are there, among trees and flowers; and over the Churchyard brood melancholy and pain.

An Englishman whom I questioned concerning the feeling of the natives in Delhi about the Mutiny, said:—

"O, they are indifferent. 'The fortunes of war,' they say. Many men are still living here who saw the fighting in the streets, and they speak of the butchery that went on then. Now the people of Delhi submit to the inevitable; but they do not believe that British Rule will last forever in India."

"What then?" I asked.

He shrugged his shoulders and said:—

"O, Japan, perhaps. Many young Indians are now going to Japan to be educated. Who can say what may happen a hundred years hence?"

The Jumma Musjid, at Delhi, which is the second largest mosque in the world, opens its front doors to royalties only; and people in Delhi say: 'Lord Curzon had to go in by the back door.' Lord Curzon is not liked in Delhi, although he has done much to preserve there the remains of the Mogul Empire. A hair of the Prophet's beard is said to be in the Jumma Musjid, and from its lofty minarets the surrounding country can be seen to great advantage. Outside, I noticed fat-tailed sheep, shorn, and painted pink and blue. These curious animals resemble a six-legged sheep, with the two last legs caught up behind and tied where a tail ought to be. Their gambles are grotesque; but the people of Delhi think them sacred animals and they are much petted and caressed. At the Kutab Minar, about twelve miles from Delhi, the sites of six Delhis are pointed out. A Mahomedan Delhi has now been succeeded by a Christian Delhi; and who can say that another Delhi will not one day replace the Delhi that American tourists now delight to visit? Thanks to Lord Curzon, the marble tombs of many historical Mahomedans are kept in a good state of preservation; and I visited a white marble cemetery, with white marble tombs, white marble floor and white marble doors. There I saw the tomb of Muhammed Shah, the proud possessor of the Peacock Throne; and a simple, narrow tomb, containing the dust of Jehanara, the favourite daughter of Shah Jehan. This Princess lived at the time when the Mogul Empire had reached the zenith of its greatness; but the pomp and grandeur of palaces did not make her happy; and she asked for a simple grave.

"Let only grass grow over my head," she said.

CHAPTER XIX

Cawnpore and Lucknow

Very early one morning, I visited the well at Cawnpore, into which 206 women and children, murdered by the order of Nana Sahib, were thrown on the 11th of July, 1857. Sir Evelyn Wood said lately in *The Times*:—

"On July 1 the British prisoners had been moved to a small house containing two rooms, twenty feet by ten feet, with servants rooms at the back, and a narrow verandah running along the front. With them were some Christians, captured when flying from Fathpur and other stations. In all 5 men, 206 women and children were crowded into this building, unfit for an English family, without furniture or even straw for bedding. They were fed on unleaven bread (chupatties) and lentil soup. Twenty-eight died in a fortnight, and then some better food was provided. On July 10 the defeated General, Bala Rao, returned from Aong, with a bullet in his shoulder, and a council was held to decide on future action. There were conflicting views as to fighting, but a unanimous opinion that all prisoners should be put to death. At five o'clock in the afternoon, the Nana sent for the men, and had them put to death in his presence; and an hour later, he ordered the Sipahi Guard to shoot the women and children, through the doors and windows of the house. Some of the Guard refused, although threatened with death at the mouth of the cannon; others fired without aim, and eventually five of the Nana's Marathi Guard and some Mahomedan butchers from the city, slaughtered our unhappy people with swords and knives and closed up the building at night. Early the next morning, tbe dead and dying (some of the women were able to speak and three or four of the children were but little hurt) were thrown into the adjacent well. There was no mutilation, no dishonour attempted, but the horrible massacre, which appalled the whole civilized world, induced reprisals on many thousands who had never been to Cawnpore."

The well is now surrounded by a beautiful garden, and there birds were singing in trees and shrubs when I left the carriage (only pedestrians are allowed in the garden) and walked between cyprus trees to the Memorial. An English soldier sat at a little table, reading a newspaper; and he rose when I approached, and unlocked the iron gate. He removed his hat and led the way to the beautiful Gothic screen, designed by the late Sir H. Yule, R. E., C. B., that surrounds the well; and he said, with characteristic British brevity, 'This is the place where they were thrown in—206 women and children—and that cross yonder marks the place where they were cut up.' Above the well is a beautiful Angel of the Resurrection, in white marble, given by Queen Victoria. The artist, Marochetti, shows the tall, majestic angel with arms folded over two crossed palm leaves. The angel is sleeping, and on its face is an expression of protective love that makes it one of the most beautiful memorials in the world. Over the arch is written: 'These are they that came out of great tribulation'; and on the well is an inscription, detailing the massacre. A simple, white marble cross marks the spot where the butchery took place.

I visited the Memorial Church, and read on a slab outside, an inscription 'to those who were the first to meet their death'. I saw the well in Wheeler's Entrenchment, and on a cross there, I read: 'In a well under this cross were laid by the hands of their fellows in suffering the bodies of men, women and children who died hard by during the heroic defence of Wheelers's Entrenchment, when beleaguered by the rebel Nana, June 6th to 27th, A. D. 1857.' I stood on Massacre Ghat (Suttee Chowra Ghat), and recalled the awful story of Cawnpore. I remembered that Sir Hugh Wheeler was in command at Cawnpore when the Mutiny broke out, and had under him only 660 European soldiers, while the rest of the garrison consisted of 3,000 natives. Reinforcements were sent by Sir Henry Lawrence; but Sir Henry Wheeler despatched some of his troops to Lucknow, although his own state was a desperate one. The 2nd Native Infantry rose on the 4th of July, and were followed by the 1st Native Infantry. The 53rd and the 56th joined them. After robbing the Treasury, and throwing open the Jail and sacking the Government Buildings, the mutineers started for Delhi; but Nana Sahib persuaded them to return and invest the British, whose strength had been reduced to 700 fighting men. A general attack was made by the mutineers, and repulsed by the English, with a loss of over 200 soldiers. An armistice followed; and relying on the Nana's promises, the remainder of the garrison, barely 450 men, women and children, marched down to the boats at Suttee Chowra Ghat, with 60 rounds of ammunition per man. The boats stuck in the mud; and the occupants were immediately fired upon by the Nana's soldiers. Some boats took fire. One floated down the river. Only four men in that boat lived to tell the tale; all the rest were shot. The women and children were taken back to Cawnpore; and there massacred by order of Nana Sahib.

Nana Sahib's bitterness against the English arose from the following facts, endorsed by Sir Evelyn Wood in his articles on 'The Revolt in Hindustan 1857,' published in 1907, in *The Times*. Baji Rao, the Ruler of what is now the Bombay Presidency, on being defeated in 1818, abdicated his position as Peshwa in return for the titular rank, a pension of £80,000 and a residence at Bithur, 12 miles from Cawnpore. He adopted Nana Sahib, and later petitioned the Governor that his adopted son might succeed to the title and pension. To this petition he received a vague reply. As no Hindu can hope for a future world unless his heir, begotten, or adopted, performs for him certain funeral ceremonies, it is obvious that Hindus must have resented it. When Baji Rao died in 1851, Nana Sahib applied for a portion of the pension for the support of the late Peshwa's descendants; but this was refused, and Azim Ullah Khan, his representative, failed to get the Calcutta decision reversed in London. Nana Sahib, who was regarded as Peshwa by all Hindus, visited Kalpi, Lucknow and Delhi in 1857. He had seldom previously quitted Bithur, where he had entertained many officers of the Cawnpore garrison, lending them elephants, horses and carriages. He was generally regarded as a kind, inoffensive but dull native; nevertheless he was very astute, and had never forgotten what he considered the confiscation of his estates; and although the Government could not discern the signs of impending trouble, he and other Marathi nobles had been plotting for years against their over-lords. The conspirators received but little encouragement from reigning princes, or from the Bengal Army until the annexation of Oudh caused general alarm at all native Courts and grave dissatisfaction among the Sipahis.

I went from Cawnpore to Lucknow—a beautiful, well-laid-out city; but the chief interest of Lucknow centred for me in the records of the Mutiny. At the Residency, which lies about two miles from the railway station, I was beset by Eurasian guides, demanding *backsheesh*; and an Eurasian, who said that he had been through the siege, was yet more importunate. He showed me a shabby silver watch, saying that it was a present from H. R. H. the Prince of Wales; and when I looked dubious, he remarked: 'Anything from Royalty is acceptable.' The Residency is called by many English writers 'a beautiful ruin,' but to my mind it lacks the solemnity due to such a place—it is a show and nothing more. No doubt, Lord Curzon, who speaks of 'happy hours passed in the Residency Gardens', was not pestered by Eurasian guides; but the ordinary visitor finds the Residency 'a melancholy disappointment'. He looks at the notice, 'Sir Henry Lawrence died here', 'The Hospital', and other placards, and wishes to be alone, for he is followed by Eurasian interpreters of things gone-by, who insist on giving their own versions of the siege and talk of 'our officers,' 'our enemies', 'our women', and 'our children'. 'Jessie's room', a cellar smelling of bats and rats, in which the daughter of an English soldier is said to have heard 'The Campbells are Coming,' in her dreams, is pointed out; a vain attempt is made to explain the lines of defence marked by various pillars and tablets; and the Water Gate is shown from which the gallant Kavanagh set forth on his famous mission. It is the same in the Cemetery, which lies north of the Residency and contains the graves of Sir Henry Lawrence, Major-General Neill, the Civil Chaplain and others. There native guides demand *backsheesh* ; while one walks among the dark evergreens, thinking of the epitaph :—

" Here lies Henry Lawrence, who tried to do his duty ; may God have mercy on him".

It will be remembered that on the 3rd of May, 1857, the 7th Oudh Irregulars mutinied, but were overpowered by the troops under Sir Henry Lawrence, who afterwards harangued the native soldiers and promoted two native officers that had warned the authorities of the rising. But none knew better than Sir Henry Lawrence that a Mutiny was eminent, and he collected food and fuel and ammunition, and did all that he could to prepare the Residency for a siege. The Mutiny broke out on the 30th of May; and the guns of the relievingforce were not heard before the 30th of September. Sir Henry Lawrence was wounded July 2, and died two days later; and Colonel Inglis then became Military Commander, and Major Banks was appointed Chief Commissioner. The coolies and most of the servants deserted and the English had to do the menial work themselves. Attacks and counter-attacks went on, but the attempts of the enemy to undermine the Residency were frustrated by Captain Fullerton and his men. On the 25th of July a letter was received saying that Brigadier-General Havelock was coming; but nothing further was heard until August 29, when a letter was received from Cawnpore, saying that the relief force would arrive in three weeks. On the 5th of September a furious onslaught was made by the enemy; and on the 14th of

September, Capt. Fullerton, R. E., to whose skill the Residency owed its preservation, was killed by a cannon shot. The guns of the English were heard September 23; the besieged and the relievers met September 25; but the siege went on until the arrival of Sir Colin Campbell, in November; and the women, children and non-combatants were not withdrawn before November 19. Sir Colin Campbell, who had assumed command in India on August 17, must be held responsible for the terrible reprisals of the English at Lucknow; and as the massacres at Cawnpore have been described, it is only fair to relate the capture of the Begum's Palace at Lucknow, of which Sir Colin Campbell said, 'It was the sternest struggle that occurred during the siege.'

Sir Evelyn Wood writes :—'There were several palatial buildings within the enclosure known by the name of the Begum's Koti. Each was capable of protracted defence, by desperate men ; for the houses and out-houses resembled a rabbit warren, with their twisting alleys and dim recesses, common in buildings where rich Eastern princes house their numerous women . . . Piper Major John Macleod, who was first man through the northern breach, immediately sounded the pibroch on his pipes, apparently regardless of a hail of bullets pouring through loopholes, for in the interior of the enclosure, as stated above, were a succession of courtyards, and gardens surrounded by high walls. The Highlanders tried to pass through the narrow hole made in a wall by our guns, but were checked until the men broke in through some blocked-up windows. Adrian Hope was shoved up by one of his Highlanders, and dropped, with claymore in right, and revolver in left hand, into a dark room, alighting in a group of Sipahis, who fled appalled by his huge stature and fierce demeanour. Others were more stout-hearted, and wherever a door, postern gate or window could be barricaded, there, some rebels, standing at bay, shot the leading assailants. Nevertheless, others, led by their officers, pressed on past alcoves and through dark narrow passages, until they reached a large inner courtyard, which was crowded by Sipahis. The number of Highlanders and Panjabis were insignificant in comparison with the mass of dark-faced men opposing them ; but on the command, 'Keep together—use the bayonet,' they advanced. No man asked for quarter ; no man got it. Lieutenant William McBean, Adjutant 93rd (Argyll and Sutherland) Highlanders, had many personal encounters. Regulation Willy, as he was called in kilted battalions, slew with claymore or pistol, mainly the former, II rebels, and some of the Highlanders bayoneted an equal number. The Sipahis were gradually pushed back, but stoutly defended the small dim chambers and dungeon-like cells, in which they took refuge. Bags of gunpowder with lighted matches were thrown in and the rebels then rushed out onto the bayonets of their foes. For two long hours the death struggle continued, only ceasing when all Sipahis in front of the right column were dead . . . Darkness put an end to the fighting between the left column of Highlanders and masses of the enemy, who now disappeared. The numerous women in the zenana were protected by an officers' guard of Europeans placed over their apartments. When day broke on March 12 the ghastly scenes in the Begum's Kothi were revealed. The features of corpses of men who had been bayoneted are nearly always painfully distorted, but *The Times* correspondent,

Mr. (later Sir) William Howard Russell, who, acting in a similar capacity, had visited the hospital at Sevastopol after the capture of the city in September 1855, wrote that the horrors of that charnel house were far exceeded by those in the Begum's palace. In the rooms, passages, and courtyards, dead Sipahis lay in thick heaps ; their clothes, having in many cases caught fire, had charred the corpses. A curt sentence of grim suggestiveness in Sir Colin Campbell's despatch tells the tale :—

"The capture of the Begum's Koti was the sternest struggle that occurred during the siege."

With regard to the massacres of women and children, history tells us that although the English soldiers were forbidden to kill a woman or a child, the native soldiers employed by the English were under no such command. At Delhi, many women and children were killed in the street-fighting by native soldiers, 'houses being decorated with their limbs'; and, in all probability, at Lucknow, the native soldiers killed many more defenceless women and children than Nana Sahib murdered at Cawnpore. But the Nana's deed was premeditated, as he had promised to protect the English people ; while at Delhi, and at Lucknow, the native soldiers were carried away by excitement, were mad with victory.

Lord Curzon said, not long ago, that the Mutiny is being forgotten in India. But it is not so. Both Mahomedans and Hindus have in their own languages records of those days, records they do not think it wise to publish. 'We are conquered people' they say ; 'and we must act accordingly'. A free, open discussion of the Mutiny, at a time like this, is better, far better, it seems to me, than the secret perusal of records that the Paramount Power might find unpleasant.

CHAPTER XX

VICEROYS SINCE THE MUTINY

LORD CANNING 1856-62.

Lord Canning took the Oath of Office on the 1st of August 1855, at a Court of Directors of the East India Company, and he attended that evening the banquet with which the Saib Company was wont to celebrate the out-going of a new Governor-General. He reached Calcutta on the 1st of February, 1856, and 'within five minutes after touching land' he took the customary oaths and his seat in Council. Sir James Outram welcomed his arrival in India with a telegram: 'All is well at Oudh.' But, at the beginning of 1857, the troops in Calcutta and at Berampur showed symptoms of a mutinous spirit; and soon afterwards came the news that the Sepoys at Meerut—the strongest post as to European troops in India—had murdered their officers, sacked the station, and set off to take possession of Delhi. Lord Canning soon found himself working in an atmosphere charged with electricity. "There was thunder in the air—fierce outbursts from agitated and angry Englishmen—a hostile press—violent pamphlets, violent speeches, violent acts—everything that could agitate, unnerve, provoke. Yet Lord Canning laboured on in unruffled equanimity. 'The issue is in higher hands than ours' he wrote to Bishop Wilson. He met the Mutiny with firmness, confidence, magnanimity, with calm, inflexible justice. On a stage crowded with heroic personages, he stood an impressive central figure—too unmoved and too undemonstrative, too completely master of himself to suit the excited temper and unbalanced judgments of an epoch rife with unprecedented catastrophe, but rising above the onset of ephemeral hostility with a dignity which, as the scene recedes and we are able more justly to appreciate its proportions, places him high on the list of those great officers of State whose services entitle them to the esteem and gratitude of their country. The onslaughts of Lord Ellenborough in England, the vituperation of English people who had been stirred to an agony that had gone to the very heart's core had to be met; but Lord Canning stood unmoved and immovable—just, tenacious of purpose, conscious of its rectitude. He had to lay down lines for the future, not only of the English sojourners in India, but for two hundred millions of Indians. The English in Calcutta were angered by his restrictions on the press—European as well as native—and they were angered by his rule obliging Europeans and natives alike to obtain a licence for carrying fire-arms. Distrust, dislike, resentment met Lord Canning at every turn among his compatriots in India; and the greatest journal in England denounced 'the clemency of Canning' and clamoured to have all power vested in the unfettered hands of the military authorities. But Lord Canning wrote to the Queen: 'There is a rabid and vindictive spirit abroad, even among Englishmen who ought to set a better example . . . not one man in ten seems to think that the hanging and shooting of 40,000 or 50,000 men can be otherwise than practicable and right.' On July 15, he wrote to Sir John Lawrence : ' I don't care two straws for the abuse of the papers, British or Indian. I am for ever wondering at myself for not doing so, but it really is a fact—partly from want of time to care, partly because an enormous task is before me, and all other cares look small. As long as I have breath in my body, I will pursue no other policy than that I have been following, not only for the reason of expediency and policy above stated, but because it is immutably just. I will not govern in anger. Justice, and that as stern, as inflexible as law and might can make it, I will deal out. But I will never allow an angry and indiscriminating act or word to proceed from the Government of India so long as I am responsible for it.' At the close of 1857, Lady Canning, who, also, had suffered severely, began to see that her husband could not bear up much longer. One day, after working from 2 A.M. until 2 P.M., without an interval for breakfast, he had a seizure and became for a time unconscious. The East India Company, who knew that the transference of India to the Crown was under consideration, brought a long indictment against him. He had been 'too kind,' 'too confidential.' A petition for his recall was extensively signed by the English in Bengal and Bombay, and sent to the Queen. But India passed to the Crown ; and in October 1858 Lord Canning received the Proclamation that announced the transfer, also a letter appointing him the first Viceroy of India."

In 1860 the work of reconstruction commenced : and then began the welding of India into one nation. Mr. James Wilson said in his Budget Speech in Calcutta : 'We are now one great dependency under one Sovereign, and we have one clear duty before us—to unite with all our efforts and all our means in maintaining her Empire prosperous and inviolable.' On the 18th of November, 1861, Lady Canning died; and then the stoicism of Lord Canning broke down for the first time, and he cried like a child. His successor, Lord Elgin, arrived the following year; and he left India shortly afterwards, 'in great depression of spirits—pale, wan, toil-worn, grief-stricken, and, although he did not know it, a dying man.' On his arrival in England, his sister had to tell him of his approaching death. 'What! so soon!' he said: and immediately he began to make arrangements for his end. On the 17th of July, he died; and he was buried in Westminster Abbey, beside his father. "It was discovered after death that his constitution had been far more completely undermined than there had been reason to suppose to be the case, and that toil, anxiety and the tremendous strain of nerve and brain had pronounced his doom while he was still labouring, with no apparent diminution of energy, at the completion of his arduous task."

LORD ELGIN 1862-3.

The published letters of Lord Elgin, who succeeded Lord Canning, show that he meant to carry on the policy of his predecessor. He was a man of ripe experience—genial, tactful, diplomatic. Unfortunately, he died in India after a brief Viceroyalty of twenty months. He held a Grand Durbar at Agra; and the keynote of his speech was the unity of India. 'I am willing to extend encouragement and friendship to all who labour for the good of India ' he said; ' and I am determined not to interfere with the Native States.'

Lord Lawrence 1864-9.

'John Lawrence' is an English hero, and more has been written about him than concerning any other Viceroy. He reached Calcutta on the 12th of January, 1864, and he wrote to his son-in-law: ' It was a proud moment to me when I walked up the steps of Government House, feeling as I then did that, without political interest or influence, I had been chosen to fill the highest office under the Crown, the Viceroyalty of the Queen. But it will be a happier moment when I walk down the steps with the feeling that I have tried to do my duty.' Lord Lawrence was a plain-living, plain-spoken man, rugged in appearance, but kind-hearted and generous. He worked hard—'no old bullock is worked harder', he said of himself while he was Viceroy of India. Frontier wars went on during his Viceroyalty ; but he laid down the rule of non-interference in Afghanistan, and initiated the policy of ' the neutral zone ' with the Government of Russia. He held a Durbah at Agra in 1866 and bestowed the Star of India—a new Order—on various Indian Princes. Land settlement occupied the greater part of his time —also, unfortunately, Famine. Great distress occurred in Orissa, one million out of three million persons dying there from starvation, or floods. In 1867, he presided in Calcutta over a public meeting for the purpose of raising money for the survivors, and headed the list with 10,000 Rs. Great irrigation works were then undertaken, and these have made it easier for his successors to convey rice to famine-stricken districts. Railways were taken over by the Government, telegraph and post office departments were improved. The result was a deficit of almost three and one-quarter millions of rupees. Lord Lawrence thought out a scheme for local taxation, which was developed by Lord Mayo and carried out by Lord Northbrook ; and this scheme helped future Budgets by making local economy a local necessity in the provinces. Lord Lawrence's eyesight suffered from the bright sun of India, and constant reading and writing, and he returned to England almost blind. His last act was to help the Christian Vernacular Society in London ; and he died saying : 'I am so tired !'

LORD MAYO 1869-72.

Lord Mayo arrived in Calcutta on the 12th of January, 1869. He was then forty-six years old, a genial, popular man. He carried on the policy of his predecessor ; and devoted himself more especially to making the Rulers of Border States friendly. For this purpose he met the Amir of Afghanistan ; and visited Burma, where he was killed by an Afghan convict. Mr. H. L. Adam says, in his book *Oriental Crime* :—

" It was at Hopetown that Lord Mayo was murdered by an Afridi convict named Sher Ali. The Viceroy was making a tour of the settlement and had just returned from a visit to Mount Harriet whither he had gone to judge of its suitability for a sanitorium. The hour of 7 had just been rung by the ships bells, and it was quite dark. By the jetty stairs a launch, with steam up, awaited his lordship, and upon the pier head a group of seamen stood ready to board the vessel. At length the Viceroy's party approached, headed by two torch-bearers; and Lord Mayo advanced quickly down the stairs which led to the launch. Suddenly a sound was heard, 'as though of some rushing animal', a hand was seen to rise in the air, and a knife to gleam in the torchlight; and Lord Mayo's Private Secretary, looking round, saw a native 'fastened like a tiger' upon his lordship. In a moment all was confusion. A dozen men fell pell-mell upon the assassin, who would have been summarily slain by the convict officers, who had to be kept back by force. The torches had gone out, and Lord Mayo had been pitched into the water, where he was seen to stagger to his feet, and brush his hair from his brow. His Private Secretary rushed through the surf to help him to the bank. 'Bourne', said the wounded man, 'they 've hit me.' Then in a louder voice 'I'm all right, I don't think I'm much hurt' or words to that effect. In a few minutes he was sitting on a native cart, beneath the flaring torches, which had been relit. They saw then upon his light coat a large dark patch. Blood poured out; and in vain they tried to staunch it with their handkerchiefs. For a moment he sat up, then he fell backwards. Finally he muttered 'Lift up my head'—and sank into the arms of death."

Lord Northbrook 1872-6.

Lord Northbrook reached Calcutta in May 1872; and resigned in 1876, on the question of sending British representatives to the Court of Kabul, against the wish of the Amir. The present King-Emperor visited India during his administration. The Mayo College for

Indian nobles was opened, because Native States had begun to copy institutions in British India, and it was thought advisable to train young Indian Chiefs on English lines. Sir Syed Ahmed Khan, in spite of much Muslim opposition, visited Europe, and on his return to India opened the Mahomedan College at Aligarh. Those who desire to understand the recent advances made by Mahomedans in India on western lines, should read the life of this remarkable man, written by Col. Graham. The employment of Indians in the Public Service was extended, and Indian Judges were appointed. The Department of Public Instruction opened more colleges and schools, and these were inspected and aided by grants. It was decided that, as the Government of the country, also law and business are carried on in the English language, school-books should continue to be written in that tongue. A great increase in the sale of English books was noticed. Vernacular newspapers increased in number, and the successor of Lord Northbrook, Lord Lytton, thought it necessary to introduce stringent Press Acts—Acts that were repealed by Lord Ripon. Thanks chiefly to economies made by the Governments of provinces, the Viceroy's Budget showed in 1876 a large surplus. The Customs Tariff was reformed, and trade boomed in Bombay and in Calcutta; and, although famines occurred, Lord Northbrook—benefiting by the experiences of his predecessors—was able to cope with distress, to some extent.

Lord Lytton 1876-80.

Lord Lytton was forty-four years old when he went to India as Governor-General. He wrote after his appointment, 'The work is overwhelming and most puzzling, but intensely interesting.' He was gifted, accomplished, and affable, but rash. 'He has all the gifts of the gods except prudence,' was said of him. On the way to Calcutta, he met the present King-Emperor, who was returning home; and he wrote of the Serapis, 'As a Noah's ark was supposed by the Rabbis to be a type of the whole world, the Serapis may be regarded as a sort of picturesque epitome of the Indian Empire'; and he described the ship as, 'A floating western palace laden with the products of the East.' His administration was saddened by the murder of Sir Louis Cavagnari; and so many brave English officers at Kabul. During his administration, Queen Victoria was proclaimed Empress of India; and his daughter, Lady Betty Balfour, gives an interesting account of the ceremony in her book, '*The History of Lord Lytton's Indian Administration, compiled from Letters and Official Papers.* She tells us that the Proclamation was read in English, and in Urdu, at a Durbar, held at Delhi, and followed by 101 salvos of artillery, intermingled with *feux de joie* from the assembled troops. The Royal Standard was hoisted, and a message from the Queen-Empress was read. Many addresses were presented, of which the following is a specimen :—

'O Mother, O Blessed One residing in the Palace of London, the descendants of the first Emperor of Delhi are burnt in the fire of your might. Surely angels sing your Majesty's glory in the heavenly regions where Yadhish Ra, the Son of Justice, who performed the great Rajasuja festival of Pandaras 3,000 years ago at Delhi now resides.'

The Delhi Durbar and the wars in Afghanistan cost an enormous amount of money ; and the Famine Fund was drawn upon to meet expenses, although a terrible famine was in the land. Grain riots followed ; and the vernacular papers wrote violently against the Government. A Commission was appointed to investigate the causes and cures of Indian famines ; and a proposal was made to abolish duties on foreign goods—a proposal carried into effect by Lord Ripon. Owing to changes at Downing Street, Lord Lytton resigned in 1880 and went home.

LORD RIPON 1880-84.

The administration of Lord Ripon is much discussed, but unfortunately, so far, very little has been written about it, and the character and work of Lord Ripon are still buried in official documents and official letters. Peace reigned in India when he arrived, and he had time to attend to the internal affairs of the country. Mr. Gladstone was Prime Minister of England, and the Liberal Party there was powerful and united. At the instigation of Mr. Gladstone (so it is said), Lord Ripon extended to Indians a place on Municipal institutions, and by so doing he made himself extremely unpopular among English people in India, as these things had previously been entirely in the hands of persons called by Lord Lytton 'white Brahmins.' Englishmen in India said that under the new regulations Indians would fetter District officials without relieving these persons of any responsibility; and Indians asked what they were to be paid for doing public work? No doubt, a good deal of friction arose when English people and Indians first began to work together on an equal footing, for while the Englishman is quick, incisive, businesslike, the Indian likes to turn a matter over and over, and then he asks, 'Can't it be put off until to-morrow?' In working together, Englishmen should try to remember that Indians are adapting themselves to a foreign mode of procedure ; and Indians should not forget that the hot climate of India has an irritating effect on an Englishman, and that in nine cases out of ten he is 'in a hurry.' The Englishman has been brought up on the creed : 'One life, and after that the Judgment.' The Indian thinks that a million lives lie before him, and that there is plenty of time to reform and plenty of time to sleep, and that, after all, nothing really matters much. That Indians have appreciated the reforms of Lord Ripon is proved by the fact that in 1903, the Municipal affairs of the four capital cities in India were conducted by 1,340 Englishmen and 8,860 Indians. Lord Ripon developed a Department of Agriculture devised by Lord Mayo, and carried out educational reforms proposed by Lord Northbrook. His Budget of 1882 showed a surplus of two-and-a-half millions of rupees.

Lord Dufferin 1884-7.

Lord Dufferin was a moderate, firm, quiet man ; and he said of his Government, when his term of administration was over, 'We have done more than anyone imagines.' He initiated the Indian Councils Act; and said, 'Native Councillors ought to be increased in number, and elected members admitted into the Legislature and even into the Executive.' The Indian National Congress came into existence during Lord Dufferin's administration ; and he smiled at it. After his return to England, he denounced it severely. The Indian National Congress was convened, in the first instance, 'for the removal of certain alleged grievances by constitutional methods.' It asked that the elective principle should be introduced into the Legislature, that Indians might be admitted to the Volunteer ranks, and that the judicial branch of the Public Service should be separated from that which discharges executive functions. The Marchioness of Dufferin and Ava instituted in 1885 the well-known Dufferin Fund, to provide female medical relief, hospitals, dispensaries, doctors and nurses for the women of India. This Fund which was under the direct patronage of the Queen-Empress, has been consecrated by the praises, prayers and tears of our Indian sisters.

LORD LANSDOWNE 1887-93.

During the administration of Lord, Lansdowne, the Legislative Councils were enlarged, and their powers were extended. A considerable portion of the members were then, for the first time, elected by local bodies, such as Municipal Corporations, District Boards, Chambers of Commerce and University Senates. The Legislative Councils were then permitted to discuss the annual financial statements made by the Government and to put questions to the Government or any administrative, judicial, fiscal or other question concerning the Empire of India, or the province, 'subject to certain restrictions in regard to matters that cannot be discussed consistently with public interest.' Five Members of the Viceroy's Legislative Council were henceforth to be elected by the non-official Members of the Provincial Legislative Councils and by the Chamber of Commerce.

Lord Elgin 1893-8.

During the administration of Lord Elgin, Plague and Famine stalked the land; and Hindus, for the first time, raised the question of the share of rent paid to the Government. Lord Elgin replied that it was less than it had ever been before. Lord Curzon said, in his Budget Speech of 1901, that the average yearly income of the native of India is Rs. 30 (£2), and the average yearly income of the agriculturist is Rs. 20 (£1-6-8). Each native has to pay in taxation and land revenue 3/3¼ per annum. He admitted that taxation is as high as it can reasonably be carried; but he declared that the average income in India has increased since 1880 from Rs. 27 to Rs. 30, and the income of the cultivator from Rs. 18 to Rs. 20. It will be seen that, out of his income of a penny a day, the peasant has to pay 3/3¼ per annum to the Government. The figures are, in the words of Lord Curzon, 'neither brilliant nor gratifying.' In the time of Lord Elgin, a Public Service Commission recommended that posts reserved for the superior Civil Service, Forest Service, and Engineering Service, that had previously been set apart for members of the Provincial Civil Service, should be recruited more or less exclusively from the natives of India. In this way the employment of Indians in the more important offices of the Government was extended; and now the subordinate Civil Service is recruited almost entirely from natives of India. In the Police, Survey, Salt, Opium and Financial Departments, Europeans are still to some extent employed; but it is no unusual thing to hear an Englishman in India say to-day: 'I must educate my sons for openings elsewhere; for by the time they grow up, all posts here will be filled by Indians.'

LORD CURZON 1898-1905.

Lord Curzon was thirty-six years old when he became Viceroy of India. He said at a dinner given to him by his old Etonian schoolfellows before he left England:—

"It is the duty of a Viceroy, first and foremost to represent the Queen-Empress, whose name, revered more than the name of any living Sovereign by all races from Cape Comorin to the Himalayas, is in India both a bond of union and the symbol of power; and to associate with the personal attributes that cling about that name, the conviction that the justice of her Government is inflexible, that its honour is stainless, and that its mercy is in proportion to its strength. Secondly, he should try to remember that all those peoples are not the sons of our own race, or creed, or clime, and it is only by regard for their feelings, by respect for their prejudices—I will even go so far as to say by deference to their scruples—that we can obtain the acquiescence as well as the submission of the governed."

Lord Curzon went to India full of earnestness and enthusiasm. He had a strong, driving spirit in a feeble frame.

"O! Papa, how beautifully you did pray!" his little daughter is reported to have said to him after the Delhi Durbar.

He was a hard worker—fourteen hours daily and night work was the rule with him when he was well enough to sit in his chair. He was able, versatile, enthusiastic, indefatigable; but he lacked the noble self-forgetfulness that has made his successor such a blessing to India. He reformed many abuses. 'It was no unusual thing for an English Resident to keep a racing-stable at the expense of an Indian Prince when Lord Curzon came to India', I was told at Hyderabad. Lord Curzon was disliked by English civilians, and hated by English soldiers; but Indians liked him, at first. 'We have never had a Viceroy so anxious to learn the real wishes of the children of the soil, so scrupulous in giving a patient hearing to their grievances, so full of schemes for the development of the resources of the Empire, so firmly resolved to leave India at the end of his term of office, a better, a more contented, and a more prosperous land than he found it,' wrote an Indian Prince, after Lord Curzon had been for a few years in India. When Famine raged, he visited the famine camps at a time when (in the words of Lord Lytton), 'the plains of India were hotter than the furnaces of Nebuchadnezzar.' But the glamour of the East took hold of him; and what was the result? At the Indian National Congress of 1908, every delegate had a stone to fling at 'the Conscript Father of Indian Nationality'—'the man who repudiated his bastard son, the Partition of Bengal, and tried to father it on Lord Ampthill'; who said, 'Many thanks, but I decline the compliment.'

LORD MINTO 1905.

The administration of Lord Minto has been marked by the first outbreak of anarchism ever known in India.

These things are too recent to be written about. No doubt, 'the passing of John Morley' will be one of the most interesting features of the present Viceroy's administration in the eyes of historians. Lord Morley of Blackburn has done nothing to mend, or to end, the House of Lords since he went there; and some people say that he sacrificed his principles because the King-Emperor thought that Indian Princes should find a 'Lord' at the office of the Secretary of State for India when they visited the capital of the British Empire. The appointment of two Indians to the Secretary of State's Council has been an innovation; but the developments in the local Legislature, proposed by Lord Minto, and adopted by Lord Morley, were already accepted in principle by Lord Dufferin, and enunciated by Lord Lansdowne and Lord Elgin as a legitimate continuation of words contained in Queen Victoria's Proclamation of 1858:—

"And it is our further will that, so far as may be, our subjects of whatever creed and race be freely and impartially admitted to offices in our service, the duties of which they may be qualified by their education, ability and integrity duly to discharge."

The developments carried on during the administration of Lord Lansdowne in the Councils of the Presidencies are to be developed further, it appears; and, if Lord Morley remains in, or goes out of office, the same policy will doubtless be pursued, because its a natural evolution. The elective principle, introduced into the Legislative Councils by Lord Lansdowne, is to be made stronger; and official majorities in the Legislative Councils are to be abolished. Indians will henceforth be admitted into the Executive Councils of the Governors of provinces. The Viceroy is still to be absolute in India ; and evidently what India has to fear, in the immediate future, is not 'wild cat Bills,' but a 'wild cat' Governor-General. Indians seem to think that until the masses are educated, and the people of India have greater political knowledge, it would be a mistake to move faster ; and some of their leaders hope by means of the promised developments, 'to guide the policy of provincial and supreme Governments, to shape legislature, and generally to control the administration of India.'

CHAPTER XXI

INDIAN PROGRESS ON WESTERN LINES

WHILE writing a brief summary of the Viceroys who have been in India since the Mutiny, I realised how little can be gathered from English books concerning the progress made by Indians during the past fifty years. We see clearly what has been done by Englishmen in high positions to introduce into India western ideas and the advantages of modern civilization; but the welding of Hindustan into a nation has come about through the will and by the consent of the peoples of India, who have adopted as their own the English language, and English manners, customs and habits. When Mr. Tilak said, during his protracted trial in Bombay, in June, 1908, that nationalism has been growing in India ever since the Mutiny, I agreed with him; because English histories show how much Viceroys and other English officials have done to foster a spirit of nationalism in India. Mr. Tilak ignored altogether that without a common language and rapid means of communication by post, telegraph and train, the welding together of many peoples, with many languages and several religions, could not have come about. If Mr. Tilak, who has a retentive memory, great knowledge of the past, and a ready pen, would, in his enforced idleness, trace the growth of nationalism in India during the last half-century, then we might see, perhaps, how the possibility of unity, introduced into India by the Proclamation of Queen Victoria, in 1858, has become so strong that some Indians now call it *Swadeshism*. The history of India by Mr. H. G. Keene, C.I.E., (new ed. 1906) is a very valuable book; but Mr. Keene, like other English historians, has ignored altogether the work done by Indians in subordinate positions during the last fifty years—work that has enabled Englishmen to become a credit to themselves and to England. Slowly, but surely, since 1858, Indians have copied English models, have formed themselves and their children on English patterns; and we find to-day (I quote the latest edition of the *Imperial Gazetteer* of India) that Indians fill the greater number of the executive, magisterial and judicial posts in India. 'They are in the Public Works of India Department, the Survey of India, the Police, Jails, Salt, Education and Civil Medical Department . . . Everywhere the European element, consisting in most cases of officers appointed in England, is confined within the limits essential for efficiency and guidance. The extent to which European agency is employed varies with the nature of the work, being greater where special knowledge and acquirements are needed of which the supply in India is still deficient, or where, as in the case of the Police, a large measure of European control is necessary.'

It seems to me that, owing to the want of a good history of India for the past fifty years, Indians do not realise to-day the enormous progress that they have made on western lines; and that they must now move in the direction their fathers, grandfathers and great-grandfathers have gone. The livelihoods of Indians, in all parts of India, depend on a continuation of the present system. Indians, of all people in this world, follow most easily 'the line of least resistance.' Why this is so, I shall attempt to point out when I speak of the religion of Hindus. A study of the last half-century makes me believe that Indians will follow the British Flag, and not set up a Flag of their own. The last half-century has seen the erection of a mighty edifice in India. Englishmen have placed the bricks; but Indians themselves have supplied the mortar.

What do we see to-day ?

Hindu lawyers suffer from no legal disabilities—they can become Judges. A Hindu Judge sat for the first time on the High Court Bench during the administration of Lord Northbrook, 1872-6. Mahomedans and Parsees are now, also, High Court Judges. Hindu lawyers in Bombay have said to me, 'The Government of India is niggardly in the matter of Indian Judgeships'. Does not this show that the present discontent is largely a matter of further progress ? In medical colleges and in hospitals throughout India, Indians of both sexes meet with encouragement; and, at the present time, so many Eurasian, Hindu, and Parsee girls receive a gratuitous medical education, aided by scholarships, that Indians are beginning to forget the things done for their grandmothers and great-grandmothers by the Dufferin Fund. In order to pass the Indian Medical Service examination, Indians, as well as country-born Englishmen, must go to England. Report says that Lord Morley intends to make alterations in this direction ; and perhaps he will before long do away with military titles in the I. M. S. A well-known writer on Indian affairs said some years ago, 'The Indian Medical Service as it now exists is a singular instance of the vitality of old institutions.

It originated with the staff attached by the East India Company to its military establishment and though at present the greater proportion of its members are employed in duties of a purely civil character, all of them are still ranked as Military Surgeons, wear uniform on certain occasions, and are under the order of the Commander-in-Chief of their respective Presidencies. It is difficult to see what good can be gained by the perpetuation of a system belonging to conditions of Indian Government which have long passed away, or why the present Indian Medical Service should not be treated as a purely civil administration.' As 'side' and 'aloofness' on the part of the English people in India have made more enemies for England than anything else, it might be well, perhaps, to abolish idle military titles now among doctors and clergymen in India.

The Indian Civil Service is open to Indians ; but in order to pass the examinations they must go to England and compete there with Englishmen. The *Imperial Gazetteer* of India says : 'The age limit for the I. C. S. examinations is from twenty-three to twenty-four, and the selected candidates undergo a year's special training in England, which they are encouraged by a special grant to spend at a University. On arriving in India, the young civilian is posted to the headquarters of a District, to learn his work, and is given the powers of a Magistrate of the lowest class. After passing the prescribed examinations, namely, in law, languages and revenue procedure, he becomes a first-class Magistrate, and is eligible for promotion to higher grades.' As English civilians are few in number, and are appointed while still young, could not the Bishop of London, who has such happy manners and is so universally popular, give them some lessons before they leave home? English civilians have greater opportunities than other English people of making England liked, or disliked, in India ; and, unfortunately, many of them leave an unpleasant impression on the minds of Indians when they return to their own land. They seem often to forget that India is the home of Indians; and that the presence of Englishmen in India is sometimes called by Hindus, 'A necessary evil', 'An infliction of Providence.' In his evidence before the Decentralization Commission, the Hon'ble Babu Bhupendra Nath Bose said last year, 'The young English civilian comes to India with all the feelings of a ruling race, and that is much worse than a ruling caste. He is at once placed in a vicious atmosphere; he generally forms an extravagant idea of his own importance, and thinks a great deal too much of personal prestige ; and he is led to believe that freer intercourse with the people would diminish it. He generally invests himself with such a coating of dignity and aloofness that self-respecting people as a rule avoid him ; he is generally intolerant of opposition, and he wields such large powers that he cannot be crossed with impunity. The result is that the District officer has hardly any personal knowledge of the people under his charge. He has not got his fingers on the pulse of the people. He has generally some sort of European society at headquarters: the Station Club rigidly excludes Indians'. An eminent living Englishman has called India,' a school for English character'; and Indians sometimes ask how much longer millions of their compatriots are to form the character of English civilians—a character they do not admire ? Certainly English civilians receive credit for a great deal that is done by Indian officials who work under their direction, and would be in a sorry plight if such helpers were taken away and they were left to themselves. Their knowledge of the languages spoken in their Districts is slight, in many cases; and in other ways they must depend on Indians in order to carry out their multifarious duties. All the same, it is not difficult to see that jealousy prompts a good deal of the Indian criticism that they receive at the present time. As I said before, in India to-day Eurasians are at the heels of Englishmen, and Indians follow close behind Eurasians. This is so in all directions; and I was amused to hear a young Indian clergyman say, while speaking about Nazareth, the Indian Christian Settlement in Southern India :—

"We are tired of letting English missionaries get all the credit and all the pay; so now we are going to have Swadeshi Christianity."

Indians occupy positions as station-masters, guards, engineers and engine-drivers on railways; but the Railway Companies seem to prefer English engine-drivers for long distances. I am inclined to think that Indians do not care to hold dangerous and responsible positions. The Swadeshi Steamship Company employs English captains for its steamers. There is no legal reason why Indians should not become sea captains; but only about half-a-dozen Mahomedans now command steamers, and their certificates will not allow them to be out at sea for more than 24 hours at a time. Indians want to go straight from college to the bridge of a steamer; they do not care to qualify for the position of sea captain according to English regulations; and Hindus of good caste have been debarred from becoming sea captains by their religion, long voyages to distant lands making them social outcastes. As officers on the Swadeshi boats, Indians have done very well. Lascars will go anywhere ; and they are, in the words of an old Scotch sea captain, 'good on the sea and better in it.' Indians are in post-offices, telegraph-offices, and savings-banks; but Eurasians seem to obtain most of the good billets in these places. Many Eurasian women are employed in post-offices; and a woman holds an important position in the Calcutta G.P.O.. Indian women are ousting their Eurasian sisters from some occupations—for instance, a station-master told me that Hindu women are now engaged by some Railway Companies to enter purdah carriages and examine railway tickets, and that as this work was done formerly by Eurasian women, and at double the pay given to Hindu women, a good deal of discontent is felt, and expressed, in consequence.

"The 'niggers' are getting all the work", said to me a young Eurasian whom I had taken to be a native Christian.

"Why do you call Indians 'niggers' "? I asked.

"Well, what else are they ?" he demanded.

"A 'nigger' is an inhabitant of tropical Africa" I told him.

"O!" he said, with a sneer "all Indians are 'niggers.' "

From one profession in India, English people are rigidly excluded, and that is begging. The police can, by the Vagrant Act, arrest any English person wandering about without visible means of support; and send him back to his own parish in England. Indian beggars abound in cities, and many Eurasians beg in the streets; but no English face is seen in their ranks.. European women of the 'unfortunate class' are generally Germans; and the English police keep a strict watch on English people out-of-doors, and such people are seldom allowed to disgrace themselves in public.

From the higher positions in the King-Emperor's Army, Indians are excluded ; and I believe that another fifty years will have to pass by before much alteration is made in that direction. The Mutiny is too recent, for one thing ; and, for another, India is the only part of the British Empire in which a Mutiny has taken place. In talking with Indians, I find that they do not at-all understand what the feeling of Englishmen really is about the Mutiny. If women and children had not been murdered at Cawnpore, then it would be a different matter. Queen Mary of England said, that after her death, 'Calais' would be found written upon her heart. 'Cawnpore' is still written upon the heart of England; and if Indians cannot understand this, then let them look at the cartoon called, 'Justice', that appeared in *Punch* after the Cawnpore tragedy. That cartoon shows 'Justice' with the women and children of India behind her shield; and the men of India before her sword. There has never been an Age of Chivalry in India. Such an Age was made possible in Europe by the Christian religion and the worship of the Virgin Mary. In order to understand the feeling of Englishmen about the Mutiny, Indians should read the old romances of Europe and study the Age of Chivalry there. I am convinced that time, and only time, will heal the wounds that I speak about. For the rest, the Indian soldier is a contented person, especially since the Commander-in-Chief increased his pay. He receives more money than other villagers ; his religious customs are respected ; and he is allowed to have a wife and children. I have talked with officers in the Nizam's Army; and they have assured me that while

Indian gentlemen find it a great hardship to be excluded from the Army of the King-Emperor, the ordinary Indian soldier in British India, is satisfied; and that the present 'unrest' has not touched the native troops, although it is much talked about in the mofussil.

Americans and Australians, who go to India, show no interest in the Mutiny; and Indians have said to me that these people take 'a more reasonable view' of the Mutiny than English people are wont to do. Indians seem to forget that Americans and Australians had no relatives in India in 1857; while almost every English gentleman to-day has a relation who suffered, and in every household of the aristocracy and the gentry of England someone was an eye-witness of the Mutiny, or knows a man, or a woman, who lived through its agonizing days. I myself find it difficult to forget old ladies in England who have been forced to spend their lives in seclusion owing to mutilations received during the Mutiny. Such people live on still, and talk to others who have never been in India. For the rest, although we find Hindus sharing with Mahomedans the highest positions—both civil and military—in the time of Akbar, we should remember that India has been a part of the British Empire for only half-a-century, and that, in all probability, Hindus had no positions at-all under the Mahomedans for centuries after the followers of the Prophet set foot in India. Also, it is wise to bear in mind that England has often had to hold the scales of Justice between Hindus and Mahomedans, while Mahomedans had only themselves and Hindus to consider. It is not very long since Mahomedans threw a cow into the Ganga-ji, and English officials in Benares had to persuade broken-hearted Hindus not to starve themselves to death, in consequence.

CHAPTER XXII

EDITORS AND NEWSPAPERS

JOURNALISM in India is rapidly drifting into the hands of Hindus; and the prosecution of so many small Hindu papers for seditious writing has proved a God-send to some little Anglo-Indian papers that circulate chiefly among Eurasians. The editors of the larger Hindu papers are shrewd, well-educated men, and their papers are a credit to Indians. But most of the small Hindu papers are a disgrace, being printed on inferior paper, and having in their columns countless clerical errors. I am sure, if Hindus possessed more of the salt of life—humour—very few of the small Hindu papers that are published to-day would come into existence. They do not pay. They murder the King's English. Their proprietors would do well, I think, to lay aside pen and ink, and to undertake a little, humble, educational work. How can they expect to find readers while among 226,000,000 persons of all races and creeds in British India only a little over 625,000 are literate in English, and only about 8,500,000 are literate in the vernaculars? Mrs. Bradlaugh Bonner said lately, at a public meeting in England: 'Western civilization only touches the fringe of the great population of India, only 16 millions out of 294 millions being able to read and write, and the total expenditure on education, including private donations, school fees, and State expenditure, being only 3 millions compared with the 20 millions spent by Great Britain from State funds alone upon a population of 40 million people.' Indians sometimes say, 'It is a shame that the Government does not pay for the education of the masses.' But they do not suggest how the money for universal education is to be found by the Government. And they forget that, so far, a Government education, without religious and moral training, has not proved of much benefit to India. No doubt, when more Indians are in the Legislative Councils, then questions will be asked about imports and exports, the cost of the Army, and the ways in which railway receipts—which exceed by several crores the money taken in land tax—are expended. Many Hindu editors who undertake to instruct the public in English, want more education themselves. I have no wish to laugh at people who use a foreign language; but I think that men, who write and print for the public, should know the language they use while earning a living, that is to say, while taking other people's money. Only lately, I saw George Eliot's novel, 'The Mill on the Floss,' printed as, 'Milk on the Floor,' and 'Moss on an old Manse,' set up as 'Moses on an old Mouse.' Hindu printers are often paid by native papers, and in native printing establishments, worse than coolies, and have but little knowledge of the language they put into type. More work is taken in than can be done well; and then excuses are made for bad workmanship. I have heard Mrs. Besant, who has a great deal of printing done in India, say, publicly, that she is often tempted to take work away from Indians and give it to Englishmen, because the latter are businesslike and keep their word. No doubt, many small Hindu papers covet to-day the notoriety of prosecution, for a martial spirit is in the air, and the raiding of a newspaper office by English constables, the prosecution and imprisonment of an editor or a manager, and the confiscacation of type, etc., make heroes of men who would otherwise pass their little lives unnoticed. The recent prosecutions for seditious writing have been compared with 'a lion catching mosquitoes', the circulation of the papers being very small, and the proceedings in the Law Courts very elaborate. I will, later on, give the account of a typical trial, the case of *The Kal.* The proprietor and editor of *The Kal* is now in prison; and so is also, the man who carried on his work after he went there. As soon as one little paper is suppressed, another springs up to take its place; and the Hindu mind is so adaptive, so ingenious, that if all the vernacular papers in India were suppressed, then some other mode of communicating and circulating thought would be discovered. An Englishman, in Calcutta, told me last year that his mother—a very old lady—had seen (or fancied that she had done so?) trees at Darjeeling marked with the signs and signals that were used during the Mutiny; and that she had been very much upset, in consequence. Many a young Hindu reads to-day into the *Bagavad Gita*, which is his Bible, the history of the present time ; and, in case any western reader may be ignorant of that pearl of Hindu literature, I will quote the following description of it given in a little book, written for the Society for Promoting Christian Knowledge, by Sir Monier Monier-Williams, and published in 1906. He says:—

"The whole composition is skilfully thrown into the form of a dramatic poem, something after the manner of the Book of Job, or a dialogue of Plato. The speakers are the two most important personages in the Mahabharata—Arjuna and Krishna. At the commencement of the *Bagavad Gita*, two contending armies are supposed to be drawn up in battle array; and Arjuna is struck with sudden compunction at the idea of fighting his way to a kingdom through the blood of his kindred, and asks Krishna's opinion as to his proper course of conduct. Krishna's reply is made the occasion of the long philosophical dialogue known as 'The Song of the Adorable One,' and venerated as one of the most sacred portions of Hindu literature, as it is certainly one of the most beautiful. As Arjuna belongs to the military caste, he is exhorted to perform his appointed work without the least thought about consequences, and without the slightest question as to the propriety of slaughtering his relations."

London editors seem to forget that every word of importance written in England is cabled to India and becomes common property there a few hours after leaving the pens of writers. It is, indeed, astonishing to see the things that are written on current events in India by responsible London editors. Many of these gentlemen seem to write for English people only, and to ignore altogether their Indian fellow-subjects—people who are easily pained, quickly offended.

"If London writers and speakers would only keep quiet, what a blessing it would be for India", is sometime said by Anglo-Indian newspapers.

The Times is the chief hornet; and although *The Thunderer* has not now the weight that it carried in days gone-by, still its opinions are cabled to India and held out there 'at the point of the bayonet.' Take its comments on Mr. Roosevelt's eulogium on Englishmen in India, for instance ! Mr. Roosevelt has never been in India, I believe; at any rate he takes a very one-sided view of modern India. As *The Times* has now sent a member of its staff to study 'unrest' in India, on the spot, we may hope to see its attitude toward 'the apple of England's eye' improve ; in fact, of late the tone of *The Times* as regards the aspirations of the people of India has been a little less unsympathetic than it was formerly.

The Pioneer still ranks as the premier Anglo-Indian newspaper. I visited its offices at Allahabad one very hot day, during last summer; and I found 1,000 Hindus and Mahomedans busy there, for the paper does a large jobbing business. Wet tatties were hanging outside open doors, punkahs were going, and æreated waters bubbled in tumblers half-filled with ice. *The Pioneer* is the best advertising medium in India, and memsahibs in the mofussil take it in for shopping purposes ; in fact, its reading matter is so hidden in advertisements that one has some difficulty in discovering in its columns the news of the day. Its offices are built in a large square; and, in the open centre, I saw a stone platform —the *puja* place. There many workmen were praying, while others mended machinery and set up type. If people in England desire to understand how different India is to their own little island, then let them try to imagine a large yard at the back of *The Daily Mail*, and, in the centre, a platform dedicated to prayer and used by workmen while all around is noise, confusion and the bustle of a newspaper office. The English staff of *The Pioneer* looked fagged, when I was there; but I was told that, in the cold weather, tennis, polo, dancing and other amusements make life at Allahabad 'quite bearable,' and that it is possible to meet there during the Season 'quite two hundred *pucka* people'.

The Statesman: The Friend of India is the most popular Anglo-Indian paper with Hindus and Mahomedans. English people prefer *The Civil and Military Gazette*, a paper that is in bad odour with Indians. *The Times of India* is widely read in the Bombay Presidency ; and its illustrated edition circulates all over India and Ceylon. I did not find a single Englishman on the staff of a native newspaper. The salaries paid by Hindu editors are small, for one thing; and, for another, to write in an Indian newspaper would be considered anti-British in English communities. I met an English journalist who had contributed a few articles to a large Hindu newspaper ; and he told me that his English fellow-journalists had accused him of 'ratting', and enquiries had been made into his antecedents by Eurasian policemen. Considering how strong the feeling against England is among Hindu journalists, and the things that are written against the Government in native newspapers, it might be both wise and politic on the part of Englishmen to write in Indian papers to-day. Mahomedan papers are small and unobnoxious ; but Hindu papers have a wide-spread influence. Almost every Anglo-Indian newspaper employs Hindu reporters; and, as clerical work is cheap in India, these men receive very small salaries in many offices. Native F. A.'s and B. A.'s abound, as I said before; and, as they must marry while very young and support a wife and children, such men find life in modern India a severe struggle. The most discontented men in India to-day are babus who can find no careers in intellectual occupations and who are unfit for the work that their forefathers carried on without an English education. The Missionary Societies have been the prime promoters of this glut in the intellectual market ; for they tacked on to Christianity a cheap English education. Hindus nibbled at the bait, but did not swallow the hook ; and then the Government stepped in, and gave a cheap English education without religious instruction, or moral training. The *Imperial Gazetteer* of India (new edition) tells us that when the English went to India all education given there was connected with the religions of the country. The Christian missionaries—often at great cost to themselves and to others, and with the best intentions—tried to make converts by means of a western education, given with, or without, instruction in the teachings of Jesus Christ. This was the thin edge of the wedge ; and the Government sent the wedge in deeper by offering a cheap English education without any religion at-all. Now, Mahomedans, and Hindus, are giving in their own Colleges a modern education in connection with their own religions; and Parsees propose to open a Central Parsee College in Bombay, on the same lines.

Several little vernacular newspapers were being prosecuted while I was in Bombay; and among them a Marathi weekly green sheet, called *The Kal.* I went to see the editor, printer and proprietor of *The Kal* brought before the Chief Presidency Magistrate at the Bombay Police Court, and charged under Sections 124-A and 153-A of the Indian Penal Code, with publishing an article on the 15th of May, 1908, and thereby 'bringing or attempting to bring into hatred and contempt, and exciting, or attempting to excite disaffection, disloyalty, and feelings of enmity towards His Majesty and the Government established by law in India'. The Acting Public Prosecutor prosecuted; and the accused was defended by a Hindu pleader. Bail was refused, although security up to a lakh of rupees was offered.

Dangerous means had been advocated; and the penalty, if the offences were proved, might be transportation for life. The accused, who was an M. A. of the Bombay University, had owned and edited *The Kal* for twelve years; and his name and title were 'Shivram Mahadev Pranjape, M. A.'. I found very few people at the Police Court. At a long table, in front of the Magistrate, say about twenty lawyers and reporters—Englishmen, Hindus and Parsees; and the accused occupied a chair directly behind his pleader. He was a tall, clean-shaven, muscular person; and he wore a long, white shirt, open at the neck, over a white muslin cloth that was caught between the legs to make trousers. A wisp of white and pink muslin was thrown over his right shoulder, and on his head was a small, pink, shell-shaped turban. His expression was slightly defiant; and he followed the proceedings with evident difficulty, his English being deficient. The English Magistrate was courteous, and the English Public Prosecutor spoke politely to the little Indian pleader. Several witnesses were called to prove that *The Kal* was actually owned, edited and published by the accused; and afterwards he was committed to take his trial at the Criminal Sessions. Asked by the Magistrate if he understood English, he answered, 'Yesh'. Asked whether he had any questions to put, he said, 'I resherve my defensh'. A Parsee interpretor translated the evidence of witnesses for the Magistrate, and explained matters to the accused; and the greater number of the people at the table wore turbans and shiny-black hats. The incriminating article (translated by the Government Translator) commented on the prizes given to the native policemen who arrested the perpetrators of the first bomb outrage in Bengal, prizes varying from 500 to 1,250 rupees, and said :' Natives are verily worthless in political matters. They have yet to acquire fitness. How can they perform acts of such importance? Verily they require the supervision of Europeans over them. Since such is the case it cannot at-all be likely that European police officers had not the chief hand in the work of detecting such a serious offence as the bomb outrage. Theirs alone must have been this sagacity, this shrewdness and this far-sightedness. Though such is the case, the names of these poor fellows are nowhere to be found in the prize-list. And all the prizes go to natives only. Is it not sheer injustice that Europeans should rack their brains as the detectives of offences while the native police should obtain the rewards ? Such being the case, why were these rewards given to natives only ? Can there be some object in this? When did the Europeans become so generous as to exert their own intelligence and physical powers and suffer the rewards to go to the natives ? And when did they begin to feel so much sympathy towards natives ? But might not the case be as follows ? Might not this reward be given for treachery against one's countrymen and to encourage the perpetration of such good deeds in the future ? Is it possible a doubt should arise whether this does, or does not constitute, treachery towards one's brethren ? . . . Before deciding to commit all sorts of improper and thoughtless acts through irritation caused by the bomb outrage, Government should carefully consider what support they can derive from public opinion, and how far they can rely on what little support they believe to be still left. Otherwise such an intolerable state of things may arise that while Government supplies such remedies for suppressing the newly-found anarchists, the entire population being irritated by these remedies should turn against Government.'

The article went on to say that few meetings had been held to express regret for the outrage, and at such meetings Englishmen, maharajas and rajas had been present. "It has been known to all that maharajas and rajas have been generally reduced to a very dependent position. They nod their heads just as they have been told to do. Not a genuine particle of sympathy has been seen anywhere. News has been published of the Mahomedans belonging to the Moslem League at Poona and Behar having observed one more ceremony of expressing sorrow. But on this side men can rarely be found who do not know that Mahomedans, in order to gain their own ends, say ditto to whatever the English may say. How long will the '*Jabric*' of the British Empire remain tottering on the insecure foundation of such bogus sympathy? Public opinion has undergone a terrible change. Starting from humble petitions, the stage of bombs has been reached. What does this signify? Fear of Government has fled from the people's minds. The British Government has acquired dominion over India by committing treachery and throwing a spell of delusion over the people. The days for the people acting in accordance with the tendency of Government are now gone. The people want their rights, and if they cannot be got by straightforward means, the people are determined to secure them by crooked devices. The only proper thing is that at such a time, the English considering the above should conciliate the people by granting them important rights, like that of *Swaraj*. If, however, this is not done, it is highly probable that the trial of strength may arrive in a short time. Thoughts of the people have undergone a very great change. There are now very few people pronouncing such sentences as, 'We have received immense benefit from the British rule', and 'British rule has been set over us by Providence.' The language used now-a-days is as follows: 'We want *Swaraj* and we shall do whatever we like for acquiring *Swaraj*.' In short this means that there is now no question about internal fear, and the only question now left is about the pressure of an external force."

The accused was afterwards held to bail by order of the High Court, because his pleader pointed out that the article complained of was written in High Marathi, and it was necessary for the accused to give instructions about it to his counsel personally. Application was also made that the case should not be tried before a Special Jury, as the accused would prefer a Common Jury. 'Under the rules there is a majority of Englishmen on the Special Jury list' said the pleader; 'Englishmen do not understand Marathi, and in this case it is entirely a question of the construction of Marathi.' The Judge, however, fixed the case for a Special Jury, saying the translations had been made by the officers of the Court and the practice of the Court had always been, when there were cases of importance to be tried, to have the services of a Special Jury. Before the case came on for trial, at the Criminal Sessions, Mr. Tilak was arrested; and the fact that he was found with the accused at the time of his arrest, gave to *The Kal* case increased interest. As a mob had thrown stones at policemen, injured a Roman Catholic priest, and molested English people in trams while Mr. Tilak was brought before the Presidency Magistrate at the Police Court, it was thought necessary to place bars before the entrance to the High Court and to station mounted constables in the precincts. The wildest rumours were afloat; and with my own ears I heard English soldiers say: 'We will shoot the natives down like dogs, if we get a chance.' Idle English soldiers in India pine to-day for a 'shindy' of any sort; and some have said, in my presence: 'We will shoot the English civilians who have insulted us first, if there is another mutiny; and the natives who have followed their lead afterwards.' However, when the trial came on for hearing, rain fell in torrents, and very few people went near the High Court. The galleries were locked; and only privileged spectators were allowed to be present. A Parsi Judge took his seat under a picture of the King-Emperor. A Jury was empanelled, consisting of Mahomedans, Englishmen and Parsees, but no Hindus. Neither Judge nor Jury knew high Marathi; and some of the Jury could not have passed an examination in English. The Advocate-General, supported by the English Public Prosecutor and two English lawyers, opened the case for the Crown; and he spoke learnedly for nearly three hours on the law of seditious journalism. He read the article complained of, and ended by saying, 'every word of the article is clamorous for a conviction under Section 124-A'. The accused, being slightly deaf, had been given a seat at the bar-table; and he read the following defence: 'I am editor, printer and proprietor of *The Kal* newspaper, which is published in Poona every Friday morning; and I am prepared as such to accept the legal responsibility of all matters published therein. The aim and object of my paper has always been to help in improving the condition of my fellow-countrymen. As regards the articles, I never thought, and I do not think even now, that I was transgressing any law in British India. They were intended as comments on certain official acts and to voice the general opinion of the people on the topics of the week. I sincerely believed, and I believe still that the act of rewarding public officers at the particular time was premature and ill-advised. The remarks about the meeting held anent the bomb outrage were intended to caution Government against being misled by proposals for repressive measures. I honestly believe that the granting of political rights and privileges to the people of India is the only remedy for allaying public discontent. As regards the remaining matters contained in the articles, they are merely auxiliary to prove the main conclusion. My criticisms of the public officers and the higher authorities were based on official facts; and cannot therefore be referred to as creating any hostility or ill-feeling between communities. I therefore submit that I ought to be acquitted of both the charges laid against me.'

'Is that all?' the Judge asked; and when the accused answered, 'Yes', his Parsi lordship said: 'I will give you an opportunity to address the Jury.'

Then, to the astonishment of Judge, Jury, solicitors and spectators, the accused made a long and eloquent speech. He took the fullest responsibility; he called no witnesses; he pointed out that the Advocate-General and the Public Prosecutor had not attempted to refute one of his statements. The Advocate-General scoffed at his little *Kal*: why then did the Government prosecute him? He read from Sir Henry Cotton's writings the sentiments expressed in the second part of his article; and asked to be told who is, and who is not, an English Statesman? He regretted that neither

Judge nor Jury understood Marathi—the language in which the articles were written—because his article could easily be misrepresented in English; and also because he was a poor speaker in a foreign tongue.

After tiffin, the accused continued his address; and spoke for almost two hours. He asked the Parsi Judge to correct him if he made legal errors. 'I am a layman like the Jury', he said.

"Go on, old man," said the Parsi Judge, who was paring his nails with a penknife, "You are doing very well."

The Advocate-General suggested that the Court had had enough of him; but the Judge let him go on until, at last, he said, 'Gentlemen of the Jury, I expect you are tired. I am tired, too. Before God I am innocent.'

The Judge, in shiny-black hat, and crimson gown, with lace at the wrists of small, womanly-looking hands, afterwards addressed the Jury. He said that no lawyer could have defended the accused better than the accused had defended himself; but—

The following day the Jury unanimously found the accused guilty on both charges; the majority of the Jury being of opinion that he had been actuated by motives of patriotism and for that reason recommending him for mercy; and he was sentenced to nineteen months' rigorous imprisonment.

CHAPTER XXIII

BOMBAY TO-DAY

MOST English people who visit India, land in Bombay; and I can imagine their hearts swelling with racial pride and satisfaction when they look at the Apollo Bunder, which is called, 'The Gate of India,' and remember that England rules over 'our Indian Empire.' Bombay is the most anglicised city in India; and an Englishman may go there to an hotel that will compare very favourably with hotels in London, read the latest English Cables, and meet English persons who hold his own opinions. He need not speak to Mahomedan, Hindu, or Parsee; but may travel in an English train, with English people, to Calcutta, or any other place that he may desire to visit.

The beginnings of Bombay were quaint.

The Times of India tells us that Bombay had no history before the Portuguese landed there in 1509. In 1529 the Portuguese visited the harbour again and christened it, 'The Island of Good Life.' A Portuguese traveller, who went there in 1538, wrote, " The land of this island is very low, and covered with great and beautiful groves of trees. There is much game, and an abundance of meat and rice, and there is no remembrance of any scarcity. Now-a-days it is called 'The Island of Good Life', a name given to it by Heiter da Silveira, because, when his fleet was cruising on the coast, his soldiers enjoyed rest and refreshment there.' In 1640, the Council of the East India Company, at Surat, pointed out to the directors at home that Bombay would make a splendid station for the Company on the western coast of India, and suggested that it should be bought from the Portuguese. Possibly negotiations were then opened up with the King of Portugal, for, twenty years later, Bombay was offered to Charles II as part of the dowry of Catherine of Braganza. The Portuguese in India begged their King not to carry out this part of the marriage contract ; and the Portuguese Viceroy wrote to his Sovereign : 'I foresee the great trouble that from this neighbourhood must result to the Portuguese, and that India will be lost the same day in which the English nation will be settled in Bombay.' But he wrote too late ; and, to his mortification, the Island was handed over to Humphry Cooke, 'whom I remember as a grocer in Lisbon' he wrote to the King of Portugal. 'In 1665, the said Humphry Cooke, who had been appointed Vice-Governor of Bombay, took to himself possession and delivery of the said Port and Island of Bombay, walking thereupon, taking in his hand earth and stones, entering and walking upon its bastions, putting his hands to the walls thereof, and walking also on the said island, taking into his hand the earth and stones thereof, and making all other like acts which in right were necessary, without any impediment or contradiction.' Humphry Cooke was later on accused of fraud and embezzlement by Sir Gervase Lucas, the first Governor of Bombay, and thrown into prison. At that time the Island yielded about £2,000 a year ; and as the cost of the settlement was greater than the revenue, Charles II made it over to the East Company in March, 1668, 'as of the manner of East

Greenwich, at a farm rent of £10 a year, payable on the 23rd of September.'

A visitor passing through Madras would say: 'A City of Hindus'; through Calcutta: 'A City of Mahomedans'; through Bombay: 'A City of Parsees.' Parsees were in Bombay long before the English went there; and the Portuguese described them all as 'shopkeepers'. To-day they seem to possess Bombay. Their shiny-black hats are seen in every direction. They talk of opening a Parsee College, on the lines of the Central Hindu College at Benares and the Mahomedan College at Aligarh; and people who have been to Udvada, and seen there a fanatical priesthood, guarding a fire that is said not to have been rekindled for 1,200 years, wonder why such a College has not been opened in India before? The sacred fire at Udvada was taken from Persia to India by men who walked all the way, and is now in a Fire Temple that neither Prince nor Viceroy may enter, is fed with sandalwood only, and kept in a silver urn.

It is an impressive sight to see the Parsees gather on the Bombay beach at sunset, unloosen the Sacred Cord, and read their prayers. They stand there—men, women and children—while the sun sinks westward; and their thoughts being centred in their religion, their faces assume a rapt and melancholy expression. They have been, for the sake of their religion, 'out-law'd people', and the sufferings of their forefathers seem to linger in their eyes. Look into the dark eyes of these fire-worshippers and you will often see there yearning, resignation and pain. The Parsees whom I met in Bombay seemed to possess earthly shrewdness mixed with other-worldliness; and on one occasion a young Parsee startled me.

'We thought you had lost your way,' I remarked, when he came in late.

'The soul is never lost' he answered.

Parsees 'set the pace' in Bombay ; so one sees there, in the streets, sombre liveries, good horses, and soberly-dressed men and women. But one notices, also, in this 'unveiled' city much that tends to thought concerning the future.

"I want to see education given behind the purdah, before the purdah is taken away," said Mrs. Sarojini Naidu, who had been staying with the Governor of Bombay before I met her in Hyderabad. "I hope that the purdah will not be taken away before Indian women can face the world with a curtain made of their innate modesty and reserve."

These words came back to me sometimes, at sunset, while I stood beside the sea, watching carriages roll by. In the carriages I saw Hindu and Parsee ladies with hair puffed and frizzed in European style, a veil fastened anywhere above the nape of the neck, gay clothes, and flashing jewels. I saw, too, dancing black eyes, ogles and smiles. Sometimes an Indian lady drove alone in a smart, modern carriage ; and on her face I saw none of the reserve and unself-consciousness that form an Englishwoman's protection when her husband, father, or brother are absent. And I wondered much then what India will be like when not only men, but, also, women there clamour for freedom.

An English lady, who has lived in Bombay for twenty-five years, told me that she notices great changes going on among Indian women there.

"Parsee ladies have only of late years taken to driving in open carriages," she said. "Now they would dress like English women, if only their fathers and husbands, would allow them to do so. They would like to marry English men ; and they are exceedingly angry and jealous when a Parsee man brings home a European wife."

"If I can't marry an Englishman, then I will never marry at-all," said lately a handsome Parsee lady doctor, who has been educated in England.

I was surprised to find in Bombay no public library. Calcutta and Madras have fine Government libraries, open to all who desire to read books on the premises ; but a Bombay branch of the Bengal Royal Asiatic Society and a Mechanics Institute are the only places in Bombay where English people can read ancient and modern literature. I wanted to see Volume IV of the *Imperial Gazetteer* of India ; and in the Nizam's public library, at Hyderabad (Deccan), the book had been available ; and I had imagined that it could be obtained in Bombay without any difficulty. So I enquired for the public library.

"What!" exclaimed a resident, "Do you expect to get anything in Bombay without paying for it?"

I went to the Bengal Royal Asiatic Society ; but I was told there that a member in the mofussil had the book I wanted, and it was impossible to say when the book would be sent back to the library. At the Mechanics Institute, the book had not been even heard about. And at the library of the Secretariat, I was told, 'We had a copy of Volume IV of the *Imperial Gazetteer* of India, but a member of the Royal Commission on Decentralization has taken the book with him to England. Perhaps you can find a copy of the book at *The Times of India* office. I mention this incident to show how much a public library is needed in Bombay.

While I was in Bombay, a bomb scare had possession of the place. An itinerant preacher, who sang the *Bande Mataram* in the streets, was sent to prison for a month; and a Hindu, who said in public, 'India expects every man to do his duty,' received a similar sentence. Exhortations in favour of bombs were written on the seats of railway compartments in some chemical preparation that would not wash out; and every pistol in the place had been bought up by English residents. The trial of Mr. Tilak was going on; and the mill hands were in an excited and angry condition. An Anglo-Indian paper said: 'There is scarcely one per cent. of English women in India that cannot use arms of precision; and scarcely an English schoolboy who cannot use a carbine; and in this lies the explanation of the remarkable placidity which prevails to-day, and the complacency with which the European population of this country regards the the apparent inactivity of the Government.' The pistols of English women and the carbines of English schoolboys in India would avail them very little, it seems to me, if Lord Kitchener did not control the cannon.

My visit to Bombay was drawing to a close when a Parsee gentleman took me in his motor to see 'White Street', which is said to be, 'the worst street in the whole world.' On the way there, the Parsee told me that since Mr. Stead, the late Mrs. Josephine Butler, and other English social reformers stopped 'registration', things have gone from bad to worse as regards prostitution in British India. It was about 11 P. M. when we came to the place that is known as 'Devil's Point' among English soldiers and sailors in Bombay.

Imagine, if you will, a street as long as Fleet Street, in London, lined on either side with brilliantly-lighted houses; and in these houses, at windows, and outside, on balconies and verandas, European and Japanese women, and many little Eurasian girls. The women are slightly dressed, and covered with paint, powder, false hair and false jewelry. They smoke, shout, scream, sing, play cards and twang musical instruments. Japanese Jezebels, who have painted their faces and tired their heads, look out of windows and call to men in the street, 'Come up here', 'Come up here.' Few of the women, let us hope, are English; but some of them have fair faces and fair hair. Little Eurasian girls, with hair hanging down their backs and frocks reaching to their knees, sit in rooms with older women; and these children run out into the street, lay hold of English soldiers and sailors, and try to drag them into houses. Parsee boys are drawn in, also French and German sailors; and members of His Majesty's Forces pass in and out. No policeman is in White Street, but police-soldiers watch to see that no soldier 'gets into a drunken row.' Look up, and you will see rooms lined with looking-glass; and in these rooms Englishmen in evening dress, and European women in diaphanous clothing. The street is filled with gharries and private carriages; and a horrible smell of garbage and filth chokes the air. Some of the women flaunt their degradation with brazen faces and mocking words; men in evening dress hurry up and down side streets; many English soldiers and English sailors are there. From 'White Street' we went into 'Black Streets' where, behind iron bars Indian women bargain for rupees and annas. Men and boys press against the bars; and the highest bidders are dragged inside cages by women that neither reptile nor beast would call sister, or friend.

The Sunday before I left Bombay, I went to a Parade

Service at the Church of St. John the Evangelist, commonly called 'The Memorial Church,' because it was built in memory of the officers and men of the British Army who fell in the campaigns of Sind and Afghanistan. The Church was half-filled with English soldiers, looking smart and fresh in their white tunics; and a military band replaced the ordinary white-surpliced choir. But I thought of an officer in His Majesty's Army, who was sent at the age of eight to a preparatory school in England, and who heard then, for the first time, the Athanasian Creed read in Church. He wrote to his father, begging to be removed, at once. 'This school' he said, 'goes to a Church where I hear cursing and swearing, and is quite unfit for the son of a gentleman.' I heard the Athanasian Creed read in 'The Memorial Church' that Sunday morning; and I listened to a six minutes' sermon in which the clergyman talked of the everlasting punishment in store for sinners. He said that soldiers used sometimes disgusting language in his hearing; and he hinted at sins that, in his opinion, justified God in condemning sinners to everlasting damnation. I was not surprised to hear him say that the collection taken at the Parade Service held on the previous Sunday had amounted to two annas. After the sermon was over, 'God Save the King' was sung, and the little clergyman walked to the Vestry with the money-bags. The Colonel led the way out of Church, followed by the officers, the officers' wives, and the soldiers. I stood on the steps for a minute, listening to the deep haw-haw of the officers, and looking at the pretty faces and frocks of their wives; and then I told a gharry-wallah to take me to the Jain Hospital for sick and wounded animals. On the way there, I read an article about the British soldier in India. The writer said that while a major may thrash a syce in front of the orderly room, and a subaltern can kick a native out of the pay-office, thanks to a 'one time household name in India' a native may be as insulting as he pleases to a British soldier. "The native will laugh in the face of a British soldier and say 'Can't touch me Sahib,' for there is an Indian regulation, 'All cases of soldiers striking natives will be dealt with by court-martial.' Travel the Bombay mail route on the Great Indian Pacific Railway and note the reception a British soldier receives from the Eurasian guard, the nondescript hybrid waiters, and even the unclean coolie. If he is in uniform, they will be condescending to a point of impertinence; in mufti they treat him like a god. The native is only aping the despicable snobbery of inexpressibly vulgar Anglo-Indian civilians who have presumably accepted the cue of a certain lady who is alleged to have said:–'The ugliest things in India are a water buffalo and a British soldier.'

There are many ugly things in India.

The British soldier has a rententive memory, and is well aware to whom he owes his present unenviable status in India, where, if he ever wants a drink, he has to beg for it more often than not, and he is smuggled into a back room and has to pay an exorbitant price. The gratuitous insult, 'no soldier served here', is the peculiar pride of India, which is built upon the bleaching bones of the British soldier, and was bought with his blood. Moreover, the community that snubs him so conspicuously, and the persons that make the petty laws that demean him, are those whose existence in India is only rendered possible, and the means of livelihood assured, by that despised individual, the British soldier. If endowed with sufficient intelligence to appreciate him, at his intrinsic value, setting aside all questions of sentiment, they would take off their hats to this British soldier, not only in gratitude for services rendered, but mindful of possible future services required."

Then I thought about the many unmarried, homeless English soldiers in India; and I said to myself, "If the Government of India had given half of the money lavished upon colleges and schools in India to English soldiers here, enabling them to live as respectable, married men, how much better it would have been for India! Mahomedan soldiers never sank as low as many English soldiers do in India, never became so brutalised, so degraded, because their religion forbids them to touch intoxicating liquour. The British soldier need not blame Lord Curzon for his position in India. He must blame the Government of India and the War Office for the difficulties placed in his way when he desires to marry, for the temptations with which he is surrounded. He thinks himself too good to associate with Indian soldiers, and he imitates the officers of some English regiments who will not condescend to call on the wives of English officers who command native regiments, but send their cards to these ladies through the post office; and Indians look on the British soldier with horror and contempt. Why? Because Indians cannot understand the economies of the War Office.

CHAPTER XXIV

VEDANTISM

ONCE more I stood beside the tank at Mylapore, looking at the green leaves on the surface of the water, and the pink lotus flowers. It was Sunday morning, and temple bells—very like Church bells in England—reminded me that my compatriots had gone to Christian places of worship. 'The dew was on the lotus,' for the sun had not yet made itself felt, and sun-rays were playing between the drooping leaves of the palms. I had come to Mylapore for the seventy-sixth Birthday Anniversary of Bhagavan Sri Ramakrishna, which was to be held at the Mutt there; and, standing beside the lotus-covered water, I remembered some of his sayings.

"Pray to God in any way you like. He is sure to hear you, for he can hear the footfall of an ant."

"When Egoism drops away, Divinity manifests itself."

"Meditate on God either in an unknown corner, or in the solitude of forests, or within your own mind."

"The strength of an aspirant lies in his tears. As a mother gives her consent to fulfil the desire of her impatiently weeping child, so does God vouchsafe to his weeping son whatever he is crying for."

Professor Max Muller made the life and sayings of

Ramakrishna known in Europe; and Swami Vivekananda has drawn to India American women like Sister Nivedita. While I was standing beside the tank, thinking about the god-intoxicated man whose anniversary was to be commemorated that day, I saw a little, white-robed American woman glide into the Mutt, and I noticed that she carried wreaths of oleander flowers. And then I began to ask myself why India has always been the home of god-intoxicated people? Hieroglyphics and cuneiform writings tell us about the religions of Egypt and Babylon; and the records of these civilizations—the oldest in the world—say nothing concerning god-intoxication. In the Old Testament of the Jews we find little about Realisation before the time of King David. As to Greece, history tells us that its philosophy came from the East; and that the philosophers who moulded western thought drew their inspirations from Asia. India has been, from the beginning of history, the cradle of religion; and Hindus assert that still, in the snowy Himalayas, may be found beings who are more than human. Is it possible that a rung of the ladder that reached from earth to heaven may yet be resting on the tops of the highest mountains in the world? At any rate, Hindus assert that Rishis have existed in India, and exist there still; and that such people gave to the world the Vedanta, the religion in which modern science finds its conclusions hinted at, the religion professed to-day by the greater number of the King-Emperor's subjects.

What then is a Vedantist?

The *Bagavad-Gita*, which is the Bible of Vedantists, answers this question in words that might have fallen from the lips of St. Thomas a Kempis.

" He who worships the Indestructible, the Ineffable,

the Unmanifested, Omnipresent and Unthinkable, the Unchanging, Immutable, Eternal . . . He who beareth no ill-will to any being, friendly and compassionate, without attachment, without egoism, balanced in pleasure and pain, and forgiving. Ever content, harmonious, self-controlled, resolute, with mind and reason dedicated to Me. He who wants nothing, is pure, expert, passionless, untroubled, renouncing every undertaking, he, My devotee, is dear to Me. He who neither loveth nor hateth, nor grieveth, nor desireth, renouncing good and evil, full of devotion, he is dear to Me. Alike to foe and friend, and also in fame and ignominy, alike in cold and heat, pleasures and pains, destitute of attachment. Taking equally praise and reproach, silent, wholly content with what cometh, homeless, firm in mind, full of devotion, that man is dear to me. They verily who partake of this life-giving wisdom, endued with faith, I their supreme object, devotees, they are surpassingly dear to me."

A part of the programme of the day was 'Feeding the Poor,' and. while I drove to the place where seven thousand poor persons were to be fed, I said to myself, 'An ounce of Charity is worth a ton of Psychism.' So far, I had seen little done by Hindus, or their copyists, that could bear the name of Charity—the love that covers a multitude of sins. But when I came to the place where the Vedantists were feeding the poor, I thought of the multitude that Jesus the Christ fed with loaves and fishes. I was driven to some strong gates, against which pressed a hungry rabble of men, women and children. Policemen guarded the gates, and I was allowed to pass through. I found myself then in a large stone yard, and in this yard I saw stone platforms, raised about two feet from the ground, and shut in by bars. On each platform sat people who devoured rice and curry, devoured it as hungry animals devour any food that is given to them. They might not carry anything away, so they ate, and ate, and ate—I could see their bodies swelling with the food. Young men gave the food to the people, and poured into their hands buttermilk; and I was told that these young men were College students, and disciples of Ramakrishna. They had stripped off their clothes to the waist, and perspiration poured off them while they fed the poor. The sun fell on their bare heads, and I was told that after two hours of such work they could do no more. Then other students must take their places, so that the feeding might continue.

"This is the only time when they will come in contact with the very poor," I was told. "They are feeding the homeless, the hungry and the outcasts. It is a part of the teachings of Ramakrishna. The Swami in charge of the Mutt begged the money for this, and he went from house to house explaining how and why it should be done."

Everything had been well arranged ; and although policemen were numerous, and noise was great, the people were fed without confusion. After each batch went away, the platforms were washed and prepared for another set of hungry people, and each person had as much as he could eat and drink, and was then dismissed. In the kitchen, I saw stacks of boiled rice, caldrons full of curry, and tubs overflowing with buttermilk ; and I was told that cooking had been going on there all through the night. Numberless children gathered round me, begging for pice ; and, with difficulty, the students conveyed me back to the carriage. Then I went to the Mutt, a low, brick building, consisting of one large room. On the whitewashed walls of this room I saw pictures of Hindu gods and goddesses, and among them a copy of 'The Madonna and Child.' At one end of the room a table had been placed, shaped like an altar ; and on this was a picture of Ramakrishna. The little American woman, who looked Madonnalike in her white draperies, was decorating the altar with flowers; and young Hindus were hanging wreaths on pictures. Many Hindus sat on the floor, but a space had been left for some men who seemed to be directing the proceedings. Drums, cymbals, a small harmonium and a vina made deafening music ; and much singing was going on. Sacred fire was carried round, and men bathed their hands and faces in the flames. Sometimes a man rose and whirled round and round, just as an English child does when it wants to make itself giddy. Sometimes two men crossed hands and spun round and round, whirling fast, then faster and faster and faster. These men fell, at last, into the arms of others; and I was told that when they fell thus, 'the God had entered into them.'

'What God ?' I asked myself.

'The Supreme and only One', would, I know, have been the reply, if I had put the question to a Hindu. And, if I had gone further, and had asked, 'What and Who is the only One ?', then the answer would have been, 'I am the only I.'

Listen to Vivekananda, the disciple of Ramakrishna.

"The gods did not create man after their type, but man created gods."

"Men are the real, the only gods to be worshipped."

"There is no god but man."

Sometimes, while looking at a Son of the Ganges, I have thought of the stories that the Jews took out of Chaldea, stories that students can read to-day on cylinders and stones. The Serpent—and serpent worship—devil worship—is older than Hinduism—tempted the first man and the first woman (so these ancient records tell us) by the promise that, if they ate the forbidden fruit they should 'be as gods'; and the gods divided men by a diversity of language because they built a tower 'whose top may reach to heaven.' Often I have asked myself whether spiritual pride has not been, and is not to-day the chief sin of India ; and whether for that reason her head has been laid in the dust, and she has been trodden upon by religionists whose creeds are modern when compared with Vedantism, but whose Teachers have told their followers to humble themselves before Almighty God and to remember that man is 'a little lower than the angels'?

After sunset, at the Mutt, a Hindu scientist gave an interesting lecture on : 'The Realization of Sri Ramakrishna Deva in the light of Modern Psychology.' I had been particularly anxious to hear this lecture, because (so it seems to me) the most important thing for India is to-day, is to bring Realization into the calm, cold light of modern science. Sir J. R. Seeley says,' The learned Hindu, even when he uses our railways, sincerely despises us. We are not cleverer than the Hindu; our minds are not richer or larger than his. He can match from his poetry our sublimist thoughts; even our science has few conceptions that are altogether new to him. Our boast is not that we have more brilliant ideas, but that our ideas are better tested and sounder. The greatness of modern as compared with medieval or ancient civilization is that it possesses a large stock of practical power. But the poetical or mystic philosopher is by no means disposed to regard demonstrated truth with reverence, he is rather apt to call it shallow, and to sneer at its practical triumphs, while he revels for his part in reverie and the luxury of unbounded speculation.' So far, no attempt has been made to persuade Hindus to study Realisation scientifically; and I was anxious to hear what a Hindu scientist had to say to his compatriots about cosmic consciousness—a kind of consciousness that seems to be growing in the world and that is, in the West, where Vedantism is now being introduced, only too often, to-day, 'confusion worse confounded'. The room was closely packed with Hindus; and in a corner, I noticed the little American woman who is a disciple of Swami Vivekananda. The speaker stood under a swinging lamp, and he spoke for an hour. All that he said was worth repeating; but I can only notice a few salient points of his address here. He told the audience that the conception of Realisation is as vague as it can be in India at the present time, and that the reason for this is that, in books on Vedantism, there is no clear analysis of Realization on modern lines. It is given to few only to experience even a glimpse of the state of consciousness that alone clears all doubt; and it is therefore of the utmost importance that we should try to understand Realisation with a view to making conscious efforts towards its attainment, for Realisation is the goal of all religions, and the goal of human evolution. Jesus the Christ called it, 'the kingdom of heaven', owing to the peace and bliss that are, perhaps, its most characteristic features. Buddhist saints have described it as 'the highest aim, the highest good.' The speaker briefly traced the growth of consciousness in this world. He pointed out that modern science shows no sharp dividing line between the mineral, vegetable and animal kingdoms. Scientists have, however, been able to discern a fundamental distinction between the consciousness manifested by animals and that manifested by the least developed of human beings, such as, for instance, the wild man of the forest. Animals are capable of recepts, but not of concepts. Animals have only a receptual intelligence. With concepts comes self-consciousness, which has been called by Balzac, 'the glory and the scourge of the world.' The link between the receptive intelligence of the animal and the conceptual consciousness of the man has not been found yet; but language seems to mark off animals from men. Simple-consciousness is not lost when self-consciousness is attained; but the first works, as it were, mechanically, and without attracting our notice, while with the other we are always busy. But man does not stop there. Above simple-consciousness is cosmic-consciousness—a larger consciousness which is the true inheritance of man. Few, very few attain to that; but all men can walk on the road that leads to it—the road toward Realisation. The voluntary renunciation of self-consciousness would appear to be absolutely necessary in order to attain to 'the kingdom of heaven.' Sri Ramakrishna says, "The perfect Liberation of the soul is within the reach of him alone who hath learnt the lesson of complete self-abnegation and absolute forgetfulness of 'I', 'me', 'mine.'" Realisation, or Liberation, is the loftiest expression of man; the link which connects the visible to the superior worlds. There is, however, no sharp line of demarcation between the three grades of consciousness; and beings are often found in whom the attributes of two or more states of consciousness mix together. The man of genius for example, is one, who, while not transcending the bounds of self-consciousness, as in the case of 'a liberated soul,' catches glimpses of the state of supra-consciousness and brings that knowledge to bear on his thoughts and actions; and he is generally so far ahead of his time and surroundings that people call him 'mad.' But while the merging of simple-consciousness into self-consciousness comes about, so far as we know, gradually and imperceptibly, the passage from self-consciousness to cosmic-consciousness is often made suddenly. Consequently religious writers have called it 're-birth,' 'liberation' (from the bondage of egoism), 'conversion,' 'resurrection from the dead.'

The speaker then gave the experiences of some persons who have attained cosmic-consciousness. Lord Buddha exclaimed when it came to him, after six years of incessant struggle, 'Amithaba!' (unbounded light). Walt. Whitman described it as, 'ineffable light, light rare, untellable, lighting the very light beyond all signs, description and languages.' He says :—

"When I undertake to tell the best, I find I cannot.
My tongue is inefficient on its pivots.
My breath will not be obedient to its organs.
I become a dumb man."

"The reason for this is plain," said the speaker. "Speech is only a tally of self-conscious intellect; it can express that and nothing but that, it does not tally with, and therefore cannot express, the cosmic sense, or, if at-all, only in as far as this may be translated into terms of self-consciousness. Sri Ramakrishna says, 'But how shall I make it clear to thee? Suppose somebody asketh thee what is the taste of clarified butter. Is it possible to make the matter perfectly clear to him? The utmost that one can say in reply to such a question is, 'the taste of the butter is precisely like the taste of the butter.' There hath been as yet in this world no created being who hath been able to express by word of mouth the nature of the Absolute. There is unspeakable joy in the company of the Lord. Word proceeding out of mouth cannot tell it. He alone knoweth who hath felt it'.

The apparent signs of cosmic consciousness are—subjective light, ecstatic bliss, moral elevation, sense of immortality, loss of the sense of sin, intellectual illumination, additional charm added to the personality of the illumined, and transfiguration, as in the cases of Christ and Buddha.

And how is Realisation to be obtained ?

"Sell all that thou hast and follow me," said Jesus of Nazareth to the young man who desired to enter the kingdom of heaven. Professor James, the greatest psychologist of to-day, says in his book, *Varieties of Religious Experiences*: "There must be in the seeker a complete loss of consolation from things worldly and an intense and incessant longing to get peace and attain grace. It is only when such a longing amounts to madness, and the person has no other desire but to see his god and attain grace, and when the intensity of his longing has reached white heat, that the threshold is gained. And then, when he feels his utter incapacity to reach the state himself, and gives up the attempt, the veil is rent asunder and he sees face to face the object of his search and attains heaven. To attain this state a man must give up everything *at heart;* and think only of the object of his search—the peace that passeth all understanding. The abandonment of self-responsibility seems to be the fundamental act in the specifically religious, as distinguished from moral practices."

Says Sri Krishna in the *Bagavad-Gita:*—

> "Give me thy heart! Adore me! Serve me, cling
> In faith and love and reverence to me.
> So shalt thou come to me. I promise true,
> For thou art sweet and dear to me.
> And let go all
> Rites and writ duties! Fly to me alone.
> Make me thy sole refuge. I will free
> Thy soul from all its sins. Be of good cheer!"

"Let go writ duties!" The words echoed in my ears when I left the Mutt and came into the cool night air. The room had been suffocatingly hot, and filled with the scents of flowers and incense; and with unspeakable relief I stood beside the tank, where seven mystic lights, at the entrance to the temple, pointed to the heavens above, and to a solitary planet that seemed to be moving in the dark sky—moving with the golden moon. Graceful palms showed drooping leaves in the soft moonlight, and on the water slept the sacred lotus. "Let go writ duties!" I repeated to myself. Surely that command is dangerous, if misunderstood. Surely that command is bad for a country where few enjoy the advantages of education and the average income is a penny a day? Then I took from my pocket the following questions that I had sent to a Hindu reformer; and I read his replies.

Question:—"I have heard it said that centuries of priestly (Brahminical) tyranny had robbed Hindus of their independence before Mahomedans set foot in India. 'A gifted race crushed by priesthood', Hindus have been called. Hindus had been ruled by foreign despots for seven hundred years when Christians conquered Mahomedans.

in India. During all those years, 'Brahminism never passed into patriotism.' Content to rule the minds of millions of people, Brahmins, apparently, thought little about the bodies of the masses. Brahmins have from time immemorial held up to Hindus a heaven on earth that all may enjoy; and have said that that state alone is worth troubling about, and that nothing else is of any importance. The methods by which that state can be attained are opposed to worldly prosperity, to worldly progress; and, in consequence, it seems to me, India has stood still, while other nations have pressed on, and she has been trampled upon. How much has the cult of Liberation, which is now called in the West cosmic-consciousness, had to do with this?"

Answer:—"A good deal, no doubt; but the way in which *Samadism* has been understood, and not the thing itself, has been the cause of the evils that you point out. The central teaching of *The Gita* is to work unattached, that is to say, without caring for results. Let me illustrate this by a Hindu parable. It is said that an ascetic was once sitting under a tree, and a crane dropped a stone on him. He threw an angry look up at the crane, and it fell at his feet, burnt to ashes. Elated by his powers, he went to a house and asked for food; and the house-wife said, 'Please wait a minute'. This enraged him; but he waited until the woman had finished her work, which was attending on her husband. At last, she brought food to the ascetic and then she asked, 'Did you take me for the crane?' Astonished, he demanded, 'How did you come by this knowledge?' 'Go to the butcher' she replied, 'and he will explain it to you'. He went to the butcher; and the butcher said, 'So the women sent you!' 'How did you guess?' he enquired. 'Please wait a little,' said the butcher, and he went on with his work, cutting up meat and selling it. Afterwards the butcher attended to the wants of his old parents; and then, finally, he put food before the ascetic and explained that the knowledge had come to himself and to the woman while they were performing their daily duties.

As to 'neglecting the bodies of the masses,' it has been the other way with us. Our religion teaches us to give to all who ask. Every person who asks for food and lodging has a right to receive these things; and he knows it. He does not consider it 'begging'. Whether the recipient be worthy, or unworthy, makes no difference. No questions must be asked. Relief must be given. This system has, no doubt, taken away from our people the chief incentive for work, and has made them lazy. In India, every man, woman and child has the right to sleep on the open verandas of the rich, and to demand food—cooked or uncooked. It was formerly the same with education. Every boy who went to a Brahmin and asked for instruction received it gratis. A third of a medicine prepared for a rich patient was put aside for the use of a patient who had no money. Western ideas have changed these things to a great extent; but formerly everything in India was on the family system, and there was no need then for organised charity—the sort of charity that prevails in Europe and in America."

Question.—" The acquisition of India", says Sir J. R. Seeley, "was blindly, unintentionally made"; and he goes on to say that the end of England's ascendancy in India is as much beyond calculation as the beginning of it. The ambitions of a few Englishmen—partly national, but largely selfish—led to the conquest of India by an Army four-fifths Indian and one-fifth English. But the

Mutiny gave to England a terrible lesson; and at that time (so I have read in records of those awful days) English people earnestly determined to mend their selfish, careless ways, and Queen Victoria offered to Indians a place in the British Empire. Since that time Englishmen in India—not all, but not a few—have borne 'the burden and the heat of the day', and have helped to lift Indians to places won with the blood of England's noblest sons. In Sir William Lee-Warner's book, *The Citizen of India*, a picture of Charles I of England, executed 1649, is introduced, without any comment; and, as I have stood upon the spot where Charles I was beheaded, I can understand the silent lesson that that picture is meant to teach. Sir J. R. Seeley tells us that the love of independence presupposes political consciousness, and that if there should ever arise in India a nationality-movement, the English power must succumb at once. Has India evolved a political consciousness? And if so, in what direction will it work?"

Answer:—"A political consciousness, called 'the new spirit', has been born in India. So far it shows itself in a feeling of brotherhood for all who desire to make India their home; but does not extend to people who come here for a short time only, make all the money they can out of the country, and then go away again. The English have done much to helpforward a spirit of unity in India; but long before Christians or Mahomedans came here, our writings expressed a desire that all kings and princes in India should 'sit under one umbrella.' This vast country is almost entirely peopled with Hindus, and they have a common religion. Mr. Vincent Smith says that the civilization of India has many features that differentiate it from that of all other regions of the world, while they are common to the whole country or rather continent in a degree sufficient to justify its treatment as a unit in the history of human, social and intellectual development. Indians of old were led to think of their country as a unit; and attempts at unity were made in India centuries before the days of Akbar. So the idea of an united India is by no means new to Hindus. An Indian renaissance, born of a new consciousness of unity, is seen everywhere to-day. The direction in which this new consciousness of unity will move is towards the raising of the masses; and, as the depressed classes are lifted up, caste distinctions will break down, and political unity will become possible. A central Government, with the elective principle, is what the new consciousness aims at; not necessarily the system in vogue in Australia, or in Canada, because for thousands of years Hindus have been accustomed to slavishly obey; but a system that will give to all equal opportunities for making known their aspirations, needs, hopes and desires."

Question:—"People in the British self-governing Colonies think that the feeling of Englishmen is largely made up of sentiment as regards India. 'We are not sentimental,' they say. 'We know that India is a source of much anxiety to England, because any day she may become a bone of contention among European rulers, and that, consequently, India is a great expense. If England had only to defend herself, and to defend us, then she need not keep up such a large Army and Navy. Each year the great self-governing Colonies have more soldiers, and more sailors; and, before long, we shall be able to defend ourselves, and to defend, also, the Mother Country, if she cannot defend herself. England is the sun; we are lusty young planets;

but India is the moon, and why should we try to revive life in India? At any rate, we will not have Indians in our new countries. They are not of our race, or of our religion. Why should we be bound by the promises of Queen Victoria? Besides, India is discontented. Let her see if she can do better for herself than the British Empire can do for her. 'Imitation is the sincerest form of flattery'; and she has imitated us pretty closely. Now she picks holes in us. Let her go.' So say the great self-governing Colonies. If England withdrew from India to-day, what, in your opinion, would be the result?"

Answer:—"Chaos."

Personally, I have the greatest possible sympathy with Indians at the present time, for a mighty task lies before them. Alexander tried to conquer a world, Napoleon almost mastered a continent; but never before has an attempt been made to convert a country almost as large as Europe into one nation. If India were cut off from the British Empire, then, so far as I can see, the hope of uniting West with East must go, too. Then there must be war between rejuvenated Asia and middle-aged Europe; and, as Providence is said to favour the strong battalions, I cannot see how Europe, even if supported by America and the British Colonies, could, in the long run, withstand the millions of China and India, organised by Japan. But, if India be helped to fulfil her present ambition, be encouraged to make herself a self-governing portion of the British Empire, then the British Empire will be too strong for war, then the British Colonies will escape the dangers of conceit and selfishness. Christians have, no doubt, made mistakes in India; but they have not made more mistakes than Hindus and Mahomedans would have made if they had ruled over millions of Christians, in Europe. No doubt, boasting of what England has done, and is doing, for India is exceedingly bad taste on the part of Englishmen. No doubt, Indians, who now understand English modes of procedure, find plenty of holes to pick in us. But the experiment of introducing western ways into India has gone so far that Englishmen cannot turn back now, it seems to me ; so far that Indians, who have adopted these things wonderfully quickly, must go on. So I would say to Indians, 'Improve on English ways, if you can; but remember that the Indian renaissance is very young, while England is already the mother and the grandmother of nations.'

'To teach his grandson draughts
His leisure he'd employ.
Until at last the old man
Was beaten by the boy.'